# WITHDRAWN FROM STOCK

# A VIEW
# FROM THE
# DINERS CLUB

Essays 1987-1991

BOOKS BY GORE VIDAL

NOVELS
*Williwaw*
*In a Yellow Wood*
*The City and the Pillar*
*The Season of Comfort*
*A Search for the King*
*Dark Green, Bright Red*
*The Judgment of Paris*
*Messiah*
*Julian*
*Washington, D.C.*
*Myra Breckinridge*
*Two Sisters*
*Burr*
*Myron*
*1876*
*Kalki*
*Creation*
*Duluth*
*Lincoln*
*Myra Breckinridge and Myron*
*Empire*
*Hollywood*

SHORT STORIES
*A Thirsty Evil*

PLAYS
*An Evening with Richard Nixon*
*Weekend*
*Romulus*
*The Best Man*
*Visit to a Small Planet*

ESSAYS
*Rocking the Boat*
*Reflections upon a Sinking Ship*
*Homage to Daniel Shays*
*Matters of Fact and of Fiction*
*Pink Triangle and Yellow Star*
*Armageddon?*

# A VIEW
# FROM THE
# DINERS CLUB

## Essays 1987-1991

BY

# GORE VIDAL

ANDRE DEUTSCH

First published in Great Britain 1991
by André Deutsch Limited
105–106 Great Russell Street, London WC1B 3LJ

*British Library Cataloguing in Publication Data*

Vidal, Gore, *1925–*
  A view from the diners club.
  I. Title
  813.54 [F]

ISBN 0 233 98730 4

Printed in Great Britain by
St Edmundsbury Press Ltd, Bury St Edmunds, Suffolk

# CONTENTS

# PREFACE

In 1976 I was elected to the National Institute of Arts and Letters, a rather homespun American imitation of the Academie Française, with, I think, two hundred immortals. I received a telegram from the Institute's secretary congratulating me on the honour bestowed. I sent him a telegram, allowing that the Institute had indeed done itself honour by an election that I could not, alas, accept as I was already a member of the Diners Club. Later that year I went to my first and last Literary Conference, in Sofia, Bulgaria. Here I met John Cheever for the first time. He was very upset. 'How could you be so rude? After the way Isherwood, Vonnegut, Dorothy Parker and Anne Sexton led that long fight for you.' I let pass the significantly minatory noun. I quoted William James on *his* refusal to accept election: he liked neither the inclusions nor the exclusions (one inclusion was brother Henry) and, in any case, he stood 'against the world and its vanities'. Cheever looked very sad. 'Why did you have to say Diners Club? It sounds so coarse. Why couldn't you have said Carte Blanche?'

When I was young I was eager to meet famous writers. I did. By twenty-five, I had lost all interest in writers as people but never in writing itself. I then placed myself firmly outside the American literary world. I never taught at a university. I never read from my work (I can see why poets might want to perform but prose writers . . .). I never appeared on campus to speak of My Work, or Literature at all if I could help it: politics is always my subject, the

vii

changing nature of the state. I attend no literary conferences. I have no interest in prizes. Only recently, I learned that I had won the Pulitzer prize in 1985. The judges (two to one) gave the prize to *Lincoln*, but the Pulitzer Prize Committee, seasoned journalists who had served the empire well, chose to give the prize to a nice woman for a nice book, whose title I don't recall.

Finally, I have never written a book review for money. When I need money I write for the movies. This means that I only write about books or events that interest me. One of the problems with English bookchat is that everyone is spread far too thin. Books are quickly and sloppily reviewed (often by good writers) who would never dream of reading on their own the book that they have been given to review and so they often just guess at its contents as they must then hurry on to review television and cookery books and one another. 'I don't blame you,' as Bette Davis most famously said to Miriam Hopkins. 'I just pity you.'

Fortunately, I can pick and choose what I want to chat about, often in the *New York Review of Books*. By and large, Brits are dismayed by the length of our reviews. Why do we go on so? Well, I will show you why. You will note a very long piece about a writer you have not heard of, with the somewhat comical name of Dawn Powell. She is American. She has been dead for twenty years. Sounds most unpromising, doesn't it? After all, if she were any good she would be known at least to bookchatland or, certainly, up at Norwich where everything has been sorted out.

As of November 5, 1987, Dawn Powell was unknown, the books out of print, and only one doctoral dissertation attested to the fact that she had ever existed. But Powell was a brilliant and witty novelist. I took a year to read or re-read all her works, and then I described every last one of them. Whether or not you find the result interesting is beside the point. Thanks to this one piece most of her books are now in print in English and other languages, and there is another good writer for the dwindling band of voluntary readers to read. I do this sort of slogging work because I think that the only purpose to bookchat is to lead readers to writers that have been overlooked for reasons that are, in themselves, interesting to note. I get nothing out of it, not even tenure. Neither, sad to say, do the writers, since most of them are dead by the time one has got the real point to them.

Since I shall not write a memoir, I have included more personal references – or rather my personal responses to others – than one ought, strictly, to do in reviewing, although such reflections are very much a part of the essay tradition to which, as a member in good standing of the Diners Club, I belong. After all, the world might never have known that the emblematic word 'Rosebud' in *Citizen Kane* refers not to the boy's sled of the William Randolph Hearst character but to Hearst's actual name of endearment for the clitoris of his mistress Marion Davies. I think you must admit that we here at the Diners Club *deliver the goods*.

# Part I:
# Book Chat

# 1

# EVERY ECKERMANN
# HIS OWN MAN

ECKERMANN: I'm delighted that *The New York Review of Books* is still going strong after – what is it now? Fifty years?

VISITOR: Twenty-five, actually.

ECKERMANN: It seems a lot longer.

VISITOR: You appeared in one of the first issues, didn't you, Mr Eckermann?

ECKERMANN: *Ja*, as Goethe would say. *Zwei Seelen wohnen, ach! in meiner Brust.* But I am my own man now. I am free of Goethe; Wilson, too. *E pluribus meum.*

VISITOR: Only there is no piece in *The New York Review of Books* of twenty-five years ago by anyone called Eckermann. There *is* a curiosity called 'Every Man His Own Eckermann', now reprinted in their *Selections* from the first two issues, a self-interview by Edmund Wilson, discussing music and painting, two subjects that he confessed he knew very little about.

ECKERMANN: That was me, if memory serves. As I recall, he – we – knew what we didn't like. On Picasso we anticipated Stassinopoulos Huffington. Always avant-garde we were in the arts we knew nothing of. Back in Weimar, Wilson is our touchstone.

VISITOR: But surely you . . . I mean Mr Wilson can no longer contribute.

3

ECKERMANN: True. That is why, today, whenever I write art criticism, I often sign myself Susan Sontag.

VISITOR: You, Mr Eckermann, or your own man, wrote 'Malthus to Balthus, or the Geometric Art of Silkscreen Reproduction'?

ECKERMANN: In a thousand years no one will know who wrote what or why or if at all. So let's keep those questions moving right along. You would like to know my impression of a small volume called *Selections*, containing a number of pieces from the first two issues of *The New York Review*, which first appeared in 1963. At the time I said, or Wilson said – you see? it hardly matters – 'The disappearance of the *Times* Sunday book section at the time of the printers' strike only made us realize it had never existed.' Naturally, it sounds even better in the original German!

VISITOR (*quickly*): In *Selections* there are eighteen critical pieces culled from the first two issues. They are written by F. W. Dupee, Dwight Macdonald, Robert Lowell, Mary McCarthy, Elizabeth Hardwick 1, W. H. Auden, Norman Mailer, John Berryman, Irving Howe, Gore Vidal, Alfred Kazin, Elizabeth Hardwick 2, William Styron, Jason Epstein, Allen Tate, Alfred Chester, Richard Wilbur, and Edmund Wilson, and there is a poem by Robert Lowell. What is your immediate impression . . .

ECKERMANN: Of seventeen contributors, eight have fled. Fallen from the perch. Crossed the shining river. Ridden on ahead. Granted, Auden and Berryman and Lowell took early trains, but American poets are obliged to. It's in the by-laws of their union, unlike European poets. Goethe was eighty-three when he cooled it, chatty to the last. But let us look on the bright side: the nine who are still with us are still robust and able to supply bookchat by the yard. Yet *autres temps autres moeurs*. I sometimes think that the long *essai*–attempt (I lapse now into English) may be too much for today's reader, eager for large side-bars and small boxes and lots of coloured ink and numerous Opinions. Oh, how Americans – Brits too, alas – dote on Opinion. But Opinion without Demon-

4

stration is worthless. It is the discursive form which the demonstration takes that distinguished *The New York Review* from . . .

VISITOR: *The Times Literary Supplement?*

ECKERMANN: Don't interrupt. The *NYR* made it possible for those writers who don't necessarily have to knock out instant Opinion pieces for money to develop themes that interested them or – the task of criticism – allowed them the space in which to illuminate the work of a forgotten or misunderstood writer. In *Selections*, Allen Tate is splendid on the work of Ford Madox Ford. Since I regard Ford as the finest novelist in English since World War I, I am prejudiced, as well as opinionated. Here's Tate on how the critical biographer should approach Ford:

> Ford's best biographer will understand at the outset that Ford himself must be approached as a character in a novel, and that novel by Ford. The complaint, often heard today, that James, Conrad, and Ford were each in his own degree obsessed by 'form' or 'method' is of course nonsense; but if it were true, would it be less damaging to the vitality of the novel in our day than the obsession with the expressionistic egotism and disorder of American novelists since the War? Ford was not, in the pejorative sense, a formalist. Ford's technique *is* Ford, and he could have had no other.

This echo of Flaubert's 'One might almost establish the axiom that there is no such thing as subject. Style in itself being an absolute manner of seeing things.' This says a lot about Ford the novelist, Tate the critic, and, perhaps the *NYR* at the start.

VISITOR: Is there a sort of house style at the *NYR* as there is – or was – at *The New Yorker?*

ECKERMANN: Thank God, no. In *Selections* I was struck by how different the writers are from each other, unlike, say, those at the old *New Yorker*, doomed to conform to a wondrously dull style, chockablock with lots of well-checked little facts, as Gore Vidal pointed out in his review of John Hersey's collection of pieces. In

5

retrospect, Vidal was perhaps too hard on the hapless Hersey and not sufficiently hard on *The New Yorker*, where his work had been, presumably, processed to the consistency of a Kraft cheese. Of course, if Hersey actually writes like that, well . . .

VISITOR: The *NYR* reviewers have been accused of reviewing one another and behaving like any other literary clique.

ECKERMANN: How can there be a clique when hardly anyone knows anyone else? Also, at the beginning, there were far fewer school-teacher contributors than now. Of course, from time to time, poets often holed up in universities in order not to die but, even so, of the sixteen critics in *Selections*, only three were full-time academics, and academics, then and now, tend to sectarianism – hence, cliquishness. Today the wars of the Literary Theoreticians are bound to leak into the *NYR* and make one, suddenly, nostalgic for a time when Literature not Theory mattered, and Johns Hopkins was known only for its healing arts.

VISITOR: How would you classify the *NYR* politically?

ECKERMANN: Personally, I prefer the *Radical History Review* or *Mother Jones* to *NYR*. But I do think a quarter-century ago we were all a bit more to the true political point than now. Here's Dwight Macdonald on Arthur Schlesinger, Jr., the Kennedy White House apologist:

> When he is not confronted with a polemical subject that makes his style taut and forces him to think (which he can do when he has to), Schlesinger likes to slip into something more comfortable. His judgments tend to become official and reverential and to be expressed in the orotundities of the hardened public speaker.

I like that adjective, 'hardened'. Now if Macdonald were a mere hack of the sort that today fills New York's current papers and magazines, this would have been an *ad hominem* attack on Schlesinger. But Macdonald likes and respects Schlesinger even when, in absolute good faith, he wants to wring his political neck. How to

6

explain personal disinterestedness to a generation that dotes on money, publicity, and personal feuds? How to explain that there are powerful forces – even ideas – abroad that must be analyzed? – and reversed?

MacDonald, in the first issue of the *NYR*, had figured out that we had all been had by the Kennedys (the President was killed a few months later – a *non sequitur*, let me quickly add) and he also detected in Schlesinger's *The Politics of Hope* a shift from the Jefferson-Madison Bill of Rights attitude toward the citizen to the autocratic Jackson and his terrible successors, the Caesars of the National Security State, only now unravelling. Macdonald blows the whistle on Schlesinger's contention, 'While the Executive should wield all his powers under the constitution with energy, he should not be able to abrogate the constitution except in face of war, revolution or economic chaos.' Macdonald finds this a nice prescription for fascism (what is economic chaos? Black Monday of October 1987?) . . . I see your eyes are beginning to glaze. I give up. Let me put this in terms that *New York* magazine can grasp. Dwight was jealous of Arthur's success at Camelot and longed, in his heart of hearts, to be flung fully clothed into the pool at Hickory Hill by the dread Ethel Kennedy. Envy is the only credible emotion, isn't it? Never say Eckermann isn't 'with it'.

VISITOR: But is the *NYR* with it? How have they dealt with black power, gay rights, women . . .

ECKERMANN: F. W. Dupee is superb on James Baldwin's *The Fire Next Time*. Dupee is also a corrective to Flannery O'Connor's contemporary view that if Baldwin hadn't been black, no one would have put up with him*. This is wondrously stupid. If Baldwin had not been black, and gay, he would not have had to behave as he did. Dupee is wondrously subtle on this. As he describes Baldwin's mind and pain, he usefully demonstrates how Baldwin is so much more poignant and effective in his memoir than in those booming sermons of last things.

* See page 1,208 in *The Collected Works of Flannery O'Connor* (Library of America, 1988).

VISITOR: So much then for politics, Mr Eckermann. Essentially, the *NYR* is a literary paper . . .

ECKERMANN: Which came along just as literature ceased to be of any general interest. Does anyone – voluntarily – read a book nowadays? Movies are the preferred diversion.

VISITOR: The *Review* has been criticised for not . . . well, doing enough about fiction, about new writers, experimental fiction . . .

ECKERMANN: Except for the genre books, packaged like boxes of cheap Depression candy, there is no longer a novel-reading public. Of course there are the books written to be taught on campus, but they are mere Demonstrations of Theory. For the 'educated' public it is filmmaker Woody Allen, not bookmaker Philip Roth, that excites interest.

VISITOR: But if the *NYR* gave more space to 'experimental' writing . . .

ECKERMANN: The record's not too bad. In the second issue Richard Poirier was down at the wharf, greeting Pynchon's *V*, while I was startled to reread, in *Selections*, Mary McCarthy's inspired praise of Burroughs's *The Naked Lunch*, a book not much praised at that time, at least not by so celebrated a critic. I say 'inspired' because I read the book then and didn't much like it, but now I begin to see things that I had missed first time around. Well, that is what criticism is meant to do – show us what we missed or just plain didn't get.

She is particularly good on Burroughs's humour, 'peculiarly American, at once broad and sly. It is the humour of a comedian, a vaudeville performer playing in *One* . . .' Surprisingly for those days, she makes no heavy weather of the fag side of Burroughs, something that the other critics then and now, a quarter-century later, still go on howling about, like the Hilton Kramer on Robert Mapplethorpe in a recent New York paper – truly crazed bigotry of the sort that, outside certain yob papers in England, no paper in the civilized Western world would print.

8

On that subject, Alfred Chester. He was a glorious writer, tough as nails, with an exquisite ear for the false note; his review of Rechy's *City of Night* is murderously funny, absolutely unfair, and totally true, a trick that only a high critic knows how to pull off. No, I won't show you how it's done. You look tired.

VISITOR: No. No. I'm awake. What did you think of Auden's review of *Anathemata* by David Jones?

ECKERMANN: *Echt* lousy, as Goethe would say. For reasons that Berryman gave in his review of Auden's *The Dyer's Hand*. Auden did

> one of two things with books entrusted to him for comment: either he wrote about what interested him at the moment, making some spidery connection with the book in hand, or, with books he felt keen about . . . he quoted from them at agreeable length. Surely the pro sits on and breaks his brains.

It is the ability to break (one's own) brains that makes all the difference. We thought that our job then. Now . . .

VISITOR: Between then and now . . .

ECKERMANN: Then, Baldwin and the black condition, the imperial search for enemies, invasion of Cuba, the turning of 'creative' writers from the novel to actual events taken from newspapers (Elizabeth Hardwick's 'Grub Street: New York'). Now – or, rather, since – political murders, Vietnam, drugs and the mafia-ization of the society, the federal deficits, the decline of education, of quality of Life, of life of Quality . . . Twenty-five years ago the United States was the world's central economic, military, and intellectual fact. Today, we are, literally, eccentric. I think the *NYR* can take some pride in the way it has handled with a degree of comprehensive dignity a quarter-century of national decline and, law-abiding as we all are (the so-called Molotov cocktail on the cover was actually a Leonardo sketch for a space shuttle – a little leg-pull), we are now simply obeying the second law of thermodynamics, as we run down.

9

VISITOR: Will *you* be here in 2015?

ECKERMANN: No – Eckermann as his own man will be a thing of the past – rather like books. After all, our Japanese masters currently prefer comic books to book books. As they are now our role models, *The New York Review of Comic Books* will doubtless replace the old *NYR*. But there will be lots more pictures, which will be nice. In any case, the two epochs will be linked here, I hope, by comprehensiveness.

VISITOR: If I comprehend you . . .

ECKERMANN: 'Comprehension is only a knowledge adequate to our intention.'

VISITOR: Goethe?

ECKERMANN: Kant. *Ich wunsche Ihren noch einen schönen Tag. Have a nice day now.*

VISITOR: Kant?

ECKERMANN: Eckermann. On your way out, open the second shutter so that more light can come in.

*The New York Review of Books*
27 October 1988

# 2

# PEN PALS:
# HENRY MILLER
# AND LAWRENCE DURRELL

The dust-jacket of *The Durrell-Miller Letters 1935–80*, edited by Ian
S. MacNiven, shows three protagonists sprawled in a shallow
wine-dark sea – Lawrence Durrell, Henry Miller, and Henry
Miller's numinous cock. Needless to say, it is the third that not
only rivets attention but commands nostalgia and, well, let us be
honest, pity and awe. Like so many celebrities caught off-guard,
the protagonist of a million words looks slightly exhausted and
rather smaller than one recalls it from Literature; and yet even in
its fragile state one senses that humming hydraulic energy which
made it the stuff of legend in the first place. Durrell, beautiful
leprechaun in his twenties, cradles modestly – nervously? – raised
knees while on his lips there is a virginal archaic smile. The rest of
Henry Miller looks rather like a frustrated stage-mother about to
burst into a chorus of 'Everything's coming up roses' from *Gypsy*.

In the preface by Alfred Perlès, a friend of the two if not the
three, all sorts of high claims are made for their correspondence
now that 'There are more letters being written . . . than ever before
in the history of man.' This is inaccurate. For half a century, the
telephone conversation has largely replaced letter-writing; and
since only mad American presidents tape their conversations, the
unique telephone artistry of a Truman Capote, say, is for ever lost
to us except as a nasal whine in the aural memory of ageing
listeners.

Perlès does describe how he was present when Durrell came to

Paris to meet Miller in 1937. Durrell was twenty-five; Miller was forty-six. Two years earlier, Durrell had read Miller's underground success, *Tropic of Cancer*, and thus began a correspondence that was to continue to the end of Miller's life. Unalike in background, they also proved to be far more unalike as writers than either suspected. But at the beginning there is only joy as the two Outsiders plot the storming of Parnassus and the setting up of a new god that will look suspiciously like the holy ghost of their trinity.

Miller was that rarest of literary types: a true American proletarian who had somehow discovered literature and then, in a wacky autodidactic way, made himself a master of a kind. If he often sounded like the village idiot, that was because, like Whitman, he was the rest of the village as well. Durrell's background was conventional; a product of the civil service mandarin class, he was born in India and sent home to school in England. School didn't take; so he absconded with his widowed mother to Corfu and took up writing. Durrell's first letter:

> *Tropic* turns the corner into a new life which has regained its bowels . . . I love its guts. I love to see the canons of oblique and pretty emotions mopped up; to see every whim-wham and bagatelle of our contemporaries from Eliot to Joyce dunged under. God give us young men the guts to plant daisies on top and finish the job.

As a Britisher, Durrell's images here are – and continued for some time to be – related more to the water-closet and the bowels (*The Black Book* is at its most daring with the fart) than to the priapic and its conventional fodder, Miller's territory. Miller responds: 'I particularly prize your letter because it's the kind of letter I would have written myself had I not been the author of the book.' In due course, they meet. Miller is certain of his own genius. Durrell fears that he himself can never be much more than another Somerset Maugham. But priapic Miller has seriously stirred him and, as Durrell will prove to be the better writer of the two (if one can compare a lemon to a banana), the *blague* that they bat across numerous great seas and oceans for forty-five years is endearing, hilarious and sometimes wise.

The early letters are mostly about literary self-promotion, a sombre subject. They may be Outsiders but they want to be published and well reviewed by the likes of Cyril Connolly. On the other hand, George Orwell's meditations on Miller are not appreciated. Durrell: 'Orwell is a nice man, but ignorant.' Miller: 'Orwell-pfui! That man lacks nearly everything in my opinion. He hasn't even a good horizontal view.' Eliot is a problem because Durrell is a poet and Eliot is . . . Eliot. Eventually Durrell earns Eliot's praise ('Lawrence Durrell's *Black Book* is the first piece of work by a new English writer to give me any hope for the future of prose fiction'). Later Durrell arranges a meeting between Eliot and Miller; the papal benediction is somewhat coolly bestowed on the village.

The private lives of the two correspondents do not take up much space in their letters. Over the decades, a great many wives and women come and go; a number of children get born. Houses are moved into and out of. Durrell, who is very much a house-person, is forever obliged to move away from that perfect Ionian retreat (for years he was with the British diplomatic service – Argentina, Yugoslavia), while the Bohemian Miller settles down, for most of their correspondence, in California; first, at Big Sur; then on the prosperous Pacific Palisades. Their one continuing link is Anaïs Nin, with whom Miller was conducting an affair when they first met.* By profession a muse to greatness, Anaïs had powerful literary longings of her own (she kept a diary, wrote poetic prose); but she would have settled for movie stardom – Luise Rainer,

---

* 'My letters alone might be worth something should my personality create attention', Henry Miller wrote to Anaïs Nin, in a mood of fatality, uncertain as to whether he would 'not die in the next forty-eight hours' and hurriedly sorting out his effects ('Naturally it all depends on how much my books earn, after my demise . . . any manuscripts left unfinished you have my permission to complete in any way you wish . . .') The letter, though, was written in December 1933 in the early (and prolific) days of their fifty years' correspondence, now brought together in *A Literate Passion: Letters of Anaïs Nin and Henry Miller 1932-1953*, published simultaneously with Miller's *Quiet Days in Clichy*, his semi-autobiographical novel about his life in Paris during the 1920s – and his *Complete Book of Friends*.

Carmen Miranda, it made no difference – or indeed *anything* that would have made her 'a legend', as she referred to herself in later life with no trace, ever, of humour. Fortunately, to the end of her life, Anaïs was married to a wealthy and highly complaisant banker who made it possible for her to publish Miller and herself in pre-war Paris, and bemuse genius.

Durrell mailed Miller the only copy of *The Black Book*, with the airy advice to throw it away if he didn't like it. Miller replied with true feeling: 'Why not put in a carbon when you write? What's to prevent it? You will find that you save time and energy.' As it was, Henry and Anaïs typed out copies of the book. In the old pre-Xerox world, that was love, dedication. Then they got Kahane's Obelisk Press to publish Durrell in 1938. Miller himself proof-read the book: 'I would suggest now, when you receive your copy, that you re-read with an eye to reducing the verbiage . . . You will lose nothing by cutting.' In later years Durrell will *tu quoque* this with a vengeance.

Finally, in the summer of 1937, the Durrells meet Miller and Anaïs in Paris. Harmony reigns. Miller is then persuaded to come to Greece, out of which comes perhaps his best book, *The Colossus of Maroussi*, based on an outsized, in every sense, fixture in Athens, George Katsimbalis. Although no politics other than literary is touched on in the letters of this period, Miller is suddenly terrified by the international situation. September 1938:

> . . . maybe I might find a way to get to Corfu – *if it's safe there?* . . . Everything would be OK if Anaïs could depend on receiving money from London regularly . . . Five minutes alone with Hitler and I could have solved the whole damned problem. They don't know how to deal with the guy. He's temperamental – and terribly earnest. Somebody has to make him laugh, or we're all lost.

Plainly the funereal Chamberlain had insufficiently tickled the Führer's funny-bone. In any case, Miller was all for saving one's own skin: 'Don't let your countrymen play on your emotions. England hasn't a bloody chance, nor France . . .' But Miller was

consistent: *sauve qui peut* was all that one could do in a world that
he had rejected at every level.

Durrell was more conventional; he went to work for the British
Council in Greece. Miller went back to America where, except for
an occasional trip, he would end his days, a cult figure, and content
because he knew 'A hundred years from now the phrases I let drop
here and there, in the books and in the letters, will be studied to
prove this and that about me, I know it. But now, even now, I am
struck by the prophetic element which is an essential part of me.'
Well, we all have those days but Miller seems to have had them
every day.

Over the years Durrell's letters begin to sound more like himself
and less like Miller. Miller never varies; he pounds his big drum,
but he is capable of the shrewd aside, especially his curious love-
hate for his native land upon whose west coast, so close to the Asia
of his imagination, he is perched, surrounded by fellow enthusiasts
for Zen, astrology, Lao Tse. Happily, too, his psychic powers never
desert him: (1941) '. . . whether the US enters the war or not, there
will be a world-wide revolution to finish this off. *You* will yet see a
wonderful period. Neither England nor Germany will win. We're
in for the greatest change the earth has known.'

Fame comes at last to Durrell with *Justine* and the rest of the
Alexandria Quartet, much underestimated, in my view, particularly in an age when explication and literary theory are sovereign
and so much teacherly sense as well as nonsense could be made of
his works. Each master affects to find fame a drag: too many
intrusions, etc. They are not much interested in other writers
except for the ones who admire them. Miller does send Durrell
Kerouac's *Dharma Bums*. Durrell's response is sharp:

> . . . found it unreadable; no, I admire it in a way, as I admire
> *Catcher in the Rye*. It is social realism as the Russians under-
> stand it. But out of the emptiness really of this generation of
> self-pitying cry-babies . . . It is only here that I think America
> is really harming you, making you critically soft; beware of

cowboy evangelism and Loving Everything and Everybody Everywhere.

Finally, of the Beats, 'They are turning the novel into a skating rink; I am trying to make it a spiral staircase.'

Miller strikes back – *re* America: 'I loathe everything about it more and more. It's the land of doom.' He reiterates his praise for Kerouac's prose; denies he himself is critically soft because he won't read 'the celebrities'. Durrell comes back even harder: 'I found [*Dharma Bums*] really corny and deeply embarrassing (Read pages 30-33 aloud in a strong American voice); and worst of all pretentious . . . As for the writing, yes it's fluent . . . but it has that breathless wondering lisp, the prattling tone which seems to have been handed down to American writers by Anita Loos.' Durrell the critic is now zeroing in on his one-time master. But then Miller is having problems with the Quartet. 'You know with whom, in some ways, you have a kinship? Malaparte.' The *farceur* to end all *farceurs*!

In 1949 Durrell sends Miller a wire: '*Sexus* deliberately bad will completely ruin reputation unless withdrawn revised Larry.' The correspondence over *Sexus*, the first part of *The Rosy Crucifixion*, is heated but amiable. Durrell: 'What on earth possessed you to leave so much twaddle in?' Miller replies that he has put in everything, as always: 'You should be able to perceive that only a man without ego could write thus about himself (or else I'm really crazy! In which case, pray for me!)' Miller bides his time; then he writes of *Monsieur* (1974):

> Somewhere after the marvellous episode in the tent . . . the book seemed to fall apart, forgive me for saying so . . . I kept wondering as I read if you had an American publisher for it. (I can't see more than a few hundred Americans capable of reading a book like this.)

In the end the great friendship holds up even though each doesn't really much care for what the other does, a sign not of invidiousness but of mastery. If one thought that someone else could do what one did, one would not do it, for the work of any artist is, to him, by its nature and its intention incomparable; otherwise, he would not bother to write at all.

The 1960s were not as much to Miller's liking as one might have suspected. After watching the Democratic convention on television, he remarks, 'How clean a dictatorship like de Gaulle's seems.' (This is wiser than he knows. I was a delegate to that convention, chosen not by the people of New York State but by the boss of Tammany, Carmine di Sapio, with orders to vote for Kennedy.) 'If Kennedy is our next president . . . something will happen . . . and if Kennedy dies in office we'll have Johnson from Texas, about the narrowest-minded group of people in America, Texans.' For once Miller's crystal ball was functioning. He also detested the mindless violence of *Bonnie and Clyde*, an emblematic film of the day. ('Bonnie' is spelt 'Bonny' in an index where B. Rossett lacks a final letter. The occasional footnotes throughout the book are inadequate.) Durrell sees the film as

> . . . a US version of the Babes in the Wood. They knew not
> what the hell they were doing, this is what was frightening on
> the moral *plan*; its application to young America (or England
> for that matter – for England has become a sub-culture of the
> US now) was not only accurate but terrifying. To do ill
> without having any value in mind which the act represents –
> that is what flatters the young . . . they feel they are like that
> – not bad but just lost.

Whatever the ageing duo's faults, easy riding was never one of them.

In the 1970s each is more or less preoccupied by the Nobel Prize, a sort of rigged good citizenship medal, awarded by a largely monolingual club of a small nation noted for its literary taste, cuisine and criminal detection (clue: *not* Belgium). It is fascinating to learn, from Durrell, that an interesting but not exactly Great Citizen, Denis de Rougemont, 'missed the Nobel this year by very little' (1971). In 1978 Durrell writes, 'I fear your indiscretions will result in Miss De Johngh (sic) and Normal (sic) Mailer being the next. I think to get that sort of prize one must be a sort of UNESCO wire-puller and president of PEN – like Mario Praz (Premier Prix Zagreb, Prix d'Honneur Kiev, etc. etc.).' But Miller is optimistic: 'No, I wasn't robbed of Prize by Singer – my applications are for 1979.' Obviously they have come a long way from literary outlaws to literary intriguers. Miller: 'I must tell you some other time how I offended Artur Lundkvist, Swedish poet and translator (Head of Lit. Committee there!) . . . Let me only say this – there are no greater, no more colossal bores than most Scandinavians, with Sweden in the lead.' Durrell responds: 'I didn't know that Lundkvist was on the Committee – he is a Com and received the Prix Lenin; it explains why I lost that year to Steinbeck . . . What the hell.'

Towards the close each is truly bemused by the rise of their common muse, Anaïs Nin, who has begun to publish her diaries; she is also rewriting them as she goes along, paying off new as well as old scores. She is Kali incarnate, whom John Dowson describes in *A Classical Dictionary of Hindu Mythology* as 'a hideous and terrible countenance, dripping with blood, encircled with snakes, hung round with skulls and human heads, and in all respects resembling a fury rather than a goddess'. Over the years Anaïs had managed to quarrel with all her Dauphins (she was Joan of Arc), including me. As Miller grew more famous, she grew bitter. When Durrell, now celebrated too, mentioned in an article that Hugo was her husband, he 'had to do a public repentance with sackcloth and ashes'. It was Anaïs's special joy to be married to two men at the same time, and no interviewer was too humble not to be taken promptly into her confidence, and then sworn to secrecy. Miller was, until the end, more tolerant of her than Durrell or my estranged self. Miller does wonder (1975), 'Why she "denies" Hugo, who treated her so wonderfully, I can't make out. But talk of "deceivers"! She takes the cake. We are lucky to be spared, eh?' After Anaïs's death, Durrell writes (1977): 'As for Anaïs I suppose the fur will start flying now as they search for the real girl among the four or five masks she left lying about with false clues attached to them.' Of course each mask was just like the others and – *honi soit qui mal y pense* . . . Later (1979) Miller has read what purports to be an interview with his ex-wife June: 'Scurrilous and full of lies. (She even beats Anaïs at it.)' He then makes a comparison that I thought I was the only one of Anaïs's Dauphins to have noted: 'Am now reading a biography of Marie Corelli, my female favorite. Resemblance to Anaïs again. But Corelli more pure, more strong . . ..' There is a lot to this, and though Anaïs will never be more than a series of busy footnotes clacking like castanets through the biographies of others, Marie Corelli might be usefully revived. Certainly, *Sorrows of Satan* is – dare I confess it? – Bookeresque in its moral propriety.

On June 1, 1980, Henry Miller died beside the Pacific Ocean. Durrell continued. Different as the two writers are, each understood Flaubert's axiom 'that there is no such thing as subject. Style in itself being an absolute manner of seeing things. All possible prosodic variations have been discovered; but that is far from being the case with prose.' Each deployed his own prose over a lifetime, and though I would rather read Durrell than Miller, our literary landscape would be even more lunar than it is had the two of them not passed, so goonily, so cheerfully, so originally through this sad century.

*The Times Literary Supplement*
9–15 September 1988

# 3
# DAWN POWELL:
# THE AMERICAN WRITER

I

Once upon a time, New York City was as delightful a place to live in as to visit. There were many amenities, as they say in brochures. One was something called Broadway, where dozens of plays opened each season, and thousands of people came to see them in an area which today resembles downtown Calcutta without, alas, that subcontinental city's deltine charm and intellectual rigour.

One evening back there in once upon a time (February 7, 1957, to be exact) my first play opened at the Booth Theatre. Traditionally, the playwright was invisible to the audience. One hid out in a nearby bar, listening to the sweet nasalities of Pat Boone's rendering of *Love Letters in the Sand* from a glowing jukebox. But when the curtain fell on this particular night, I went into the crowded lobby to collect someone. Overcoat collar high about my face, I moved invisibly—through the crowd, or so I thought. Suddenly a voice boomed-tolled across the lobby. '*Gore!*' I stopped; everyone stopped. From the cloakroom a small round figure, rather like a Civil War cannon ball, hurtled toward me and collided. As I looked down into that familiar round face with its snub nose and shining bloodshot eyes, I heard, the entire crowded lobby heard: '*How could you do this?* How could you *sell out* like this? To *Broadway!* To *Commercialism!* How could you give up *The Novel?* Give up the *security?* The security of knowing that every two years there will be

20

– like clockwork – *that five-hundred-dollar advance!*' Thirty years later, the voice still echoes in my mind, and I think fondly of its owner, our best comic novelist. 'The field', I can hear Dawn Powell snarl, 'is not exactly overcrowded.'

On the night that *Visit to a Small Planet* opened, Dawn Powell was fifty-nine years old. She had published fourteen novels, evenly divided between accounts of her native Midwest (and how the hell to get out of there and make it to New York) and the highly comic New York novels, centred on Greenwich Village, where she lived most of her adult life. Some twenty-three years earlier, the Theatre Guild had produced Powell's comedy *Jig Saw* (one of *her* many unsuccessful attempts to sell out to commercialism), but there was third-act trouble and, despite Spring Byington and Ernest Truex, the play closed after forty-nine performances.

For decades Dawn Powell was always just on the verge of ceasing to be a cult and becoming a major religion. But despite the work of such dedicated cultists as Edmund Wilson and Matthew Josephson, John Dos Passos and Ernest Hemingway, Dawn Powell never became the popular writer that she ought to have been. In those days, with a bit of luck, a good writer eventually attracted voluntary readers and became popular. Today, of course, 'popular' means bad writing that is widely read while good writing is that which is taught to involuntary readers. Powell failed on both counts. She needs no interpretation and in her lifetime she should have been as widely read as, say, Hemingway or the early Fitzgerald or the mid O'Hara or even the late, far too late, Katherine Anne Porter. But Powell was that unthinkable monster, a witty woman who felt no obligation to make a single, much less a final, down payment on Love or The Family; she saw life with a bright Petronian neutrality, and every host at life's feast was a potential Trimalchio to be sent up.

In the few interviews that Powell gave, she often mentions as her favourite novel, surprisingly for an American, much less for a woman of her time and place, the *Satyricon*. This sort of thing was not acceptable then any more than it is now. Descriptions of warm, mature, heterosexual love were – and are – woman's writerly task, and the truly serious writers really, heartbreakingly, flunk the course while the pop ones pass with bright honours.

Although Powell received very little serious critical attention (to the extent that there has ever been much in our heavily moralizing culture), when she did get reviewed by a really serious person like Diana Trilling (*The Nation*, May 29, 1948), *la* Trilling warns us that the book at hand is no good because of 'the discrepancy between the power of mind revealed on every page of her novel [*The Locusts have No King*] and the insignificance of the human beings upon which she directs her excellent intelligence'. Trilling does acknowledge the formidable intelligence but because Powell does not deal with morally complex people (full professors at Columbia in mid-journey?), 'the novel as a whole . . . fails to sustain the excitement promised by its best moments'.

Apparently, a novel to be serious must be about very serious – even solemn – people rendered in a very solemn – even serious – manner. Wit? What is that? But then we all know that power of mind and intelligence count for as little in the American novel as they do in American life. Fortunately neither appears with sufficient regularity to distress our solemn middle-class middlebrows as they trudge ever onward to some Scarsdale of the mind, where the red light blinks and blinks at pier's end and the fields of the republic rush forward ever faster like a rug rolling up.

Powell herself occasionally betrays bewilderment at the misreading of her work. She is aware, of course, that the American novel is a middlebrow middle-class affair and that the reader/writer must be as one in pompous self-regard. 'There is so great a premium on dullness,' she wrote sadly (Robert Van Gelder, *Writers and Writing*, New York: Scribner's, 1946), 'that it seems stupid to pass it up.' She also remarks that:

> . . . it is considered jolly and good-humored to point out the oddities of the poor or of the rich. The frailties of millionaires or garbage collectors can be made to seem amusing to persons who are not millionaires or garbage collectors. Their ways of speech, their personal habits, the peculiarities of their think-

ing are considered fair game. I go outside the rules with my stuff because I can't help believing that the middle class is funny, too.

Well, she was warned by four decades of bookchatters.

My favourite was the considered judgement of one Frederic Morton (*The New York Times*, September 12, 1954):

> But what appears most fundamentally lacking is the scene of outrage which serves as an engine to even the most sophisticated [*sic*] satirist. Miss Powell does not possess the pure indignation that moves Evelyn Waugh to his absurdities and forced Orwell into his haunting contortions. Her verbal equipment is probably unsurpassed among writers of her genre – but she views the antics of humanity with too surgical a calm.

It should be noted that Mr Morton was the author of the powerful, purely indignant, and phenomenally compassionate novel, *Asphalt and Desire*. In general, Powell's books usually excited this sort of commentary. (Waugh *indignant*? Orwell hauntingly *contorted*?) The fact is that Americans have never been able to deal with wit. Wit gives away the scam. Wit blows the cool of those who are forever expressing a sense of hoked-up outrage. Wit, deployed by a woman with surgical calm, is a brutal assault upon nature – that is, Man. Attis, take arms!

Finally, as the shadows lengthened across the greensward, Edmund Wilson got around to his old friend in *The New Yorker* (November 17, 1962). One reason, he tells us, why Powell has so little appeal to those Americans who read novels is that 'she does nothing to stimulate feminine day-dreams [sexist times!]. The woman reader can find no comfort in identifying herself with Miss Powell's heroines. The women who appear in her stories are likely to be as sordid and absurd as the men.' This sexual parity was – is – unusual. But now, closer to century's end than 1962, Powell's sordid, absurd ladies seem like so many Mmes de Staël compared to our latter-day viragos.

Wilson also noted Powell's originality: 'Love is not Miss Powell's theme. Her real theme is the provincial in New York who has come on from the Middle West and acclimatized himself (or herself) to the city and made himself a permanent place there, without ever, however, losing his fascinated sense of an alien and anarchic society.' This is very much to the (very badly written) point. Wilson finds her novels 'among the most amusing being written, and in this respect quite on a level with those of Anthony Powell, Evelyn Waugh, and Muriel Spark'. Wilson's review was of her last book, *The Golden Spur*; three years later she was dead of breast cancer. 'Thanks a lot, Bunny,' one can hear her mutter as this belated floral wreath came flying through her transom.

Summer. Sunday afternoon. *Circa* 1950. Dawn Powell's duplex living-room at 35 East Ninth Street. The hostess presides over an elliptical aquarium filled with gin: a popular drink of the period known as the Martini. In attendance, Coby – just Coby to me for years, her *cavaliere servente*; he is neatly turned out in a blue blazer, rosy-faced, sleek silver hair combed straight back. Coby can talk with charm on any subject. The fact that he might be Dawn's lover has never crossed my mind. They are so old. A handsome, young poet lies on the floor, literally at the feet of E. E. Cummings and his wife, Marion, who ignore him. Dawn casts an occasional maternal eye in the boy's direction; but the eye is more that of the mother of a cat or a dog, apt to make a nuisance. Conversation flows. Gin flows. Marion Cummings is beautiful; so indeed is her husband, his eyes a faded denim blue. Coby is in great form. Though often his own subject, he records not boring triumphs but improbable disasters. He is always broke, and a once distinguished wardrobe is now in the hands of those gay receivers, his landladies. This afternoon, at home, Dawn is demure; thoughtful. 'Why,' she suddenly asks, eyes on the long body beside the coffee table, 'do they never have floors of their own to sleep on?'

Cummings explains that since the poet lives in Philadelphia he is too far from his own floor to sleep on it. Not long after, the young poet and I paid a call on the Cummingses. We were greeted at the door by an edgy Marion. 'I'm afraid you can't come in.' Behind her an unearthly high scream sounded. 'Dylan Thomas just died,' she explained. 'Is that Mr Cummings screaming?' asked the poet politely, as the keening began on an even higher note. 'No,' said Marion. 'That is not Mr Cummings. That is Mrs Thomas.'

But for the moment, in my memory, the poet is forever asleep on the floor while on a balcony high up in the second story of Dawn's living-room, a grey blurred figure appears and stares down at us. 'Who,' I ask, 'is that?'

Dawn gently, lovingly, stirs the Martinis, squints her eyes, says, 'My husband, I think. It is Joe, isn't it, Coby?' She turns to Coby, who beams and waves at the gray man, who withdraws. 'Of course it is,' says Coby. 'Looking very fit.' I realize, at last, that this is a *ménage à trois* in Greenwich Village. My Martini runs over.

2

To date the only study of Dawn Powell's is a doctoral dissertation by Judith Faye Pett (University of Iowa, 1981). Miss Pett has gathered together a great deal of biographical material for which one is grateful. I am happy to know, at last, that the amiable Coby's proper name was Coburn Gilman, and I am sad to learn that he survived Dawn by only two years. The husband on the balcony was Joseph Gousha, or Goushé, whom she married on November 20, 1920. He was musical; she literary, with a talent for the theatre. A son was born retarded. Over the years, a fortune was spent on schools and nurses. To earn the fortune, Powell did every sort of writing, from interviews in the press to stories for ladies' magazines to plays that tended not to be produced to a cycle of novels about the Midwest, followed by a cycle of New York novels, where she came into her own, dragging our drab literature screaming behind her. As doyenne of the Village, she held court in the grill of the Lafayette Hotel (for elegiasts, the

Lafayette was off Washington Square, at University Place and Ninth Street).

Powell also runs like a thread of purest brass through Edmund Wilson's *The Thirties*: 'It was closing time in the Lafayette Grill, and Coby Gilman was being swept out from under the table. Niles Spencer had been stuttering for five minutes, and Dawn Powell gave him a crack on the jaw and said, "*Nuts* is the word you're groping for."' Also, '[Peggy Bacon] told me about Joe Gousha's attacking her one night at a party and trying to tear her clothes off ... I suggested that Joe had perhaps simply thought that this was the thing to do in Dawn's set. She said, "Yes: he thought it was a social obligation."' Powell also 'said that Dotsy's husband was very much excited because the Prince of Wales was wearing a zipper fly, a big thing in the advertising business.' A footnote to this text says that 'Dawn Powell (1897–1965)' and Wilson carried on a correspondence in which she was Mrs Humphry Ward and he 'a seedy literary man named Wigmore'. Later, there is a very muddled passage in which, for reasons not quite clear, James Thurber tells Dawn Powell that she does not *deserve* to be in the men's room. That may well be what it was all about.

I have now read all of Powell's novels and one of the plays* Miss Pett provides bits and pieces from correspondence and diaries, and fragments of bookchat. Like most writers, Powell wrote of what she knew. Therefore, certain themes recur, while the geography does not vary from that of her actual life. As a child, she and two sisters were shunted about from one midwestern farm or small town to another by a father who was a salesman on the road (her mother died when she was six). The maternal grand-

---

* I have omitted an interesting short novel because it is not part of the New York cycle. Powell made one trip to Europe after the war. Although Paris was no match for the Village, Powell, ever thrifty, uses the city as a background for a young man and woman trapped in *A Cage for Lovers* (published the year that Dawn roared at me in the Booth Theatre). The girl is a secretary-companion to a monster-lady, and the young man her chauffeur. The writing is austere; there are few characters; the old lady, Lesley Patterson, keeper of the cage, is truly dreadful in her loving kindness. In a rather nice if not perhaps too neat ending, they cage *her* through her need to dominate. Thus, the weak sometimes prevail.

mother made a great impression on her and predisposed her towards boarding-house life (as a subject not a residence). Indomitable old women, full of rage and good jokes, occur in both novel cycles. At twelve, Powell's father remarried, and Dawn and sisters went to live on the stepmother's farm. 'My stepmother, one day, burned up all the stories I was writing, a form of discipline I could not endure. With thirty cents earned by picking berries I ran away, ending up in the home of a kind aunt in Shelby,Ohio.' After graduation from the local high school, she worked her way through Lake Erie College for Women in Painesville, Ohio. I once gave a commencement address there and was struck by how red-brick New England Victorian the buildings were. I also found out all that I could about their famous alumna. I collected some good stories to tell her. But by the time I got back to New York she was dead.

Powell set out to be a playwright. One play ended up as a movie while another, *Big Night*, was done by the Group Theatre in 1933. But it was the First World War not the theatre that got Powell out of Ohio and to New York in 1918, as a member of the Red Cross: The war ended before her uniform arrived. Powell wrote publicity. Married. Wrote advertising copy (at the time Goushé or Gousha was an account executive with an advertising agency). Failure in the theatre and need for money at home led her to novel writing and the total security of that five-hundred-dollar advance each of us relied on for so many years. Powell's first novel, *Whither*, was published in 1925. In 1928 Powell published *She Walks in Beauty*, which she always maintained, mysteriously, was really her first novel. For one thing, the Ohio heroine of *Whither* is already in New York City, like Powell herself, working as a syndicated writer who must turn out 30,000 words a week in order to live (in Powell's case to pay for her child's treatments). In a sense, this New York novel was premature; with her second book, Powell turns back to her origins in the Western Reserve, where New Englanders had re-created New England in Ohio; and the tone is dour Yankee, with a most un-Yankeeish wit.

The Ohio cycle begins with *She Walks in Beauty*, which is

dedicated to her husband, Joe. The story is set in Powell's youth before the First World War. The book was written in 1927. Popular writers of the day: Thornton Wilder had published *The Bridge of San Luis Rey* in the same year as Powell's first but really second novel. Louis Bromfield received the Pulitzer Prize for *Early Autumn* (a favourite Bromfield phrase, 'candy pink and poison green', occasionally surfaces in Powell) while Cather's *Death Comes for the Archbishop* was also published in 1927. The year 1925, of course, had been the most remarkable in our literary history. After satirizing life in the Midwest, Sinclair Lewis brought his hero Arrowsmith to New York City, a pattern Powell was to appropriate in her Ohio cycle. Also in that miraculous year alongside, as it were, *Whither*: Theodore Dreiser's *An American Tragedy*, Dos Passos's *Manhattan Transfer*, Fitzgerald's *The Great Gatsby*. It is interesting that Dreiser, Lewis, Hemingway, Fitzgerald, Dos Passos, and the popular Bromfield were all, like Powell, mid-westerners with a dream of some other great good place – preferably Paris, but Long Island Sound and social climbing would do.

Powell briskly shows us the town of Birchfield. Dorrie is the dreamy, plain, bright sister (always two contrasting sisters in these early novels); she stands in for Powell. Linda is the vain, chilly one. Aunt Jule keeps a boarding-house. The Powell old lady makes her debut: 'She pinned her muslin gown at the throat, dropped her teeth with a cheerful little click in the glass of water on the table, and turned out the gas.' The 'cheerful' launches us on the Powell style. The story is negligible: who's going to make it out of the sticks first. In the boarding-house there is an old man who reads Greek; his son has already made it to the big city, where he is writing a trilogy. Powell doesn't quite see the fun of this yet. But Dorrie falls for the young man, Dorrie 'with that absurd infantile tilt to her nose' (Dawn to a T). Also Dorrie's tact is very like her creator's. A theatrical couple of a certain age are at the boarding-house. The actress, Laura, tries on a hat. ' "It will look wonderful on Linda," Dorrie vouchsafed pleasantly. 'It's too young for you, Aunt Laura." ' The adverb 'pleasantly' helps make the joke, a point of contention between no-adverbs Graham Greene and myself. I look to the adverb for surprise. Greene thinks that the verb should do all the work.

Dorrie observes her fellow townspeople – nicely? 'He had been such a shy little boy. But the shyness had settled into surliness, and the dreaminess was sheer stupidity. Phil Lancer was growing up to be a good Birchfield citizen.' Points of view shift wildly in Powell's early books. We are in Linda's mind, as she is about to allow a yokel to marry her. 'Later on, Linda thought, after they were married, she could tell him she didn't like to be kissed.' The book ends with Dorrie still dreaming that the trilogist will come and take her off to New York.

In 1929 came *The Bride's House*. One suspects that Powell's own wit was the result of being obliged for so long to sing for her supper in so many strange surroundings: 'Lotta's children arrived . . . three gray, horrid-looking little creatures and their names were Lois and Vera and Custer . . "We've come to stay!" they shouted . . . "We've come to stay on the farm with Uncle Stephen and Aunt Cecily. Aren't you glad?"' No one is, alas. But these children are well-armoured egotists. '"She tells lies," Lois hissed in George's ear. "I'm the pretty one and she's the bright one. She told the conductor we lived in the White House. She's a very bad girl and mother and I can't do a thing with her . . . Everything she says is a lie, Cousin Sophie, except when it hurts your feelings then it's true."' A child after absolutely no one's heart.

Unfortunately, Powell loses interest in the children; instead we are told the story of Sophie's love for two men. The grandmother character makes a dutiful appearance, and the Powell stock company go rather mechanically through their paces. Powell wants to say something original about love but cannot get the focus right: 'A woman needed two lovers, she finally decides, one to comfort her for the torment the other caused her.' This is to be a recurring theme throughout Powell's work and, presumably, life: 'Coby versus Joe? or was it Coby *and* Joe?

\* \* \*

29

*Dance Night* (1930) is the grittiest, most proletarian of the novels. There are no artists or would-be artists in Lamptown. Instead there is a railroad junction, a factory, the Bon Ton Hat Shop, where the protagonists, a mother and son, live close to Bill Delaney's Saloon and Billiard Parlor. Like the country, the town has undergone the glorious 1920s boom; now the Depression has begun to hit. Powell charts the fortunes of the mother-milliner, Elsinore Abbott, and her adolescent son, Morry. Elsinore's husband is a traveling salesman; he affects jealousy of his wife, who has made a go of her shop but given up on her life.

Morry gets caught up in the local real-estate boom. He also gets involved with a waif, Jen, from an orphanage, who has been adopted by the saloon-keeper as a sort of indentured slave. Jen dreams of liberating her younger sister, Lil, from the home where their mother had deposited them. Jen is not much of an optimist: 'People last such a little while with me. There's no way to keep them, I guess, that's why I've got to go back for Lil because I know how terrible it is to be left always – never see people again.' It took Powell a long time to work all this out of her system. Happily, farce intrudes. A young swain in a romantic moment 'slid his hand along her arm biceps and pressed a knuckle in her armpit. "That's the vein to tap when you embalm people," he said, for he was going to be an undertaker.'

The highest work for a Lamptown girl is telephone operator, then waitress, then factory hand. Powell has a Balzacian precision about these things; and she remembers to put the price tag on everything. Money is always a character in her novels, as it was in Balzac's. In fact, Powell makes several references to Balzac in her early books as well as to his Eugénie Grandet.

Morry grows up, and his mother hardly notices him: 'She had moved over for Morry as you would move over for someone on a street car, certain that the intimacy was only for a few minutes, but now it was eighteen years and she thought, why Morry was hers, hers more than anything else in the world was.' This revelation shatters no earth for her or for him; and one can see how distressing such realism must have been – as it still is – for American worshippers of the family; Love, too.

Morry gets involved with a builder who indulges him in his dreams to create handsome houses for a public that only wants small look-alike boxes jammed together. Meanwhile, he loves Jen's sister, Lil, while Jen loves him: a usual state of affairs. The only bit of drama, indeed melodrama, is the return of Morry's father; there is a drunken fight between father and son, then a row between father and Elsinore, whom he accuses, wrongly, of philandering. Finally, 'wearing down her barriers', she reaches for a pistol: 'This was one way to shut out words . . . She raised the gun, closed her eyes and fired.' Although everyone knows that she killed her husband, the town chooses to believe it was suicide, and life goes on. So does Morry, who now realises that he must go away: 'There'd be no place that trains went that he wouldn't go.'

In 1932, Powell published *The Tenth Moon*. This is a somewhat Catheresque novel composed with a fugue-like series of short themes (the influence of her ex-music-critic husband?). Connie Benjamin is a village Bovary, married to a cobbler, with two daughters; she once dreamed of being a singer. Connie lives now without friends or indeed a life of any kind in a family that has not the art of communication with one another. Connie daydreams through life while her daughters fret. ('They went to bed at ten but whispered until twelve, remembering through all their confidences to tell each other nothing for they were sisters.') The husband works in amiable silence. Finally, Connie decides to have a social life. She invites to supper her daughter's English teacher; she also invites the music teacher, Blaine Decker, an exquisite bachelor, as adrift as Connie in dreams of a career in music that might have been.

Powell now introduces one of her major themes: the failed artist who, with luck, might have been – what? In dreams, these characters are always on stage; in life, they are always in the audience. But Blaine has actually been to Paris with his friend, a glamorous one-shot novelist, Starr Donnell (Glenway Wescott?).

Blaine and Connie complement and compliment each other. Connie realises that she has been 'utterly, completely, hideously unhappy' for fifteen years of marriage. Yet each pretends there are compensations to village life and poverty. '"Isn't it better, I've often thought," she said, "for me to be here keeping up with my interests in music, keeping my ideals, than to have failed as an opera singer and been trapped into cheap musical comedy work?"' To hear them tell it, they are as one in the contentment of failure.

But Blaine still hears his mother's voice from offstage, a Powell-esque killer: 'I sometimes wonder, Blaine, if I didn't emphasize the artistic too much in your childhood, encouraging you and perhaps forcing you beyond your real capacity in music. It was only because you did so poorly in school, dear . . .' Powell always knows just how much salt a wound requires.

Although the dreamers 'talked of music until the careers they once planned were the careers they actually had but given up for the simple joys of living', knowing 'success would have destroyed us', Connie goes too far. First, she tries indeed to sing and, for an instant, captures whatever it was she thought that she had and promptly haemorrhages – tuberculosis. Second, she confides to Blaine that she lost a career, home, virginity to Tony the Daredevil, a circus acrobat, who abandoned her in Atlantic City, where the kindly cobbler met and married her. He needed a wife; she could not go home. Blaine is made furious by the truth.

Then daughter Helen runs off with a boy, and the dying Connie pursues her. She finds that Helen has not only managed to get herself a job with a theatrical stock company but she is about to drop the boy; and Connie 'knew almost for a certainty that Helen would climb the heights she herself had only glimpsed.' Connie goes home to die, and Powell shifts to the dying woman's point of view:

When Dr Arnold's face flashed on the mirror she thought, 'This must be the way one dies. People collect on a mirror like dust and something rushes through your mind emptying all the drawers and shelves to see if you're leaving anything behind' . . . What a pity, she thought, no one will ever know these are my last thoughts – that Dr Arnold's mouth was so small.

At the end Connie is spared nothing, including the knowledge that her husband never believed that she came of a good family and studied music and only fell once from grace with an acrobat. Blaine goes off to Paris as a tour guide.

With *The Story of a Country Boy* (1934) she ends the Ohio cycle. This is the most invented of the novels. There is no pretty sister, no would-be artist, no flight from village to city. Instead Powell tells the story of a conventional young man, a country boy, who becomes a great success in business; then he fails and goes home to the country, no wiser than before. Ironically, Powell was doing the exact reverse in her own life, putting down deep lifelong roots in that village called Greenwich, far from her own origins. In a sense, this book is a goodbye to all that.

Again, one gets the boom and bust of the Twenties and early Thirties. Chris Bennett is the all-American boy who makes good. He is entirely self-confident and sublimely unaware of any limitations. Yet, in due course, he fails, largely because he lacks imagination. There is a good deal of Warren Harding, Ohio's favourite son, in his makeup. He is more striking-appearance than reality. Also, Powell was becoming more and more fascinated by the element of chance in life, as demonstrated by Harding's incredible election (those were simple times) to the presidency. 'Chris could not remember ever being unsure of himself except in little details of social life where his defects were a source of pride rather than chagrin.' He also wonders 'if pure luck had brought him his success'. He is right to wonder: it has. When he finally looks down from the heights he falls. No fatal flaw – just vertigo.

A splendid new character has joined the stock company, a former US senator who sees in Chris the sort of handsome mediocrity that, properly exploited, could be presidential. John J. Habbiman's drunken soliloquies are glorious:

33

'Tell them I died for Graustark,' said the Senator in a faraway voice. He somberly cracked peanuts and ate them, casting the shells lightly aside with infinite grace. 'What wondrous life is this I lead. Ripe apples drop about my head.'

Powell also developed an essayistic technique to frame her scenes. A chapter will begin with a diversion:

In the utter stillness before dawn a rat carpentered the rafters, a nest of field mice seduced by unknown applause into coloratura ambitions, squeaked and squealed with amateur intensity . . . Here, at daybreak, a host of blackbirds were now meeting to decide upon a sun, and also to blackball from membership in the committee a red-winged blackbird.

Unfortunately, her main character is too schematic to interest her or the reader. In any case, except for one final experiment, she has got Ohio out of her system; she has also begun to write more carefully, and the essays make nice point counterpoint to the theatricality of her scene writing.

The theatre is indeed the place for her first New York invention, *Jig Saw* (1934), a comedy. The gags are generally very good but the plotting is a bit frantic. Claire is a charming lady, whose eighteen-year-old daughter, Julie, comes to stay with her in a Manhattan flat. Claire has a lover; and a best woman friend to make the sharper jokes. Julie 'is a very well brought up young lady – easy to see she has not been exposed to home life.' Again it takes two to make a mate: 'It takes two women to make your marriage a success.' To which Claire's lover, Del, responds, 'Have it your way – then Claire and I have made a success of my marriage to Margaret.'

A young man, Nathan, enters the story. Both mother and daughter want him. Julie proves to be more ruthless than Claire. Julie moves in on Nathan and announces their coming marriage to the press. He is appalled; he prefers her mother. But Julie is steel: 'I can make something of you, Nate. Something marvelous.' When he tries to talk her out of marriage, she declares, 'I expect to go through life making sacrifices for you, dear, giving up my career for you.' When he points out that she has never had a career, she rises to even greater heights: 'I know. That's what makes it all the more of a sacrifice. I've never had a career. I never will have. Because I love you so much.' Nate is trapped. Claire wonders if she should now marry Del, but he advises against it: 'You're the triangular type . . .' With a bit of the sort of luck that so fascinated Powell by its absence in most lives, she might have had a successful commercial career in the theatre. But that luck never came her way in life, as opposed to imagination. Finally, Powell's bad luck on Broadway was to be our literature's gain.

## 3

The New York cycle begins with *Turn, Magic Wheel* (1936), dedicated to Dwight Fiske, a sub-Coward nightclub performer for whom Powell wrote special material. Powell now writes about a writer, always an edgy business. Dennis Orphen is a male surrogate for Powell herself. He is involved with two women, of course. He is also on the scene for good: he reappears in almost all her books, and it is he who writes finis to *The Golden Spur*, some twenty years later, as the Lafayette Hotel is being torn down and he realises that his world has gone for good. But in 1936 Dennis is eager, on the make, fascinated by others: 'his urgent need to know what they were knowing, see, hear, feel what they were seeing, for a brief moment to *be* them.' He is consumed by a curiosity about others which time has a pleasant way of entirely sating.

Corinne is the profane love, a married woman; Effie is sacred love, the abandoned wife of a famous writer called Andrew Callingham, Hemingway's first appearance in Powell's work. Effie is a keeper of the flame; she pretends that Andrew will come back: 'Why must she be noble, frail shoulders squared to defeat, gaily confessing that life was difficult but that was the way things were?' Dennis publishes a *roman à clef*, whose key unlocks the Callingham/

Hemingway story, and he worries that Effie may feel herself betrayed because Dennis completely dispels her illusion that the great man will return to her. As Dennis makes his New York rounds, the Brevoort Café, Longchamps, Luchow's, he encounters Okie, the ubiquitous man about town who will reappear in the New York novels, a part of their Balzacian detail. Okie edits an entertainment guide magazine, writes a column, knows everyone, and brings everyone together. A party is going on at all hours in different parts of the town, and Powell's characters are always on the move, and the lines of their extramarital affairs cross and recross. The essays now grow thoughtful and there are inner soliloquies:

> Walter missed Bee now but sometimes he thought it was more fun talking to Corinne about how he loved Bee than really being with Bee, for Bee never seemed to want to be alone with him, she was always asking everyone else to join them. In fact the affair from her point of view was just loads of fun and that was all. She never cried or talked about divorce or any of the normal things, she just had a fine time as if it wasn't serious at all.

Powell is much concerned with how people probably ought to behave but somehow never do. The drinking is copious: 'Corinne went into the ladies room and made up again. It was always fun making up after a few pernods because they made your face freeze so it was like painting a statue.' Of course, 'Walter was as mad as could be, watching the cunning little figure in the leopard coat and green beret patter out of the room.' Whenever 'cunning' or 'gaily' or 'tinkling' is used, Powell is stalking dinner, with the precision of a sabre-toothed tiger. She also notes those 'long patient talks, the patient civilized talks that, if one knew it, are the end of love.'

There are amusing incidents rather than a plot of the sort that popular novels required in those days: Effie is hurt by Orphen's portrayal of her marriage in his book; Corinne vacillates between husband and lover; the current Mrs Callingham goes into hospital to die of cancer. There are publishers who live in awe of book reviewers with names like Gannett, Hansen, Paterson. One young publisher 'was so brilliant that he could tell in advance that in the years 1934–35 and -36 a book would be called exquisitely well-written if it began: "The boxcar swung out of the yards. Pip rolled over in the straw. He scratched himself where the straw itched him."' Finally, the book's real protagonist is the city:

> In the quiet of three o'clock the Forties looked dingy, deserted, incredibly nineteenth century with the dim lamps in dreary doorways; in these midnight hours the streets were possessed by their ancient parasites, low tumble-down frame rooming houses with cheap little shops, though by day such remnants of another decade retreated obscurely between flamboyant hotels.

*That* city is now well and truly gone.

'Fleetingly, Effie thought of a new system of obituaries in which the lives recorded were criticized, mistaken steps pointed out, structure condemned, better paths suggested.' This is the essence of Dawn Powell: the fantastic flight from the mundane that can then lead to a thousand conversational variations; and the best of her prose is like the best conversation where no *escalier* is ever wit's receptacle. As a result, she is at her best with The Party; but then most novels of this epoch were assembled around The Party, where the characters proceed to interact and the unsayable gets said. Powell has a continuing hostess who is a variation on Peggy Guggenheim, collecting artists for gallery and bed. There is also a minor hostess, interested only in celebrities and meaningful conversation. She quizzes Dennis: '"Now let's talk," she commanded playfully [Powell's adverbs are often anaesthetic preparatory for surgery]. "We've never really had a nice talk, have we, Dennis? Tell me how you came to write? I suppose you had to make money so you just started writing, didn't you?"' Callingham himself comes to The Party. Powell's affection for the real Hemingway did not entirely obscure his defects, particularly as viewed by an ex-wife, Effie, who discovers to her relief 'there was no Andy left, he had been wiped out by Callingham the Success as so many men

before him had been wiped out by the thing they represented.'
Effie frees herself from him and settles back into contented
triangularity with Dennis and Corinne. Cake had; ingested, too.

In 1938, with *The Happy Island*, the Powell novel grows more
crowded and The Party is bigger and wilder. This time the rustic
who arrives in the city is not a young woman but a young man.
Powell is often more at home with crude masculine protagonists,
suspecting, perhaps, that her kind of tough realism might cause
resentment among those who think of women as the fair sex.

A would-be playwright, Jeff Abbott (related to Morry?), arrives
on the bus from Silver City; a manager has accepted his play with
the ominous telegram, CASTING COMPLETE THIRD ACT NEEDS REWRIT-
ING [like that of *Jig Saw*] COME IMMEDIATELY. Jeff has two friends in
the city. One is Prudence Bly, a successful nightclub singer; the
other is Dol, a gentleman party-giver and fancier of young men. At
the book's end, Dol gives great offence by dying, seated in a chair,
at his own party. How like him! the guests mutter.

Prudence is the most carefully examined of Powell's women. She
is successful; she drinks too much; she is seldom involved with
fewer than two men. But it is the relationships between women
that make Powell's novels so funny and original. Jean Nelson, a
beautiful dummy, is Prudence's best friend; each needs the other
to dislike. At the novel's beginning, Jean has acquired Prudence's
lover Steve. The two girls meet for a serious drunken chat over
lunch. 'You aren't jealous of me, are you, Prudence?' '*Jealous?*
Jealous? Good God, Jean, you must think this is the Middle Ages!'
Prudence then broods to herself:

> Why do I lunch with women anyway? . . . We always end up
> sniveling over men and life and we always tell something that
> makes us afraid of each other for weeks to come . . . Women
> take too much out of you, they drink too much and too
> earnestly. They drink the way they used to do china painting,
> and crewel work and wood burning.

38

In the restaurant things grow blurred: '"You're so good to everyone," sighed Jean. "You really are." Nothing could have enraged Prudence more or been more untrue.' Finally, Jean goes: 'Prudence looked meditatively after Jean as she wove her way earnestly through tables and knees. The girl did look like a goddess but the trouble was she walked like one, too, as if her legs had been too long wound in a flag.'

Prudence's forebears include, yet again, the eccentric grand-mother. This one is rich, and 'Prudence was always glad her grandmother had been neither kind nor affectionate.' The escape from Silver City had been easy. The grandmother was indifferent to everyone, including 'her surly young Swedish chauffeur'. A great traveller, Mrs Bly 'always wanted to buy one dinner with two plates, as if he were a Pekinese, and, more alarming still, to take one room in the hotels where they stayed ... After all, she explained, she always slept with her clothes on so there was nothing indecent in it.' In addition, Mrs Bly is a sincere liar, who believes that she was on the *Titanic* when it was sunk; and was courted by the Czar.

Jeff Abbott and Prudence meet. They have an affair. Jeff is sublimely humourless, which intrigues Prudence. He is also a man of destiny, doomed to greatness in the theatre. '"I never yet found anything to laugh at in this world," said Jeff. "You never heard of a great man with a sense of humor, did you? Humor's an anesthetic, that's all, laughing gas while your guts are jerked out."' Since they are not made for each other, marriage is a real possibility. Prudence is growing unsure of herself:

> She could not find the place where the little girl from Ohio, the ambitious, industrious little village girl, merged into the *Evening Journal* Prudence Bly, the *Town and Country* Bly. There were queer moments between personalities, moments such as the hermit crab must have scuttling from one stolen shell to the next one ... Prudence Bly was not so much a person as a conspiracy.

Then Powell, in a quick scuttle, briefly inhabits her own shell:

Prudence slew with a neat epithet, crippled with a true word, then, seeing the devastation about her and her enemies growing, grew frightened of revenge, backed desperately, and eventually found the white flag of Sentimentality as her salvation. For every ruinous *mot* she had a tear for motherhood.

The failure of Jeff's powerful play does not disturb him, and Prudence is somewhat awed since worldly success is the only thing that makes the island happy. But 'he belongs to the baffling group of confident writers who need no applause. For them a success is not a surprise but cause for wonder that it is less than international . . . A failure proves that a man is too good for his times.' When he says he wants to buy a farm in the Midwest and settle down and write, Prudence is astonished. When he does exactly that, she goes with him. Integrity at last. No more glamour. No more happy island. Only fields, a man, a woman. In no time at all, she is climbing the walls and heading back to New York where she belongs. Since Jean has let go of Steve, he receives her amiably (but then hardly anyone has noticed her departure). The book ends with: 'Prudence's looks, [Steve] reflected with some surprise, were quite gone. She really looked as hard as nails, but then so did most women eventually.' That excellent worldly novelist Thackeray never made it to so high a ground.

*Angels on Toast* (1940); war has begun to darken the skyline. But the turning wheel's magic is undiminished for Ebie, a commercial artist, whose mother is in the great line of Powell eccentrics. Ebie lives with another working woman, Honey, who 'was a virgin (at least you couldn't prove she wasn't), and was as proud as punch of it. You would have thought that it was something that had been in the family for generations.' But Ebie and Honey need each other to talk at, and in a tavern

> where O. Henry used to go . . . they'd sit in the dark smoked-wood booth drinking old-fashioneds and telling each other things they certainly wished later they had never told and

bragging about their families, sometimes making them hot-stuff socially back home, the next time making them romantically on the wrong side of the tracks. The family must have been on wheels back in the Middle West, whizzing back and forth across tracks at a mere word from the New York daughters.

Brooding over the novel is the downtown Hotel Ellery. For seventeen dollars a week Ebie's mother, Mrs Vane, lives in contented genteel squalor.

> BAR and GRILL: it was the tavern entrance to a somewhat medieval looking hotel, whose time-and-soot-blackened façade was frittered with fire-escapes, . . . its dark oak-wainscoting rising high to meet grimy black walls, its ship windows covered with heavy pumpkin chintz . . . Once in you were in for no mere moment . . . The elderly lady residents of the hotel were without too much obvious haste taking their places in the grill-room, nodding and smiling to the wait-resses, carrying their knitting and a slender volume of some English bard, anything to prop against their first Manhattan . . . as they sipped their drinks and dipped into literature. It was sip and dip, sip and dip until cocktail time was pro-claimed by the arrival of the little cocktail sausage wagon.

In its remoteness, this world before television could just as easily be that of *St Ronan's Well*.

It is also satisfying that in these New York novels the city that was plays so pervasive a role. This sort of hotel, meticulously described, evokes lost time in a way that the novel's bumptious contemporary, early talking movies, don't.

> Another curious thing about these small, venerable, respect-able hotels, there seemed no appeal here to the average newcomer. BAR and GRILL, for instance, appealed to seem-ingly genteel widows and spinsters on small incomes . . . Then there were those tired flashes-in-the-pan, the one-shot celeb-rities, and, on the other hand, there was a gay younger group

whose loyalty to the BAR and GRILL was based on the cheapness of its martinis. Over their simple dollar lunches (four martinis and a sandwich) this livelier set snickered at the older residents.

Ebie wants to take her mother away from all this so that they can live together in Connecticut. Mrs Vane would rather die. She prefers to lecture the bar on poetry. There is also a plot: two men in business, with wives. One has an affair with Ebie. There is a boom in real estate; then a bust. By now, Powell has mastered her own method. The essay-beginings to chapters work smartly:

> In the dead of night wives talked to their husbands, in the dark they talked and talked while the clock on the bureau ticked sleep away, and the last street cars clanged off on distant streets to remoter suburbs, where in new houses bursting with mortgages and the latest conveniences, wives talked in the dark, and talked and talked.

The prose is now less easygoing; and there is a conscious tightening of the language although, to the end, Powell thought one thing was different *than* another while always proving not her mettle but metal.

Powell is generally happiest in the BAR and GRILL or at the Lafayette or Brevoort. But in *A Time to Be Born* (1942) she takes a sudden social leap, and lands atop the town's social Rockies. Class is the most difficult subject for American writers to deal with as it is the most difficult for the English to avoid. There are many reasons. First, since the Depression, the owners of the Great Republic prefer not to be known to the public at large. Celebrities, of the sort that delight Powell, fill the newspapers while the great personages are seldom, if ever, mentioned; they are also rarely to be seen in those places where public and celebrities go to mingle. 'Where', I asked the oldest of my waiter-acquaintances at the Plaza (we've known each other forty years), 'have the nobles gone?'

He looked sad. 'I'm told they have their own islands now. Things' – he was vague – 'like that.'

As I read my way through Powell, I noted how few names she actually does drop. There is a single reference to the late Helen Astor, which comes as a mild shock. Otherwise the references are no more arcane than Rockefeller equals money (but then John D. had hired the first press agent). In a sense, Midwesterners were the least class-conscious of Americans during the first half of the twentieth century and those who came from the small towns (Hemingway, Dreiser, Powell herself) ignore those drawing-rooms where Henry James was at home amongst pure essences, whose source of wealth is never known but whose knowledge of what others know is all that matters. Powell, agreeably, knows exactly how much money everyone makes (not enough) and what everything costs (too much). As for value, she does her best with love, but suspects the times are permanently inflationary for that overhyped commodity. Powell never gets to Newport, Rhode Island, in her books but she manages Cape Cod nicely. She inclines to the boozy meritocracy of theatre and publishing and the art world both commercial and whatever it is that Fifty-seventh Street was and is.

But in *A Time to Be Born*, she takes on the highest level of the meritocracy (the almost-nobles) in the form of a powerful publisher and his high-powered wife, based, rather casually, on Mr and Mrs Henry Luce. At last Powell will have a fling at those seriously important people Diana Trilling felt that she was not up to writing about. But since one person is pretty much like another, all are as one in art, which alone makes the difference. Humble Ebie is neither more nor less meaningful than famous Amanda. It's what's made of them in art. Powell does have a good deal of fun with Julian and Amanda Evans, and the self-important grandeur of their lives. But Powell has no real interest in power or, more to this particular point, in those whose lives are devoted to power over others. Powell is with the victims. The result is that the marginal characters work rather better than the principals. One never quite believes that Julian owns and operates sixteen newspapers. One does believe Vicki Haven, who comes from the same Ohio town as Amanda, authoress of a *Forever Amber* best-seller that has been written for her by the best pen-persons and scholar-squirrels that Julian's money can buy. Ken Saunders, a reasonably failed hack, gets Powell's full attention: he is a friend of Dennis Orphen, who makes an obligatory appearance or two as does the great novelist, Andrew Callingham, still hugely at large.

Powell sets *A Time* (magazine?) *To Be Born* in that time *not* to be born, the rising war in the West:

> This was a time when the true signs of war were the lavish plumage of the women; Fifth Avenue dress shops and the finer restaurants were filled with these vanguards of war. Look at the jewels, the rare pelts, the gaudy birds on elaborate hair-dress and know that war was here; already the women had inherited the earth. The ominous smell of gunpowder was matched by a rising cloud of Schiaparelli's *Shocking*. The women were once more armed, and their happy voices sang of destruction to come . . . This was a time when the artists, the intellectuals, sat in cafés and in country homes and accused each other over their brandies or their California vintages of traitorous tendencies. This was a time for them to band together in mutual antagonism, a time to bury the professional hatchet, if possible in each other . . . On Fifth Avenue and Fifty-fifth Street hundreds waited for a man on a hotel window ledge to jump; hundreds waited with craning necks and thirsty faces as if this single person's final gesture would solve the riddle of the world. Civilization stood on a ledge, and in the tension of waiting it was a relief to have one little man jump.

I know of no one else who has got so well the essence of that first war-year before we all went away to the best years of no one's life.

. Again the lines of love and power cross and recross as they do in novels and often, too, in life. Since Julian publishes newspapers and magazines and now propaganda for England, much of it written in his wife's name, there is a Sarrautesque suspicion of language in Powell's reflections. A publisher remarks, 'A fact changes into a lie the instant it hits print.' But he does not stop there. 'It's not print, it's the word,' he declares. 'The Spoken Word, too. The lie forms as soon as the breath of thought hits air. You hear your own words and say – "That's not what I mean ..."' Powell is drawing close to the mystery of literature, life's quirky – quarkish – reflection.

Amanda's power world does not convince quite as much as the Village life of Vicki and Ken and Dennis Orphen. Earlier readers will be happy to know that cute Corinne 'had considered leaving her husband for Dennis Orphen for two or three years, and during her delay' the husband had divorced her, 'with Corinne still confused by this turn of events ... She wanted a little more time to consider marrying Dennis.' When in doubt, do nothing, is the Powellesque strategy for life. Ken goes back and forth between Amanda and Vicki. For a time Amanda is all-conquering:

> She knew exactly what she wanted from life, which was, in a word, everything. She had a genuine distaste for sexual intimacy ... but there were so many things to be gained by trading on sex and she thought so little of the process that she itched to use it as currency once again.

This time with the great writer-hunter Callingham. As it is, ironically, she gets knocked up by Ken and falls out with Julian. But she is never not practical: on the subject of writing, she believes that 'the tragedy of the Attic poets, Keats, Shelley, Burns was not that they died young but that they were obliged by poverty to do all their own writing.' Amanda's descendants are still very much with us: sweet lassies still saddened at the thought of those too poor to hire someone who will burn with a bright clear flame, as he writes their books for them.

It is plain that Powell was never entirely pleased with the Ohio cycle. She had a tendency to tell the same story over and over again, trying out new angles, new points of view, even – very occasionally – new characters. Finally, in mid-war, she made one last attempt to get Ohio (and herself) right. *My Home Is Far Away* (1944) is lapidary – at least compared to the loose early works. New York has polished her style; the essays glitter convincingly. The rural family is called Willard. A Civil War veteran for a grandfather; missing the odd eye, limb. Two sisters again: Lena the pretty one, Marcia the bright one. Powell again holds up the mirror to her past. 'The uncanniness of [Marcia's] memory was not an endearing trait; invariably guests drew respectfully away from the little freak and warmed all the more to the pretty unaffected normalcy of little Lena.' The book begins when father, mother, daughters leave a contented home. Suddenly, there is a nightmare vision: A man in a balloon floats across a starry sky. Home is now forever far away.

Too clever by more than half and too much obliged throughout a peripatetic childhood to sing for a supper prepared by tone-deaf strangers, Powell hammered on the comic mask and wore it to the end. But when the dying mother has a horrendous vision of the man in the balloon, the mask blinks – for the last time.

Aunt Lois has a boarding-house. The girls work. The old ladies are more than ever devastating. ' "A grandmother doesn't like children any more than a mother does," she declared. "Sometimes she's just too old to get out of tending them, that's all, but I'm not." ' Lena goes first. Then Marcia leaves town, as Powell left town, and catches that train 'which will go everywhere on earth that is not home'. On a foggy pane of glass, she writes, with her finger, *Marcia Willard*. Dawn Powell.

4

After the war, Powell returned to the New York cycle for good. She published a book of short stories, *Sunday, Monday and Always* (1952). There are occasional ill-omened visits back home but no longer does she describe the escape; she has escaped for good. There are some nice comic moments. Edna, a successful actress, comes home to find her rustic family absorbed in radio soap operas. Although she is quite willing to describe her exciting life, the family out-manoeuvres her. ' "Well, Edna," cackled Aunt Meg, hugging her. "I declare I wouldn't have known you. Well, you can't live that life and not have it show, they tell me." ' The 'they tell me' is masterful. Powell's ear for the cadences of real-life talk only improved with time.

The final New York novels, *The Locusts Have No King* (1948), *The Wicked Pavilion* (1954), and *The Golden Spur* (1962), demonstrate Powell's ultimate mastery of subject, art, self. Where the last two are near-perfect in execution, *The Locusts Have No King* ('yet they, all of them, go forth by bands': *Proverbs*) shares some of the helter-skelterness of the early books. It is as if before Powell enters her almost-benign Prospero phase, she wants to cut loose once more at The Party.

This time the literary scene of the Forties gets it. The protagonist, Frederick Olliver, is a young man of integrity (a five-hundred-dollar-advance man) and literary distinction and not much will. He has been having an affair with Lyle, part of a married team of writers: Lyle is all taste and charm. But Frederick Olliver meets Dodo in a bar. Dodo is deeply, unrepentantly vulgar and self-absorbed. She says, 'Pooh on you', and talks baby talk, always a sign for Powell of Lilithian evil. They meet in one of Powell's best bars downtown, off Rubberleg Square, as she calls it. The habitués all know one another in that context and, often, no other: parallel lives that are contiguous only in the confines of a cozy bar.

Frederick takes Dodo to a publisher's party (our friend Dennis is there) and Dodo manages to appal. Lyle is hurt. Everyone is slightly fraudulent. A publisher who respects Frederick's integrity offers him the editorship of *Haw*, a low publication which of course Frederick makes a success of. Lyle writes her husband's plays. There is a literary man who talks constantly of Jane Austen, whom he may not have read, and teaches at the League for Cultural Foundations (a.k.a. The New School), where 'classes bulged with middle-aged students anxious to get an idea of what it would be like to have an idea'. But under the usual bright mendacities of happy island life, certain relationships work themselves out. The most Powellesque is between two commercial artists, Caroline and Lorna:

> Ever since their marriages had exploded Caroline and Lorna had been in each other's confidence, sharing a bottle of an evening in Lorna's studio or Caroline's penthouse. In fact they had been telling each other everything for so many years over their cups that they'd never heard a word each other had said.

In an ecstasy of female bonding, they discuss their lost husbands:

> They told each other of their years of fidelity – and each lamented the curse of being a one-man woman. Men always took advantage of their virtue and Caroline agreed with Lorna that, honestly, if it could be done over again, she'd sleep with every man who came along instead of wasting loyalty on one undeserving male. After a few drinks, Caroline finally said she had slept with maybe forty or fifty men but only because she was so desperately unhappy. Lorna said she didn't blame anyone in Caroline's domestic situation for doing just that, and many times wished she had not been such a loyal sap about George, but except for a few vacation trips and sometimes being betrayed by alcohol she had really never – well, anyway, she didn't blame anyone.

Revelations bombard deaf ears. 'Frequently they lost interest in dinner once they had descended below the bottle's label and then a remarkable inspiration would come to open a second bottle and repeat the revelations they had been repeating for years to glazed eyes and deaf ears.' Finally, 'Both ladies talked in confidence of their frustrations in the quest for love, but the truth was they had gotten all they wanted of the commodity and had no intention of making sacrifice of comfort for a few Cupid feathers.' Powell was a marvelous sharp antidote for the deep-warm-sincere love novels of that period. Today she is, at the least, a bright counterpoint to our lost-and-found literary ladies.

Powell deals again with the, always to her, mysterious element of luck in people's careers. When one thinks of her own bad luck, the puzzlement has a certain poignancy. But she can be very funny indeed about the admiration that mediocrity evokes on that happy island where it has never been possible to be too phony. Yet when Frederick, free of his bondage to Dodo, returns to Lyle, the note is elegiac: 'In a world of destruction one must hold fast to whatever fragments of love are left, for sometimes a mosaic can be more beautiful than an unbroken pattern.' We all tended to write this sort of thing immediately after Hiroshima, *mon assassin*.

*The Wicked Pavilion* (1954) is the Café Julien is the Lafayette Hotel of real life. The title is from *The Creevey Papers*, and refers to the Prince Regent's Brighton Pavilion, where the glamorous and louche wait upon a mad royal. Dennis Orphen opens and closes the book in his by now familiarly mysterious way. He takes no real part in the plot. He is simply still there, watching the not-so-magic wheel turn as the happy island grows sad. For him, as for Powell, the café is central to his life. Here he writes; sees friends; observes the vanity fair. Powell has now become masterful in her setting of scenes. The essays – preludes, overtures – are both witty and sadly wise. She has also got the number to Eisenhower's American, as she brings together in this penultimate rout all sorts of earlier figures, now grown old: Okie is still a knowing man-about-town and author of the definitive works on the painter Marius; Andy Callingham is still a world-famous novelist, serene in his uncontagious self-love; and the Peggy Guggenheim figure is back again as Cynthia, an art-gallery owner and party-giver. One plot is young love: Rick and Ellenora who met at the Café Julien in wartime and never got enough of it or of each other or of the happy island.

A secondary plot gives considerable pleasure even though Powell lifted it from a movie of the day called *Holy Matrimony* (1943) with Monty Woolley and Gracie Fields, from Arnold Bennett's novel *Buried Alive*. The plot that Powell took is an old one: a painter, bored with life or whatever, decides to play dead. The value of his pictures promptly goes so high that he is tempted to keep on painting after 'death'. Naturally, sooner or later, he will give himself away: Marius paints a building that had not been built before his 'death'. But only two old painter friends have noticed this, and they keep his secret for the excellent reason that one of them is busy turning out 'Marius' pictures, too. Marius continues happily as a sacred presence, enjoying in death the success that he never had in life: 'Being dead has spoiled me,' he observes. It should be noted that the painting for this novel's cover was done by Powell's old friend, Reginald Marsh.

A new variation on the Powell young woman is Jerry: clean-cut, straightforward, and on the make. But her peculiar wholesomeness does not inspire men to give her presents; yet 'the simple truth was that with her increasingly expensive tastes she really could not afford to work . . . As for settling for the safety of marriage, that seemed the final defeat, synonymous in Jerry's mind with asking for the last rites.' An aristocratic lady, Elsie, tries unsuccessfully to launch her. Elsie's brother, Wharton, and sister-in-law, Nita, are fine comic emblems of respectable marriage. In fact, Wharton is one of Powell's truly great and original monsters, quite able to hold his own with Pecksniff:

> Wharton had such a terrific reputation for efficiency that many friends swore that the reason his nose changed colors before your very eyes was because of an elaborate Rimbaud color code, indicating varied reactions to his surroundings . . . Ah, what a stroke of genius it had been for him to have found Nita! How happy he had been on his honeymoon and for years afterward basking in the safety of Nita's childish innocence where his intellectual shortcomings, sexual cold-ness and caprices – indeed his basic ignorance – would not be discovered . . . He was well aware that many men of his quixotic moods preferred young boys, but he dreaded to expose his inexperience to one of his own sex, and after certain cautious experiments realized that his anemic lusts were canceled by his overpowering fear of gossip . . . Against the flattering background of Nita's delectable purity, he blos-

somed forth as the all-round He-man, the Husband who knows everything ... He soon taught her that snuggling, hand-holding, and similar affectionate demonstrations were kittenish and vulgar. He had read somewhere, however, that breathing into a woman's ear or scratching her at the nape of the neck drove her into complete ecstasy ... In due course Nita bore him four daughters, a sort of door prize for each time he attended.

The Party is given by Cynthia now, and it rather resembles Proust's last roundup: 'There are people here who have been dead twenty years,' someone observes, including 'the bore that walks like a man.' There is a sense of closing time; people settle for what they can get. 'We get sick of our clinging vines, he thought, but the day comes when we suspect that the vines are all that hold our rotting branches together.' Dennis Orphen at the end records in his journal the last moments of the wicked pavilion as it falls to the wrecker's ball:

It must be that the Julien was all that these people really liked about each other, for now when they chance across each other in the street they look through each other, unrecogniz- ing, or cross the street quickly with the vague feeling that here was someone identified with unhappy memories – as if the other was responsible for the fall of the Julien.

What had been a stage for more than half a century to a world is gone and 'those who had been bound by it fell apart like straws when the baling cord is cut and remembered each other's name and face as part of a dream that would never come back.'

In 1962, Powell published her last and, perhaps, most appealing novel, *The Golden Spur*. Again, the protagonist is male. In this case a young man from Silver City, Ohio (again), called Jonathan Jaimison. He has come to the city to find his father. Apparently twenty-six years earlier his mother, Connie, had had a brief fling with a famous man in the Village; pregnant, she came home and married a Mr Jaimison. The book opens with a vigorous description of Wanamaker's department store being torn down. Powell is now rather exuberant about the physical destruction of her city (she wrote this last book in her mid-sixties, when time was doing the same to her). There is no longer a Dennis Orphen on the scene; presumably, he lies buried beneath whatever glass-and-cement horror replaced the Lafayette. But there are still a few watering holes from the twenties, and one of them is The Golden Spur, where Connie mingled with the bohemians.

Jonathan stays at the Hotel De Long, which sounds like the Vanderbilt, a star of many of Powell's narratives. Jonathan, armed with Connie's cryptic diary, has a number of names that might be helpful. One is that of Claire van Orphen (related to Dennis?), a moderately successful writer, for whom Connie did some typing. Claire now lives embalmed in past time. She vaguely recalls Connie, who had been recommended to her by the one love of her life, Major Wedburn, whose funeral occurs the day Jonathan arrives at the De Long. Claire gives Jonathan possible leads; meanwhile, his presence has rejuvenated her. She proposes to her twin sister, Bea, that they live together, and gets a firm no. The old nostalgia burned down long ago for the worldly Bea. On the other hand, Claire's career is revived, with the help of a professionally failed writer who gets 'eight bucks for fifteen hundred words of new criticism in a little magazine or forty for six hundred words of old criticism in the Sunday book section.' He studies all of Claire's ladies' magazine short stories of yesteryear; he then reverses the moral angle:

'In those days the career girl who supported the family was the heroine, and the idle wife was the baddie,' Claire said gleefully. 'And now it's the other way round. In the soap operas, the career girl is the baddie, the wife is the goodie because she's better for *business* . . . Well, you were right. CBS has bought the two [stories] you fixed, and Hollywood is interested.'

Powell herself was writing television plays in the age of Eisenhower and no doubt had made this astonishing discovery on her own.

Jonathan is promptly picked up by two girls at The Golden Spur; he moves in with them. Since he is more domestic than they, he works around the house. He is occasionally put to work in bed until he decides that he doesn't want to keep on being 'a diaphragm-tester'. Among his possible fathers is Alvine Harshawe alias Andrew Callingham alias Ernest Hemingway. Alvine is lonely; 'You lost one set of friends with each marriage, another when it dissolved, gaining smaller and smaller batches each time you traded in a wife.' Alvine has no clear memory of Connie but toys with the idea of having a grown son, as does a famous painter named Hugow. Another candidate is a distinguished lawyer, George Terrence, whose actress daughter, unknown to him, is having an affair with Jonathan. Terrence is very much school of the awful Wharton of *The Wicked Pavilion*, only Terrence has made the mistake of picking up a young actor in the King Cole Bar of the St Regis Hotel; the actor is now blithely blackmailing him in a series of letters worthy of his contemporary Pal Joey. Terrence welcomes the idea of a son but Jonathan shies away: he does not want his affair with the daughter to be incestuous.

Finally, Cassie, the Peggy Guggenheim character, makes her appearance, and The Party assembles for the last time. There are nice period touches: girls from Bennington are everywhere. While Cassie herself 'was forty-three – well, all right, forty-eight, if you're going to count every lost weekend – and Hugow's betrayal had happened at birthday time, when she was frightened enough by the half-century mark reaching out for her before she'd even begun to have her proper quota of love,' Cassie takes a fancy to Jonathan and hires him to work at her gallery. He has now figured out not only his paternity but his maternity and, best of all, himself. The father was Major Wedburn, who was, of course, exactly like the bore that his mother, Connie, married. The foster-father appears on the scene, and there is recognition of this if not resolution. As for Connie, she had slept with everyone who asked her because 'she wanted to be whatever anybody expected her to be, because she never knew what she was herself.' Jonathan concludes, 'That's the way I am.' At an art gallery, he says, 'I have a career of other people's talents.'

The quest is over. Identity fixed. The Party over, Jonathan joins Hugow in his cab. 'He was very glad that Hugow had turned back downtown, perhaps to the Spur, where they could begin all over.' On that blithe note, Powell's life and lifework end; and the wheel stops; the magic's gone – except for the novels of Dawn Powell, all of them long since out of print, just as her name has been erased from that perpetually foggy pane, 'American Literature'.

*The New York Review of Books*
5 November 1987

# 4
# REMEMBERING ORSON WELLES

Although Orson Welles was only ten years my senior, he had been famous for most of my life. I was thirteen when he made his famous Martians-are-coming radio broadcast. Then, three years later, when Welles was twenty-six, there was, suddenly, *Citizen Kane*. I was particularly susceptible to *Citizen Kane* because I was brought up among politicians and often saw more of my own father in newsreels than in life, particularly *The March of Time*, whose deep-toned thundering narrator – the voice of history itself – Welles was to evoke in his first film, whose cunning surface is so close to that of newsreel-real life that one felt, literally, at home in a way that one never did in such works of more gorgeous cinematic art as *All This and Heaven Too*.

Five years later, at the Beverly Hills Hotel, I first beheld the relatively lean Orson Welles. ('Note,' Mercury Player Joseph Cotten once told me, 'how Orson either never smiles on camera, or, if he has to, how he sucks in his cheeks so as not to look like a Halloween pumpkin.') On his arm was Rita Hayworth, his wife. He has it all, I remember thinking in a state of perfect awe untouched by pity. Little did I know – did he know? – that just as I was observing him in triumph, the great career was already going off the rails while the Gilda of all our dreams was being supplanted by the even more beautiful Dolores del Rio. Well, Rita never had any luck. As for Welles . . .

As for Welles. First, who – what – was Welles? For the television generation he is remembered as an enormously fat and garrulous man with a booming voice, seen most often on talk shows and in commercials where he somberly assured us that a certain wine would not be sold 'before its time', whatever that meant. But Welles himself was on sale, as it were, long before *his* time in the sense that he was an astonishing prodigy, as Frank Brady records in *Citizen Welles*, a long biography which, blessedly, emphasises the films in detail rather than the set of conflicting humours that made up the man.

Born in Kenosha, Wisconsin, on May 6, 1915, Welles was much indulged by a well-to-do, somewhat arty family. He was a born actor, artist, writer, magician. At fifteen, he ended his schooling. At sixteen, he was acting, successfully, grown-up parts for Dublin's Gate Theatre. At eighteen, he co-edited and illustrated three Shakespeare plays and a commercial textbook, *Everybody's Shakespeare*. At nineteen, he appeared on Broadway as Chorus and Tybalt in *Romeo and Juliet*. At twenty-two, he founded his own acting company, The Mercury Theater, whose greatest success was a modern-dress *Julius Caesar* with Welles as Brutus. The Mercury Theater then took radio by storm, dramatising novels and stories, among them H. G. Wells's *War of the Worlds*, done in a realistic radio way, using the medium to report, moment by moment, the arrival of Martians in New Jersey. The subsequent national panic augurs ill for that inevitable day when Ortega drops his Señor Buén Muchacho mask and nukes Miami.

In due course RKO gave Welles a free hand, if a limited budget, to write, direct, and star in his first film. *Citizen Kane* began a new era in the movies. For those given to making lists, *Citizen Kane* still remains on everyone's list of the ten best films; often as the best film ever made. But for Welles himself things started to fall apart almost immediately. The Hearst newspapers declared war on him for his supposed travesty of Hearst's personal life. On Kane's deathbed, he whispers the word 'Rosebud'. This is thought to be the key, somehow, to his life. In the film it turns out to be a boy's sled, which Mr Stephen Spielberg recently bought for $55,000. In actual life, Rosebud was what Hearst called his friend Marion

Davies's clitoris, the sort of item that producers of children's films tend not to collect. Although the next film, *The Magnificent Ambersons* (1942), might have been even better than *Citizen Kane*, there was trouble with the editing – largely because Welles was in South America, failing to make a film.

For the rest of his life Welles moved restlessly around the world, acting on stage, in movies, on television. As director-actor, he managed to make *Macbeth, Othello, Chimes at Midnight* (the world from Falstaff's point of view). He also invented, as much as anyone did, the so-called film noir with *Journey into Fear* (1943), *The Lady from Shanghai* (1948), *Touch of Evil* (1958).

Everything that Welles touched as a director has a degree of brilliance, here and there, but he was always running out of money not to mention leading ladies, who kept mysteriously changing in his films, because he was often obliged to shut down for long periods of time, and then, when he started again, actors would be unavailable. In *Othello* Desdemona, finally, is a most expressive blonde wig. Meanwhile, Welles took every acting job he could to finance his own films and pay American taxes. We got to know each other in the Sixties, a period which Mr Brady regards as 'the nadir' of Welles's acting career. Well, all I can say is that there was an awful lot of nadir going around in those days. In fact, Welles acted in a nadir film that I had written called *Is Paris Burning?* (it wasn't, to the eternal dismay of Michel Tournier).*

In later years we appeared on television together. 'You see, I have to do the talk shows to keep my lecture price up at the universities.' Orson always acted as if he were broke and, I suppose, relative to the Business, he was. He seemed to live in Spain as well as Hollywood and Las Vegas, 'where I am near the

* I was astonished to read in Frank Brady's *Citizen Welles* that Orson was offered the starring role in *Caligula*, 'but when he read the Gore Vidal script and found it to be a mixture of hard-core pornography and violence, he peremptorily turned it down on moral grounds.' Since Brady also gets the plot to *The Big Brass Ring* wrong, I assumed that he was wrong about Caligula, a part Orson could not have played even if my script for the picture had been used as written. But now, suddenly, I recalled Kenneth Tynan telling me that Orson had been upset by my original script. 'You must never forget what a Puritan he is when it comes to sex.'

airport', he would say mysteriously. 'Also there are no death duties in Nevada unlike, shall we say, Haiti.'

Orson's conversation was often surreal and always cryptic. Either you picked up on it or you were left out. At one point, he asked me to intervene on his behalf with Johnny Carson because there had been a 'misunderstanding' between them and he was no longer asked to go on *The Tonight Show* and his lecture fees had, presumably, plummeted. I intervened. Carson was astonished. There was no problem that he knew of. I reported this to Orson in the course of one of our regular lunches at a French restaurant in Hollywood where Orson always sat in a vast chair to the right of the door. There was a smaller chair for a totally unprincipled small black poodle called Kiki.

'There is more to this than Johnny will ever tell you,' he rumbled. 'Much, much more. Why', he turned to the waiter with cold eyes, 'do you keep bringing me a menu when you know what I must eat? Grilled fish.' The voice boomed throughout the room. 'And iced tea. How I hate grilled fish! But doctor's orders. I've lost twenty pounds. No one ever believes this. But then no one ever believes I hardly eat anything.' He was close to four hundred pounds at the time of our last lunch in 1982. He wore bifurcated tents to which, rather idly, lapels, pocket flaps, buttons were attached in order to suggest a conventional suit. He hated the fat jokes that he was obliged to listen to – on television at least – with a merry smile and an insouciant retort or two, carefully honed in advance. When I asked him why he didn't have the operation that vacuums the fat out of the body, he was gleeful. 'Because I have seen the results of liposuction *when the operation goes wrong*. It happened to a woman I know. First, they insert the catheter in the abdomen, subcutaneously.' Orson was up on every medical procedure. 'The suction begins and the fat – it looks like yellow chicken fat. You must try the chicken here. But then the fat – hers not the chicken's – came out unevenly. And so where once had been a Rubensesque torso, there was now something all hideously rippled and valleyed and canyoned like the moon.' He chuckled and, as always, the blood rose in his face, slowly, from lower lip to

58

forehead until the eyes vanished in a scarlet cloud, and I wondered, as always, what I'd do were he to drop dead of a stroke.

We talked mostly of politics and literature. At our last lunch, I was running in the Democratic primary for Senate. Orson approved. 'I too had political ambitions, particularly back in the FDR days. I used to help him with speeches and I like to think I was useful to him. I know he thought I should have a serious go at politics some day. Well, some day came. They wanted me to run for the Senate in my home state of Wisconsin, against Joe McCarthy. Then I let them – another "them" – convince me that I could never win because', and the chuckle began again, 'I was an actor – hence, frivolous. And divorced – hence, immoral. And now Ronnie Reagan, who is both, is president.' Eyes drowned in the red sea; laughter tolled; then, out of who knows what depths of moral nullity, Kiki bit a waiter's sleeve.

When I observed that acting – particularly old-time movie acting – was the worst possible preparation for the presidency because the movie actor must be entirely passive so that he can do and say exactly what others tell him to do and say, Orson agreed that although this might be true in general (we both excluded *him* from any generality), he had known two movie actors who would have been good presidents. One was Melvyn Douglas. The other was Gregory Peck. 'Of course', he was thoughtful, 'Greg isn't much as an actor, which may explain why he has so good a character.'

During the last year of our occasional meetings, Orson and I were much preoccupied with Rudy Vallée. The popular singer of yesteryear was living in the mansion 'Silvertip' high atop that Hollywood hill halfway up which I sometimes live. When the maestro heard that I was his neighbour, he sent me a copy of his memoirs *Let The Chips Fall* . . . Like a pair of Talmudic scholars, Orson and I constantly studied this astonishing book. Parts of it we memorised:

> Somehow I have never inspired confidence. I don't think it is
> due to any weakness particularly evident in my face, but there

is something about me, possibly a quiet reserve or shyness, that gives most people the impression that I can't do anything very well.

Each of us had his favourite moments. Mine was the telegram (reproduced) that Rudy sent the relatively unknown radio announcer, Arthur Godfrey, in 1940, to show what a keen eye and ear Rudy had for talent (for a time Vallée ran a talent agency). Orson preferred the highly detailed indictment of Rudy's protégé 'The Ungreatfulcholy Dane', Victor Borge, complete with reproductions of inter-office memoranda, telegrams sent and received, culminating in two newspaper cuttings. One headline: 'VICTOR BORGE SUED FOR $750,000'; the other: 'BORGE SUED BY THE IRS'.

As professional storytellers, we were duly awed by Rudy's handling of The Grapefruit Incident, which begins, so casually, at Yale.

> Ironically, the dean was the father of the boy who, nine years later, was to hurl a grapefruit at me in a Boston theater and almost kill me.

Then the story is dropped. Pages pass. Years pass. Then the grapefruit motif is reintroduced. Rudy and his band have played for the dean; afterward, when they are given ice cream, Rudy asks, 'Is this all we're having . . .'

> Apparently one of [the dean's] sons noticed my rather uncivil question . . . and resolved that some day he would avenge this slight. What he actually did later at a Boston theater might have put him in the electric chair and me in my grave but fortunately his aim was bad. But of that more later.

Orson thought this masterful. Appetites whetted, we read on until the now inevitable rendezvous of hero and grapefruit in a Boston theatre where, as Rudy is singing – *Oh, Give Me Something to Remember You By,*

> 'a large yellow grapefruit came hurtling from the balcony. With a tremendous crash it struck the drummer's cymbal

. . .', but 'if it had struck the gooseneck of my sax squarely where it curves into the mouth it might have driven it back through the vertebra in the back of my neck.'

Of this passage, the ecstatic Orson whispered, 'Conrad' – what might have been *if* Lord Jim had remained on watch.

Finally, in a scene reminiscent of Saint-Simon's last evocation of the Duchess of Burgundy, Vallée tells us how he had got the Chairman of the Board himself to come see his house and its rooms of memorabilia. Frank Sinatra dutifully toured room after room of artefacts relating to the master. Although an offending journalist gave 'the impression that most of the pictures portrayed my likeness, actually, one third of the pictures are of neutral subjects or of personalities other than myself.' Even so, 'as Frank Sinatra rather snidely put it as we left this particular corridor, "You would never guess who lived here."'*

In literary matters, Orson was encyclopaedic, with an actor's memory for poetry. I have known few American writers who have had much or, indeed, any enthusiasm for literature. Writers who teach tend to prefer literary theory to literature and tenure to all else. Writers who do not teach prefer the contemplation of Careers to art of any kind. On the other hand, those actors who do read are often most learned, even passionate, when it comes to literature. I think that this unusual taste comes from a thorough grounding in Shakespeare combined with all that time waiting around on movie-sets.

When we had finished with politics and literature and the broiled fish, Orson told me a hilarious story of a sexual intrigue in Yugoslavia during the shooting of Kafka's *The Trial*. How was

* Rudy Vallée scholars will search in vain for the adverb 'snidely' in *Let the Chips Fall* . . . I have taken the liberty of using an earlier version of the Sinatra visit as recorded in *My Time is Your Time* (1962). Even though Rudy Vallée always wrote the same book, he was given to subtle changes, particularly in his use or omission of adverbs, reminiscent, in their mastery, of the grace notes in Bach. A synoptic edition of Vallée's three memoirs is long overdue, as well as a meticulous concordance.

Orson to manoeuvre a willing young woman away from her escort
in a bar that was connected by a dark and creaking staircase to
Orson's room, and then . . . ? Each detail of this labyrinthine tale
was lovingly recounted right up until the final victory in the wrong
bed or room – or something. Orson was a superb dramatizer. As
an actor, he was limited by his unique physical presence and that
great booming conman's voice. But when it came to storytelling,
he was as exciting at a corner table, talking, as he was on the
screen itself in a work all his own. But the tragedy of Welles
('How', I can hear him say, eyes theatrically narrowed to slits in
that great round pudding of a face, 'do you define tragedy?') is
that more time was spent evoking movies at corner tables than in
a studio. Yet he was always seriously at work on a number of
projects that he could never get the financing for.

'This time I've written a political script. Rather your kind of
thing.' He puffed on a cigar. He looked like Harry Lime. 'You
know Paul Newman. Can you put in a word for him? Because if I
don't have one of the Six Bankable Boys, there's no financing.
What one has to go through.' He patted his stomach as if it were
his dog. He looked like Falstaff. 'They always ask me, aren't you
glad, *cher maître*, that the old studio system is finished, that there
are no more vulgar furriers controlling your films? And I say, my
God, how I miss them! Even Harry Cohn. When you make fifty-
two pictures a year on an assembly-line basis there is always room
for an Orson Welles film. But now there is no room anywhere.' He
smoothed the dog's fur as if it were his stomach. Then he chuckled.
'I have made an art form of the interview. The French are the best
interviewers, despite their addiction to the triad, like all Carte-
sians.' I took this well: triad=trinity, but *versus*, I would have
thought, Descartes.

Orson was now in full flow. 'They also have the gift of the
unexpected let-down. The ultimate Zinger. "There are only three
great directors in the history of the film," they will announce. I
smile shyly.' Orson smiles. Cotten was right. Though he doesn't
seem to be sucking in his cheeks, the corners of his mouth are
drawn not up but down. 'There is D. W. Griffith. I roll my eyes

toward Heaven in an ecstasy of agreement. There is Orson Welles. I lower my lids, all modesty – little me? Then,' his voice drops, basso profundissimo, 'there is – Nicholas Ray!' Orson erupts in laughter. We meditate on the interview as art form as well as necessity for Orson, 'because I don't lecture any more.'

'Then why,' I asked, 'did you ask me to ask Carson to get you back on *The Tonight Show* so that you could get more lecture dates when you've given up lecturing?' He looked at me in true surprise. 'Surely I told you I've stopped lecturing because I can't walk from the airport terminal to the gate.' You can use a wheelchair, I said. 'But that would be the end of me as an actor. Word would spread I was terminally ill. Besides there is no wheelchair large enough unless I bring my own, which would make a truly bad impression.'

Orson never knew that I knew how, the previous week, Orson's driver had delivered him to the restaurant's parking lot, only to find that Orson was so tightly wedged in the front seat that the car had to be taken apart so that he could get out.

'If not Newman, there's Nicholson or Beatty. Warren has consented to give me an audience. But Nicholson would be better. The story's called *The Big Brass Ring*, about a senator who's just been defeated by Reagan for president – two years from now, of course. Really right down your alley . . .'

Three years after our last lunch, Orson died at the age of seventy. He had not been able to get one of the Bankable Boys to agree to do *The Big Brass Ring* and so it is now just one more cloudy trophy to provoke one's imagination. What would Welles's Don Quixote have been like if he had been able to finish it? But then it is pleasurable to imagine what he might have done with any theme because he was, literally, a magician, fascinated by legerdemain, tricks of eye, forgeries, labyrinths, mirrors reflecting mirrors. He was a master of finding new ways of seeing things that others saw not at all.

Happily, I now know something about *The Big Brass Ring*, which was published obscurely in 1987 as 'an original screen-play by Orson Welles with Oja Kodar.' Wellesian mysteries begin to swirl.

Who is Oja Kodar? The dust jacket identifies her as Welles's 'companion and collaborator (as actress and screenwriter, among other capacities) over the last twenty years of his life. She is a Yugoslav sculptor who has had one-woman shows in both Europe and the US. The lead actress in *F for Fake* [which I've never seen] and *The Other Side of the Wind* [unreleased], she collaborated on the scripts of both films as well as many other Welles projects' . . . all unmade.

Orson never mentioned her. But then, come to think of it, except for bizarre dreamlike adventures, he never spoke of his private life. In all the years I knew him, I never set foot in any place where he was living, or met his wife, Paola Mori, who died a year after he did. I invited Orson several times to the house where I lived within megaphone distance of the Rudy Vallée shrine and he always accepted, with delight. Then the phone calls would start. 'I know that it is the height of rudeness to ask who will be there, so my rudeness is of the loftiest sort. Who will be there?' I would tell him and he'd be pleased to see so many old friends; finally, an hour before the party began, he'd ring. 'I have an early call tomorrow. For a commercial. Dog food, I think it is this time. No, I do not eat from the can on camera but I *celebrate* the contents. Yes, I have fallen so low.'

Further mysteries: there is an afterword published to the script by Jonathan Rosenbaum, who tells us that Welles left two estates, 'one of them controlled by his wife Paola Mori and daughter Beatrice, . . . the other controlled by Kodar.' Now the two estates appear to be in equilibrium; hence, 'the publication of *The Big Brass Ring* represents a major step forward in the clarification of the invisible Orson Welles, even though it comprises only a piece of the iceberg (or jigsaw puzzle, if one prefers).' I prefer jigsaw puzzle. And now, for me, an essential piece is at hand: the screenplay, which is purest Welles. He is plainly at the top of his glittering form, which was as deeply literary as it was visual.

What, precisely, is 'purest Welles'? Although every line sounds like Welles, we are told that he based some of the story on an autobiographical sketch by Kodar. Thus, they collaborated. But the germ of the story, one of Welles's few 'originals' (a word in this context never to be let out of quotes), was first expressed by Welles in a conversation with the film director Henry Jaglom. Welles said that there was a story that 'he'd been thinking about for years, about an old political adviser to Roosevelt who was homosexual, and whose lover had gotten crippled in the Spanish Civil War fighting the fascists. Now he was in an African kingdom, advising the murderous leader – and back in the US, a young senator who'd been his protégé was going to run against Reagan in 1984, as the Democratic nominee.' So far so Wellesian. The fascination with politics, particularly the New Deal; with homosexuality to the extent that it involves masks and revelation; and, finally, with the relationship between the teacher and the taught.

The action is swift. A series of images – fading campaign posters: the defeated presidential candidate, Pellarin, walks through a restaurant where he is recognised and cheered: he is a combination of Texas Good-Ole-Boy and Harvard Law School. The wife, Diana, is edgy, long-suffering, rich. Then we are aboard a yacht. Pellarin is bored. Diana plays backgammon with a woman friend. Pellarin goes into their bedroom and finds a girl – a manicurist – stealing his wife's emerald necklace. To his own amazement, he tells her, 'Keep it.' With this Gidean *acte gratuit* the story takes off. When a shipwide search for the necklace begins, Pellarin realises that it will be found on the girl; so he makes her give him the jewels; then he promises her that he will turn them over to a fence at the next port, which is Tangiers.

At Tangiers Pellarin books a flight to the African country where his old mentor, Kimball Menaker, is advising the local Idi Amin. At the airport, he is ambushed by Cela Brandini, a superb portrait of the dread Oriana Fallaci in the terminal throes of requited self-love. 'I am Cela Brandini,' she declares with all the authority of a bush afire. 'Of course you are,' he says, mildly. Brandini: 'And I have never asked you for an interview.' Pellarin: 'Guess I'm just plain lucky.' Now Welles can use this second art form, the interview with tape recorder. Brandini has just interviewed Menaker, a figure that Pellarin must never see again because . . . The plot of the emerald necklace crosses with that of the search for Menaker, to be played by Welles at his most oracular, not to mention polymathematical.

As they wait in the airport lounge, Brandini plays for him some of Menaker's dialogue on her recorder, a nice narrative device. Menaker: 'A message? Do I wish to send a message to the Senator from Texas? ex-chairman of the Foreign Affairs Committee? former vedette of the Hasty Pudding Club Review, our future President, and my former friend?' Brandini has interviewed Menaker as background for a piece she wants to do on Pellarin. She is aware that Menaker is the skeleton in Pellarin's closet. Had they been lovers? What glorious scandal! Brandini: 'The way he speaks of you – he seems to think he's your [father].' Pellarin is pleased. She strikes, 'And yet, politically – he almost killed you off.' Pellarin demurs: 'He didn't quite do that, you know – He killed himself.' Mysteries within mysteries. A quest. Nothing now is what it seems. Pellarin, pilgrim.

Pellarin finds Menaker in the Batunga Hilton; he is in bed with a sick monkey while two naked black women play backgammon as they keep guard over him. Although the scene is about finding a fence for the emeralds (Menaker is the author of *The Criminal Underworld Considered as a Primitive Culture – An Anthropological View*: 'I'm an authority on everything,' he says), the subtext concerns a woman, Pellarin's lost love, a Cambodian beauty, last seen by Menaker in Paris.

Pellarin departs with the sick monkey knotted about his neck, hiding the emeralds. He joins the yacht at Barcelona. Brandini is also there. She declaims: 'I'm an anarchist.' Pellarin: 'I wish you were a veterinarian.' Brandini: 'I do not think that monkey has very long to live.' Pellarin: 'Neither do I.' Brandini: 'Interesting.' Pellarin: 'Death? The subject doesn't capture my imagination.' Brandini: 'I know something about it, Pellarin. I've seen it in Vietnam, Central America – in Greece.' Pellarin: 'I know. There's a lot of that stuff going around.' Back on the yacht, Pellarin tries to get the monkey off his neck: it falls into the sea, the emeralds clutched in its fist. How is Pellarin to get the money he 'owes' to the girl?

Meanwhile, Menaker is out of Africa and again in the clutches of Brandini. A reference is made to Menaker's Harvard rival, Henry Kissinger, 'chief brown-noser to the Rockefellers'. Menaker is concerned about Kissinger because: 'He *is* getting *shorter* – Have you noticed that? He's positively *dwindling* with thwarted ambition: Metternich as the incredible shrinking man. They ought to give poor shrinking Henry one last go at State. As a foreigner, there's no higher he can go – and who knows how much smaller he can get.' They speak of Menaker's influence on Pellarin. Menaker seems to him triumphant despite their association, not to mention that of Harvard. These are only minor limitations. Brandini: 'You've spoken of his limitations – What are yours?' Menaker: 'I'm an old man, Miss Brandini – and a faggot. I couldn't use another limitation.'

Pellarin and Menaker meet. Menaker says not to worry about the emeralds: they are false. Diana sold the originals to help get Pellarin elected to Congress. She has worn paste copies ever since. So Pellarin must cash a cheque in order to give money to the girl for the worthless jewels that she stole and Pellarin lost. This is exquisite Welles. And he brings it off with Wildean panache.

Now the story of the emeralds again crosses the story of the lost love in Paris. Apparently, she is in Madrid. She wants to see Pellarin. Menaker will take him to her. Meanwhile they meditate upon identity. Menaker: 'Even the great ones must have sometimes felt uncomfortable in their own skins. Caesar must have dreamt of Alexander, and Napoleon of Caesar.' Pellarin: 'Shit, Professor – I couldn't make their weight.' Menaker: 'Then think of poor Dick Nixon – mincing about inside his fortress in the Oval Room, all bristling with bugs – hoping a playback would eventually inform him who he was . . . He told us often what he *wasn't*, but he never really got it figured out.' Pellarin: 'Neither have I . . . You sly old son of a bitch, so *that's* what you've been getting at.' Menaker: 'In a perfect world, all of us should be allowed some short vacations from our own identities. Last week you were Bulldog Drummond, gentleman jewel thief. Soon you'll be hoping to sneak down that rabbit hole again to where it's always Paris in the spring.' Orson Welles, who was known to all the world as Orson Welles, could never be anyone else in life but, in art, he could saw a lady in half, pull a rabbit from a hat, arrange shadows on celluloid in such a way as to be any number of entirely other selves.

Menaker leads Pellarin to 'The Old Dark House'. A *feria* is in progress; fireworks. Only Pellarin goes inside the house: 'The scene is strange, almost surreal . . . (The action must be given in synopsis . . . The climax of this sequence is strongly erotic: to spell out its specific details would be to risk pornography) . . . A man searching and searching – up and down, from floor to floor, from room to room of an empty house, comes to discover (in a lightning flash of fireworks breaking through a shuttered window) that all along there has been someone watching him: – naked, in a shadowed chair.' This is much the same scene that Orson told me at our last lunch as having happened to him. Did it? Or was he trying out the scene on me? She is found; they speak in French; make love; then she vanishes. Although the film was to be shot in black and white, Orson intended the fireworks to be in colour; at the scene's end 'The colored lights fall into darkness.'

Pellarin faces Menaker in the street. Menaker never delivered the letter that Pellarin had written asking the girl to marry him. Menaker did not deliver it because he wants Pellarin to go to glory. Pellarin: 'Screw Pennsylvania Avenue.' Menaker: 'Boysie – There's nowhere else for you to go.' Later, the ubiquitous Brandini strikes. She tells Pellarin that 'during his sexual fantasizing about you – Dr Menaker would masturbate into a handkerchief . . . Then, when it was stiff with his dried semen, he mailed it to his crippled friend, as . . . I don't know what: a sentimental souvenir.' I must say that even at the lively fun-court of Tiberius and of his heir, Caligula, neither Suetonius nor I ever came up with anything quite so – dare I use so punitive a word? – icky. But Orson needed an emotional trigger for a nightmare flight through the city and an encounter with a blind beggar who menaces Pellarin and whom he kills. Let it come down. The police suspect; but cover for him.

Pellarin re-enters the world. A speech must be given in Brussels. Menaker is on the train, which Brandini satisfactorily misses – 'dressed as usual: semi-safari with a strong hint of battle fatigues'. They sing, jointly, Menaker's 'hit number from the Hasty Pudding Show of nineteen twenty-nine'. Then Orson adds, with his usual flourish: 'If you want a happy ending, that depends, of course, on where you stop your story.'

In a statement to Henry Jaglom (May 20, 1982), Orson wrote of Pellarin.

> He is a great man – like all great men he is never satisfied that he has chosen the right path in life. Even being President, he feels, may somehow not be right. He is a man who has within him the devil of self-destruction that lives in every genius ... There is this foolish, romantic side of us all ... That is what the *circumstances* of the film are about – the theft of the necklace, the situation with the monkey, etc. All these idiotic events that one's romantic nature leads one into.

But of course Orson is describing Menaker, not Pellarin, and, again of course, Orson is describing his own 'romantic nature' which led him down so many odd roads, to our enduring delight if not always his.

I have a recurring fantasy that if one were to dial the telephone number of someone in the past, one would hear again a familiar voice, and time would instantly rewind from now to then. I still have Orson's telephone number in my book (213–851–8458). Do I dare ring him and talk to him back in 1982, where he is busy trying to convince Jack Nicholson to play Pellarin for two not four million dollars? Should I tell him that he'll not get the picture made? No. That would be too harsh. I'll pretend that I have somehow got a copy of it, and that I think it marvellous though perhaps the handkerchief was, from so prudish a master, a bit much? Even incredible.

'Incredible?' The voice booms in my ear. 'How could it be incredible when I stole it from *Othello*? But now I have a real treat for you. Standing here is your neighbour ... Rudy! Overcome "that quiet reserve or shyness". *Sing.*'

From out of the past, I hear 'My time is your time', in that reedy highly imitable voice. The after-life's only a dial tone away. 'What makes you think that this is the after-life?' Orson chuckles. 'This is a recording.' Stop story here.

*The New York Review of Books*
1 June 1989

# 5
# MAUGHAM'S
# HALF & HALF

I

Mr Robert Calder has written a biography of W. Somerset Maugham in order to redress, nicely, I think, some recent studies of the man who was probably our century's most popular novelist as well as the most successful of Edwardian playwrights. Maugham's last biographer, Mr Ted Morgan, concentrated morbidly on the incontinences and confusions of a mad old age while scanting works and bright days. Doubtless, he was influenced by the young Maugham's remark:

> I cannot understand why a biographer, having undertaken to give the world details of a famous man's life, should hesitate, as so often happens, to give details of his death . . . Our lives are conditioned by outer circumstances but our death is our own.

Not, as it proves, with Mr Morgan on the case. But then, as demonstrated by Mr Morgan and other biographers of known sexual degenerates (or merely suspected – Lennon, Presley, by one A. Goldman, the master of that expanding cottage industry, Bioporn), a contemptuous adversarial style seems to be the current . . . norm. Despite the degenerate's gifts, he is a Bad Person; worse, he is Immature; even worse, he is Promiscuous. Finally, he is demonstrably more Successful than his biographer, who is Married, Mature, Monogamous, and Good.

Although Mr Calder is MMM&G, he does believe that

> Morgan's antipathy to the man is most damaging. Though his treatment of Maugham's homosexuality is more explicit than anything previously published, it always emphasizes the nasty procuring side of his homosexual life.

Yet even a gentle schoolteacher in Saskatchewan like Mr Calder must know that the men of Maugham's generation paid for sex with men or women or both (the last century was prostitution's Golden Age – for the buyer, of course). Would Mr Calder think it relevant to note and deplore as immature if Joseph Conrad, say, had visited women prostitutes? I doubt it. Obviously a double standard is at work here. What is sheer high animal spirits in the roaring boy who buys a pre-feminist girl is vileness in the roaring boy who buys another boy.

To Mr Calder's credit, he does his best to show the amiable side to the formidable Mr Maugham – the side that Mr Calder terms 'Willie', as he was known to friends. But our schoolteacher also distances himself from 'nastiness' in his acknowledgements where he notes 'the unqualified encouragement of my parents, and my children – Alison, Kevin, Lorin, and Dani'. (Did they pipe 'What's rough trade, Daddy?' with *unqualified* encouragement?) No matter. By and large, children, your Daddy has done the old fruitcake proud.

Maugham spent his first twenty-six years in the nineteenth century and for the subsequent sixty-five years he was very much a nineteenth-century novelist and playwright. In many ways he was fortunately placed, though he himself would not have thought so. He was born in Paris where his lawyer father did legal work for the British Embassy, and his mother was a popular figure in Paris society. Maugham's first language was French and although he made himself into the premier English storyteller, his prose has always had a curious flatness to it, as if it wanted to become either Basic English or Esperanto or perhaps go back into French.

Maugham's self-pity, which was to come to a full rather ghastly flowering in *Of Human Bondage*, is mysterious in origin. On the demerit side, he lost a beloved mother at eight; lost three older brothers to boarding school (all became lawyers and one Lord Chancellor); lost, at eleven, a not-so-well-loved father. He was then sent off to a clergyman uncle in Whitstable – home of the oyster – and then to the standard dire school of the day. On the credit side, under his father's will, he got £150 a year for life, enough to live on. He was well-connected in the professional upper middle class. He had the run of his uncle's considerable library – the writer's best education. When he proved to be sickly, he was sent to the south of France; when, at seventeen, he could endure his school no more, he was sent to Heidelberg and a merry time.

On balance, the tragic wound to which he was to advert throughout a long life strikes me as no more than a scratch or two. Yes, he wanted to be taller than five foot seven; yes, he had an underslung jaw that might have been corrected; yes, he stammered. But . . . *tant pis*, as he might have observed coldly of another (used in a novel, the phrase would be helpfully translated).

Yet something *was* gnawing at him. As he once observed, sardonically, to his nephew Robin Maugham, 'Jesus Christ could cope with all the miseries I have had to contend with in life. But then, Jesus Christ had advantages I don't possess.' Presumably, Jesus was a six-foot-tall blond blue-eyed body-builder whereas Maugham was slight and dark with eyes like 'brown velvet', and, of course, Jesus's father owned the shop. On the other hand, Maugham was not obliged to contend with the sadomasochistic excitement of the Crucifixion, much less the head-turning rapture of the Resurrection. It is the common view of Maugham biographers that the true tragic flaw was homosexuality, disguised as a club foot in *Of Human Bondage* – or was that the stammer? Whatever it was, Maugham was very sorry for himself. Admittedly, a liking for boys at the time of Oscar Wilde's misadventures was dangerous but Maugham was adept at passing for MMM&G: he *appeared* to have affairs with women, not men, and he married and fathered a daughter. There need not have been an either/or for him.

\* \* \*

73

Maugham's career as a writer was singularly long and singularly successful. The cover of each book was adorned with a Moorish device to ward off the evil eye: the author knew that too much success over-excites one's contemporaries, not to mention the gods. Also much of his complaining may have been prophylactic: to avert the Furies if not the book-chatterers, and so he was able to live just as he wanted for two thirds of his life, something not many writers – or indeed anyone else – ever manage to do.

At eighteen, Maugham became a medical student at St Thomas's Hospital, London. This London was still Dickens's great monstrous invention where 'The messenger led you through the dark and silent streets of Lambeth, up stinking alleys and into sinister courts where the police hesitated to penetrate, but where your black bag protected you from harm.' For five years Maugham was immersed in the real world, while, simultaneously, he was trying to become a writer. 'Few authors,' Mr Calder tells us, 'read as widely as Maugham and his works are peppered with references to other literature.' So they are – peppered indeed – but not always seasoned. The bilingual Maugham knew best the French writers of the day. He tells us that he modelled his short stories on Maupassant. He also tells us that he was much influenced by Ibsen, but there is no sign of that master in his own school of Wilde comedies. Later, he was awed by Chekhov's stories but, again, he could never 'use' that master because something gelled very early in Maugham the writer, and once his own famous tone was set it would remain perfectly pitched to the end.

In his first published novel, *Liza of Lambeth* (1897), Maugham raised the banner of Maupassant and the French realists but the true influence on the book and its method was one Arthur Morrison, who had made a success three years earlier with *Tales of Mean Streets*. Mr Calder notes that Morrison,

> writing with austerity and frankness . . . refused to express sympathy on behalf of his readers so that they could then avoid coming to terms with the implications of social and economic inequality. Maugham adopted this point of view in

his first novel, and was therefore, like Morrison, accused of a lack of conviction.

In general, realists have always been open to the charge of coldness, particularly by romantics who believe that a novel is essentially a sermon, emotional and compassionate and so inspiring that after the peroration, the reader, wiser, kinder, *bushier* indeed, will dry his eyes and go forth to right wrong. This critical mindset has encouraged a great deal of bad writing. The unemotional telling of a terrible story is usually more effective than the oh, by the wind-grieved school of romantic (that is, self-loving) prose. On the other hand, the plain style can help the dishonest, pusillanimous writer get himself off every kind of ideological or ethical hook. Just the facts, ma'am. In this regard, Hemingway, a literary shadow-self to Maugham, was our time's most artful dodger, all busy advancing verbs and stony nouns. Surfaces coldly rendered. Interiors unexplored. Manner all.

For someone of Maugham's shy, highly self-conscious nature (with a secret, too) the adoption of classic realism, Flaubert with bitters, was inevitable. Certainly, he was lucky to have got the tone absolutely right in his first book, and he was never to stray far from the appearance of plain story-telling. Although he was not much of one for making up things, he could always worry an anecdote or bit of gossip into an agreeable narrative. Later, as the years passed, he put more and more effort – even genius – into his one triumphant creation, W. Somerset Maugham, world-weary world-traveller, whose narrative first person became the best-known and least wearisome in the world. At first he called the narrator 'Ashenden' (a name carefully chosen so that the writer would not stammer when saying it, unlike that obstacle course for stammerers, 'Maugham'); then he dropped Ashenden for Mr Maugham himself in *The Razor's Edge* (1944). Then he began to appear, as narrator, in film and television dramatisations of his work. Thus, one of the most-read novelists of our time became widely known to those who do not read.

Shaw and Wells invented public selves for polemical reasons, while Mark Twain and Dickens did so to satisfy a theatrical need, but Maugham contrived a voice and a manner that not only charm and surprise in a way that the others did not, but where they were menacingly larger than life, he is just a bit smaller (5′ 7″), for which he compensates by sharing with us something that the four histrionic masters would not have dreamed of doing: inside gossip. It is these confidences that made Maugham so agreeable to read: *nothing*, he tells us with a smile, *is what it seems*. That was his one trick, and it seldom failed. Also, before D. H. Lawrence, Dr Maugham (obstetrician) knew that women, given a fraction of a chance, liked sex as much as men did. When he said so, he was called a misogynist.

In October 1907, at thirty-three, Maugham became famous with the triumphant production of *Lady Frederick* (one of six unproduced plays that he had written). Maugham ravished his audience with the daring trick of having the eponymous lady – middle-aged with ardent unsuitable youthful admirer – save the boy from his infatuation by allowing him to see her un-made-up at her dressing-table. So stunned is the lad by the difference between the beauty of the *maquillage* and the crone in the mirror that he is saved by her nobleness, and right before our eyes we see 'nothing is what it seems' in spades, raw stuff for the theatre of those days.

By 1908 Maugham had achieved the dream of so many novelists: he had four plays running in the West End and he was financially set for life. In that same year, the sixty-five-year-old impecunious Henry James was having one last desperate go at the theatre. To Edith Wharton he wrote that he was

> working under a sudden sharp solicitation (heaven forgive me!) for the Theatre & that I had, as a matter of life or death, to push through with my play, or rather with my 2 plays (for I'm doing two), the more important of which (though an abject little cochonnerie even *it*, no doubt!) is to be produced ... I have been governed by the one sordid & urgent consideration of the possibility of making some money ...

76

Forgive so vulgar a tale – but I am utterly brazen about it;
for my base motive is all of that brassy complexion – till
sicklied o'er with the reflection of another metal.

But it was to Maugham, not the Master, that the other metal
came.

Maugham enjoyed his celebrity; he was a popular diner-out; he
was, when he could get the words out, something of a wit. He was
eminently marriageable in Edwardian eyes. So which will it be –
the lady or the tiger/man? Mr Calder cannot get enough of
Maugham the faggot in conflict with Maugham the potential
MMM&G. Will good drive out evil? Maturity immaturity?

Unhappily, the witch-doctor approach to human behaviour still
enjoys a vogue in academe and Mr Calder likes to put his subject
on the couch, while murmuring such Freudian incantations as 'loss
of a beloved mother, the lack of a father with whom to identify . . .
followed a common pattern in the development of homosexuality.'
That none of this makes any sense does not alter belief: in matters
of faith, inconvenient evidence is always suppressed while contradictions go unnoticed. Nevertheless, witch-doctors to one side,
witches did – and do – get burned, as Oscar Wilde discovered in
1895, and an entire generation of same-sexers were obliged to go
underground or marry or settle in the south of France. I suspect
that Maugham's experiences with women were not only few but
essentially hydraulic. Writers, whether same-sexers or other-sexers,
tend to have obsessive natures; in consequence, they cross the
sexual borders rather less often than the less imaginative who
want, simply, to get laid or even loved. But whereas a same-sexer
like Noel Coward never in his life committed an other-sexual act
('Not even with Gertrude Lawrence?' I asked. 'Particularly not
with Miss Lawrence' was the staccato response), Dr Maugham
had no fear of vaginal teeth – he simply shut his eyes and thought
of Capri.

At twenty-one Maugham was well and truly launched by one
John Ellingham Brooks, a littérateur who lived on Capri, then
known for the easy charm of its boys. 'The nasty procuring side' of

Maugham started in Capri and he kept coming back year after year. At ninety, he told a reporter, 'I want to go to Capri because I started life there.' In old age, he told Glenway Westcott that Brooks was his first lover. This is doubtful. Maugham told different people different things about his private life, wanting always to confuse. Certainly, for sheer energetic promiscuity he was as athletic as Byron; with a club foot, what might he not have done! Even so, 'He was the most sexually voracious man I've ever known,' said Beverley Nichols, the journalist and one-time Maugham secretary, who knew at first hand. Robin Maugham and the last companion, Alan Searle, agreed.

Ironically, within a dozen years of Wilde's imprisonment, Maugham was the most popular English playwright. Unlike the reckless Oscar, Maugham showed no sign of ever wanting to book so much as a room at the Cadogan Hotel. Marriage it would be. With Syrie Barnardo Wellcome, an interior decorator much liked in London's high bohemia. Fashionable wife for fashionable play-wright. A daring woman of the world – an Iris March with a green hat *pour le sport* – Syrie wanted a child by Maugham without wedlock. Got it. As luck – hers and his – would have it, Maugham then went to war and promptly met the great love of his life, Gerald Haxton.

For a time Maugham was a wound dresser. Gerald was in the Ambulance Corps. They were to be together until Gerald's death twenty-nine years later, 'longer than many marriages,' observes the awed Mr Calder. But there was a good deal of mess to be cleaned up along the way. Haxton could not go to England: he had been caught by the police in bed with another man. Maugham himself did not want, finally, to be even remotely MMM&G. Syrie suffered. They separated. Toward the end of his life, Maugham tried to disinherit his daughter on the ground that she was not his but, ironically, he had got a door prize for at least one dutiful attendance and she was very much his as anyone who has ever seen her or her descendants can attest: the saturnine Maugham face still gazes by proxy upon a world where nothing else is ever what it seems.

During the war, Maugham was hired by the British secret service to go to Moscow and shore up the Kerensky government. He has written of all this in both fiction (*Ashenden* – literary ancestor to Eric Ambler, Ian Fleming, John le Carré) and two books of memoirs. Unfortunately, the mission to Moscow was aborted by the overthrow of Kerensky.

Maugham developed tuberculosis. During twenty months in a Scottish sanatorium he wrote four of his most popular plays, including *The Circle* and the highly successful novel *The Moon and Sixpence*, where a Gauguin-like English painter is observed by the world-weary Ashenden amongst Pacific palms. Maugham wrote his plays rather the way television writers (or Shakespeare) write their serials – at great speed. One week for each act and a final week to put it all together. Since Mr Calder is over-excited by poor Willie's rather unremarkable (stamina to one side) sex life, we get far too little analysis of Maugham's writing and of the way that he worked, particularly in the theatre. From what little Mr Calder tells us, Maugham stayed away from rehearsals but, when needed, would cut almost anything an actor wanted. This doesn't sound right to me but then when one has had twenty play productions in England alone, there is probably not that much time or inclination to perfect the product. In any case, Mr Calder is, as he would put it, 'disinterested' in the subject.

In 1915, while Maugham was spying for England, *Of Human Bondage* was published. Maugham now was seen to be not only a serious but a solemn novelist – in the ponderous American manner. The best that can be said of this masterpiece is that it made a good movie and launched Bette Davis's career. I remember that on all the pre-Second War editions, there was a quotation from Theodore Dreiser to the effect that the book 'has rapture, it sings'. Mr Calder does not mention Dreiser but Mr Frederic Raphael does, in his agreeable picture book with twee twinkly text, *Somerset Maugham and His World* (1977). Mr Raphael quotes from Dreiser, whom he characterises as 'an earnest thunderer in the cause of naturalism and himself a Zolaesque writer of constipated power'. Admittedly,

Dreiser was not in a class with Margaret Drabble but – constipated?*

The Maugham persona was now perfected in life and work. Maugham's wit was taken for true evil as he himself was well known, despite all subterfuge, to be non-MMM&G. Mr Calder is disturbed by Maugham's attempts at epigrams in conversation. Sternly, Mr Calder notes: 'Calculated flippancy was none the less a poor substitute for natural and easy insouciance.' But despite a near-total absence of easy insouciance, Maugham fascinated everyone. By 1929 he had settled into his villa at Cap Ferrat; he was much sought after socially even though the Windsors, the Churchills, the Beaverbrooks all knew that Haxton was more than a secretary. But the very rich and the very famous are indeed different from really real folks. For one thing, they often find funny the MMM&Gs. For another, they can create their own world and never leave it if they choose.

It is a sign of Maugham's great curiosity and continuing sense of life (even maturity) that he never stopped travelling, ostensibly to gather gossip and landscape for stories, but actually to come alive and induge his twin passions, boys and bridge, two activities far less damaging to the environment than marriages, children, and big-game hunting. Haxton was a splendid organiser with similar tastes. Mr Calder doesn't quite get all this but then his informants, chiefly nephew Robin Maugham and the last companion, Alan Searle, would have been discreet.

During the Second War, Maugham was obliged to flee France for America. In Hollywood he distinguished himself on the set of *Dr Jekyll and Mr Hyde*. George Cukor had explained to Willie how, in this version of the Stevenson story, there would be no horrendous make-up change for the star, Spencer Tracy, when he turned from good Dr Jekyll into evil Mr Hyde. Instead, a great actor, Tracy, would bring forth both evil and good from within. Action! Tracy

---

* Mr Raphael has many opinions about books that he has not actually read. You will see him at his glittering best in the *Times*, in his obituary of Gore Vidal (date to come).

menaces the heroine. Ingrid Bergman cowers on a bed. Tracy simpers, drools, leers. Then Maugham's souciant voice is heard, loud and clear and stammerless. 'And which one is he supposed to be now?'

During this time, the movie of *The Moon and Sixpence* was released – the twenty-third Maugham story to be filmed. Maugham himself travelled restlessly about the East coast, playing bridge. He also had a refuge in North Carolina where, while Maugham was writing *The Razor's Edge*, Haxton died. For a time Maugham was inconsolable. Then he took on an amiable young Englishman, Alan Searle, as secretary-companion, and together they returned to the Riviera where Maugham restored the war-wrecked villa and resumed his life.

One reason, prurience aside, why Mr Calder tells us so much about Maugham's private life (many kindnesses and charities are duly noted) is that Maugham has no reputation at all in North American academe where Mr Calder is a spear-carrier. The result is a lot of less than half-praise: 'His career had been largely a triumph of determination and will, the success in three genres of a man not naturally gifted as a writer.' Only a schoolteacher innocent of how literature is made could have written such a line. Demonstrably, Maugham was very talented at doing what he did. Now, this is for your final grade, *what* did he do? Describe, please. Unfortunately, there aren't many good describers (critics) in any generation. But I shall give it a try, presently.

At seventy-two, Maugham went to Vevey, in Switzerland, where a Dr Niehans injected ageing human organisms with the cells of unborn sheep, and restored youth. All the great and not-so-good came to Niehans, including Pius XII – in a business suit and dark glasses, it was said – an old man in no hurry to meet his Jewish employer. Thanks perhaps to Niehans, Maugham survived for nearly fifteen years in rude bodily health. But body outlived mind and so it was that the senile Maugham proceeded to destroy his own great invention, W. Somerset Maugham, the teller of tales, the man inclined to the good and to right action and, above all, to common sense. By the time that old Maugham had finished with himself, absolutely nothing was what it seemed and the double self-portrait that he had given the world in *The Summing Up* and *A Writer's Notebook* was totally undone by this raging Lear upon the Riviera, who tried to disinherit his daughter while adopting Searle as well as producing *Looking Back*, a final set of memoirs not quite as mad as Hemingway's but every bit as malicious. With astonishing ingenuity, the ancient Maugham mined his own monument; and blew it up.

For seven decades Maugham had rigorously controlled his personal and his artistic life. He would write so many plays, and stop; and did. So many short stories . . . He rounded off everything neatly, and lay back to die, with a quiet world-weary smile on those ancient lizard lips. But then, to his horror, he kept on living, and having sex, and lunching with Churchill and Beaverbrook. Friends thought that Beaverbrook put him up to the final memoir, but I suspect that Maugham had grown very bored with a lifetime of playing it so superbly safe.

2

It is very difficult for a writer of my generation, if he is honest, to pretend indifference to the work of Somerset Maugham. He was always so entirely *there*. By seventeen I had read all of Shakespeare; all of Maugham. Perhaps more to the point, he dominated the movies at a time when movies were the lingua franca of the world. Although the French have told us that the movie is the creation of the director, no one in the Twenties, Thirties, Forties paid the slightest attention to who had directed *Of Human Bondage, Rain, The Moon and Sixpence, The Razor's Edge, The Painted Veil, The Letter*. Their true creator was W. Somerset Maugham, and a generation was in thrall to his sensuous, exotic imaginings of a duplicitous world.

Although Maugham received a good deal of dutiful praise in his lifetime, he was never to be taken very seriously in his own country or the United States, as opposed to Japan where he has been for two thirds of a century the most read and admired Western writer. Christopher Isherwood tells us that he met Maugham at a Bloomsbury party where Maugham looked most ill-at-ease with the likes of Virginia Woolf. Later Isherwood learned from a friend of Maugham's that before the party, in an agony of indecision, as the old cliché master might have put it, he had paced his hotel sitting room, saying, 'I'm just as good as they are.'

I suspect that he thought he was probably rather better *for what he was*, which was not at all what they were. Bloomsbury disdained action and commitment other than to Art and to Friendship (which meant going to bed with one another's husbands and wives). Maugham liked action. He risked his life in floods, monsoons, the collapse of holy Russia. He was worldly like Hemingway, who also stalked the big game of wild places, looking for stories, self. As for what he thought of himself, Mr Calder quotes Maugham to the headmaster of his old school: 'I think I ought to have the OM [Order of Merit] . . . They gave Hardy the OM and I think I am the greatest living writer of English, and they ought to give it to me.' When he did get a lesser order, Companion of Honour, he was sardonic: 'It means very well done . . . but.'

But. There is a definite but. I have just reread for the first time in forty years *The Narrow Corner*, a book I much admired; *The Razor's Edge*, the novel on which the film that I found the ultimate in worldly glamour was based; *A Writer's Notebook*, which I recalled as being very wise; and, yet again, *Cakes and Ale*. Edmund Wilson's famous explosion at the success of Maugham in general and *The Razor's Edge* in particular is not so far off the mark.

The language is such a tissue of clichés that one's wonder is finally aroused at the writer's ability to assemble so many and at his unfailing inability to put anything in an individual way.

Maugham's reliance on the banal, particularly in dialogue, derived from his long experience in the theatre, a popular art form in those days. One could no more represent the people on stage without clichés than one could produce an episode of *Dynasty*: Maugham's dialogue is a slightly sharpened version of that of his audience.

Both Wilde and Shaw dealt in this same sort of realistic speech but Shaw was a master of the higher polemic (as well as of the baleful clichés of the quaint working-man, rendered phonetically to no one's great delight) while Wilde made high verbal art of clichés so slyly crossed as to yield incongruent wit. But for any playwright of that era (now, too), the *mot juste* was apt to be the correctly deployed *mot banal*. Maugham's plays worked very well. But when Maugham transferred the tricks of the theatre to novel writing, he was inclined not only to write the same sort of dialogue that the stage required but in his dramatic effects he often set his scene with stage directions, ignoring the possibilities that prose *with* dialogue can yield. The economy won him many readers, but there is no rapture, song. Wilson, finally, puts him in the relation of Bulwer-Lytton to Dickens: 'a half-trashy novelist who writes badly, but is patronized by half-serious readers who do not care much about writing.' What ever happened to those readers? How can we get them back?

Wilson took the proud modernist view that, with sufficient education, everyone would want to move into Axel's Castle. Alas, the half-serious readers stopped reading novels long ago, while the 'serious' read literary theory, and the castle's ruins are the domain of literary archaeologists. But Wilson makes a point, inadvertently: if Maugham is half-trashy (and at times his most devoted admirers would probably grant that) what, then, is the other half, that is not trash? Also, why is it that just as one places, with the right hand, the laurel wreath upon his brow, one's left hand starts to defoliate the victor's crown?

*A Writer's Notebook* (kept over fifty years) is filled with descriptions of sunsets and people glimpsed on the run. These descriptions are every bit as bad as Wilson's (in *The Twenties*) and I don't see why either thought that writing down a fancy description of a landscape could – or should – be later glued to the page of a novel in progress. Maugham's descriptions, like Wilson's are disagreeably purple while the physical descriptions of people are more elaborate than what we now put up with. But Maugham was simply following the custom of nineteenth-century novelists in telling us whether or not eyebrows grow together while noting the exact placement of a wen. Also, Dr Maugham's checklist is necessary for diagnosis. Yet he does brood on style; attempts to make epigrams. 'Anyone can tell the truth, but only very few of us can make epigrams.' Thus, young Maugham, to which the old Maugham retorts, 'In the nineties, however, we all tried to.'

In the preface, Maugham expatiates on Jules Renard's notebooks, one of the great delights of world literature and, as far as I can tell, unknown to Anglo-Americans, like so much else. Renard wrote one small masterpiece, *Poil de Carotte*, about his unhappy childhood – inhuman bondage to an evil mother rather than waitress.

Renard appeals to Maugham, though 'I am always suspicious of a novelist's theories, I have never known them to be anything other than a justification of his own shortcomings.' Well, that is commonsensical. In any case, Maugham, heartened by Renard's marvellous notebook, decided to publish his own. The tone is world-weary, modest. 'I have retired from the hurly-burly and ensconced myself not uncomfortably on the shelf.' Thus, he will share his final musings.

There is a good deal about writing. High praise for Jeremy Taylor:

> He seems to use the words that come most naturally to the mouth, and his phrases, however nicely turned, have a colloquial air . . . The long clauses, tacked on to one another in a string that appears interminable, make you feel that the thing has been written without effort.

Here, at twenty-eight, he is making the case for the plain and the flat and the natural sounding:

> There are a thousand epithets with which you may describe the sea. The only one which, if you fancy yourself a stylist,

you will scrupulously avoid is *blue*; yet it is that which most satisfies Jeremy Taylor . . . He never surprises. His imagination is without violence or daring.

Of Matthew Arnold's style, 'so well suited to irony and wit, to exposition . . . It is a method rather than an art, no one more than I can realize what enormous labour it must have needed to acquire that mellifluous cold brilliance. It is a platitude that simplicity is the latest acquired of all qualities . . .' The interesting giveaway here is Maugham's assumption that Arnold's style must have been the work of great labour. But suppose, like most good writers, the style was absolutely natural to Arnold and without strain? Here one sees the hard worker sternly shaping himself rather than the natural writer easily expressing himself as temperament requires:

> My native gifts are not remarkable, but I have a certain force of character which has enabled me in a measure to supplement my deficiencies. I have common sense . . . For many years I have been described as a cynic; I told the truth. I wish no one to take me for other than I am, and on the other hand I see no need to accept others' pretences.

One often encounters the ultimate accolade 'common sense' in these musings. Also, the conceit that he is what you see, when, in fact, he is not. For instance, his native gifts for narrative were of a very high order. While, up to a point, he could tell the truth and so be thought cynical, it was always 'common sense', a.k.a. careerism, that kept him from ever saying all that he knew. Like most people, he wanted to be taken for what he was not; hence, the great invention W. Somerset Maugham.

Maugham uses his Moscow experience to good literary advantage. He reads the Russians. Marvels at their small cast of characters. Notes that no one in a Russian book ever goes to an art gallery. Later, he travels through America, wondering what the people on the trains are really like. Then he reads, with admiration, *Main Street*, where he detects the emergence of a complex caste system: 'The lip service which is given to equality occasions a sort

86

of outward familiarity, but this only makes those below more conscious of the lack of inward familiarity; and so nowhere is class-hatred likely to give rise in the long run to more bitter enmity.'

Maugham was alert to the persisting problem of how to be a writer at all: certainly the writer 'must never entirely grow up . . . It needs a peculiar turn of mind in a man of fifty to treat with great seriousness the passion of Edwin for Angelina.' Or Edmund for Daisy. 'The novelist is dead in the man who has become aware of the triviality of human affairs. You can often discern in writers the dismay with which they have recognized this situation in them-selves.' He notes how Flaubert turned from *Madame Bovary* to *Bouvard et Pécuchet*, George Eliot and H. G. Wells to 'sociology', Hardy to *The Dynasts* – a step farther up Parnassus but no one thought so then.

Maugham's great enthusiasm is for Chekhov, a fellow doctor, playwright, and short-story writer:

> He has been compared with Guy de Maupassant, but one would presume only by persons who have read neither. Guy de Maupassant is a clever story-teller, effective at his best – by which, of course, every writer has the right to be judged – but without much real relation to life . . . But with Chekhov you do not seem to be reading stories at all. There is no obvious cleverness in them and you might think that anyone could write them, but for the fact that nobody does. The author has had an emotion and he is able so to put it in words that you receive it in your turn. You become his collaborator. You cannot use of Chekhov's stories the hackneyed expression of the slice of life, for a slice is a piece cut off and that is exactly the impression you do not get when you read them; it is a scene seen through the fingers which you know continues this way and that though you only see a part of it.

Mr Maugham knows very well what literature is, and how great effects are, if not made, received.

Finally, he makes a bit of literature in one of the notebook entries. A popular writer of the day, Haddon Chambers, is dead.

He is known for one phrase, 'the long arm of coincidence'. Maugham does a short amusing sketch of Chambers, the man and the writer; then he concludes: 'I seek for a characteristic impression with which to leave him. I see him lounging at a bar, a dapper little man, chatting good-humouredly with a casual acquaintance of women, horses and Covent Garden opera, but with an air as though he were looking for someone who might at any moment come in at the door.' That is very fine indeed, and Mr Chambers still has a small corner of life in that bar, in that paragraph.

My only memory of *The Razor's Edge* (1944) was that of an American lady who threw a plate at the narrator, our own Mr Maugham, with the cry, 'And you can call yourself an English gentleman', to which Mr Maugham, played urbanely in the movie by Herbert Marshall, responded niftily, 'No, that's a thing I've never done in all my life.' The scene has remained in my memory all these years because it is almost the only one in the book that has been dramatised. Everything else is relentlessly told. The first-person narrator, so entirely seductive in the short stories, is now heavy, garrulous, and awkward, while the clichés are not only 'tissued' but Maugham even cocks, yes, a snook at his critics by recording every one of an American businessman's relentless banalities. Of course, the author is sixty-nine. Maugham's view of the world was consistent throughout his life. Intrigued by religion, he remained an atheist. Vedanta was attractive, but reincarnation was simply not common sense. If you had no recollection of any previous incarnations, what was the point? For all practical purposes the first carnation was extinct when it died, and all the others random. But during the Second War there was a lot of musing about the meaning of it all, and out of that age's anxiety did come Thomas Mann's masterpiece, *Dr Faustus*.

Maugham stalks similar game. Again, the narrator is our Mr Maugham, the all-wise, all-tolerant Old Party who knows a thing or two. Nearby, on the Riviera, lives Elliot Templeton, an elegant snobbish old queen whose identity was revealed for the first time in the pages of *The New York Review of Books* (September 29, 1983) as Henry de Courcy May. (Mr Calder thinks that the character is, in part, Chips Channon, but Chips is separately present as Paul Barton, another American social climber.) Elliott is an amusing character (Mr Calder finds him 'brilliant') but Maugham can't do very much with him other than give him a Chicago niece. And money, Paris. Love. The niece is in love with Larry Darrell – why a name so close to real life Larry Durrell? Maugham's names for characters (like Hemingway's) are standard for the time – highly forgettable Anglo-Saxon names. Why? Because novels were read by a very large public in those days and any but the most common names could bring on a suit for libel.

Larry does not want to go to work, he wants to 'loaf'. This means that he has spiritual longings: what does it all mean? He want to know. He loses the girl to a wealthy young man who doesn't care what it may or may not mean. In pursuit of *it*, Larry becomes very learned in Germany; he works in a coal mine; he goes to India and discovers Vedanta. He returns to the world perhaps with *it* or perhaps not since *it* is an illusion like all else.

Maugham and Larry sit up all night in a bistro while Larry tells him the entire story of his life, much of which Maugham has already told us: it is very dangerous to be your own narrator in a book. Finally, as the dawn like a frightened Scottish scone peeps through the bistro window, Larry tells and tells about India. And Vedanta.

Larry wants nothing less than Enlightenment. Does he achieve it? Maugham teases us. Yes, no, it's all the same, isn't it? There are several short stories intercut with Larry's passion play: a brilliant poetic girl becomes a drunken drug-ridden hag and ends up on the Riviera and in the Mediterranean, murdered by a piece of trade. Proof to Mr Calder and his Freudian friends that because Maugham liked males he (what else?) hated females. This is one of the rocks on which the whole Freudian structure has been, well . . . erected. For the witch-doctors, Maugham's invention of such a woman is *prima facie* evidence of his hatred of the opposite sex, which vitiated his work and made it impossible for him to be truly great and married. Yet in real life it is the other-sexers (Hemingway) who hate women, and the same-sexers (Maugham) who see them not as women but, as someone observed of Henry James's response to the ladies, as people. Finally, even the most confused witch-doctor must have stumbled upon that essential law of human behaviour: one cannot hate what one cannot love. Nevertheless, as members of chemistry departments still search for cold fusion, so dedicated English teachers still seek to crack the fairy code.

Depressed, I move on to *The Narrow Corner*. On the first page, the energy is switched on. First chapter: 'All this happened a good many years ago.' That's it. One settles in. Second chapter begins. 'Dr Saunders yawned. It was nine o'clock in the morning.' An English doctor (under a cloud in England – abortion? We are not told). He practises medicine in the Chinese port of Fu-chou. There is no Mrs Saunders. There is a beautiful Chinese boy who prepares his opium pipes. Sentences are short. Descriptions of people are never tedious. We inhabit Dr Saunders's mind for most of the book though, as always, Maugham will shift the point of view to someone else if for some reason Dr Saunders is not witness to a necessary scene. This is lazy but a lot better than having someone sit down and tell you the story of his life, in quotation marks, page after page.

Dr Saunders is offered a great deal of money to operate on a rich Chinese opium trafficker, domiciled on the island of Takana in the distant Malay archipelago (a trip as momentous and hazardous in those days as one from Ann Arbor to East Anglia today). By page seven the trip has been made and a successful operation for cataract has been performed. Now Dr Saunders and beautiful Chinese boy are looking for a ship to get them home again. Enter Captain Nichols, a man under numerous clouds, but a first-class English skipper. Dr Saunders is amused by the rogue who has arrived aboard a lugger out of Sydney, destination vague. They spar. Each notes the other's cloud. Will Dr Saunders leave the island aboard Nichols's boat?

Dr Saunders was not a great reader. He seldom opened a novel. Interested in character, he liked books that displayed the oddities of human nature, and he had read over and over again Pepys and Boswell's Johnson, Florio's Montaigne and Hazlitt's essays ... He read neither for information nor to improve his mind, but sought in books occasion for reverie.

In 1938, George Santayana dismissed Maugham's stories; 'They are not pleasing, they are not pertinent to one's real interests, they are not true; they are simply plausible, like a bit of a dream that one might drop into in an afternoon nap.' Yet, perhaps, that is a necessary condition of narrative fiction, a plausible daydreaming. Although Maugham could never have read Santayana's letter to a friend, he returns the compliment in *A Writer's Notebook*:

> I think Santayana has acquired his reputation in America owing to the pathetically diffident persuasion of Americans that what is foreign must have greater value than what is native ... To my mind Santayana is a man who took the wrong turning. With his irony, his sharp tongue, common-sense and worldly wisdom, his sensitive understanding, I have a notion that he could have written semi-philosophical romances after the manner of Anatole France which it would have been an enduring delight to read ... It was a loss to American literature when Santayana decided to become a philosopher rather than a novelist.

Kindly vocational guidance from Uncle Willie; or it takes one to ...

The plot: aboard the lugger is an edgy young Australian beauty (this was Maugham's one and only crypto-fag novel). Fred Blake is also under a cloud but where Doctor and Skipper each wears his cloud *pour le sport*, Fred seems ready to jump, as they say, out of his skin. It is finally agreed that the Doctor accompany them to one of the Dutch islands where he can find a ship for home. They embark. There is a storm at sea, not quite as well rendered as that in *Williwaw*, but Maugham's influence permeates those chaste pages, even down to the annoying use of 'i' and 'ii' as chapter heads. Plainly, the book had a large effect on the youthful war writer.

Finally, they arrive at the Dutch island of Banda Neira. There are substantial Dutch houses with marble floors, relics of a former prosperity, as well as nutmeg trees, all the props. They encounter a noble Danish youth, Erik Christessen, who in turn introduces them to a one-time English school teacher, Frith, and his daughter, Louise. The saintly Eric is in love with beautiful Louise, who is enigmatic. Dr Saunders sees the coming tragedy but the others are unaware, particularly the trusting Eric, who says, early on, how much he likes the East. 'Everyone is so nice. Nothing is too much trouble. You cannot imagine the kindness I've received at the hands of perfect strangers.' I was not the only American writer to be influenced by this book.*

Fred and Louise couple for a night. Eric finds out and kills himself. Louise is sad but confesses to the doctor that she really did not love Eric, who had been enamoured not so much of her as of her late mother. She is, in her quiet way, a startling character. The lugger sails away. Then Fred's cloud is revealed: by accident, he murdered the husband of an older woman who had been hounding him. Fred's lawyer father is a great power in the corrupt government of New South Wales (*tout ça change*, as we say in Egypt), Fred is whisked away by Captain Nichols. In due course, it is learned that Fred is supposed to have died in a flu epidemic. So he is now a nonperson under two clouds. Dr Saunders leaves them. Some time later, Dr Saunders is daydreaming in Singapore when Nichols reappears. Fred fell overboard and drowned. Appar-

---

* In 1948, after Tennessee Williams had read my 'bold' novel, *The City and the Pillar*, we tried to remember what books we had read that dealt, overtly or covertly, with same-sexuality. Each had a vivid memory of *The Narrow Corner*. According to Mr Calder, Maugham himself was somewhat nervous of his romantic indiscretion. 'Thank heavens nobody's seen it,' he said to his nephew Robin at about the same time that Tennessee and I were recalling a novel each had intensely 'seen'. Another novel that each had read was James M. Cain's *Serenade* (1937), where bisexual singer loses voice whenever he indulges in same-sex but gets it back when he commits other-sex, which he does, triumphantly, in Mexico one magical night in the presence of – get cracking, Williams scholars – an iguana.

ently all his money was in his belt which so weighed him down . . . Worse, he had won all of Nichols's money at cribbage. Plainly, the doomed boy had been killed for his money which, unknown to Nichols, he took with him to Davy Jones's locker. Nothing is . . .

The novel still has all of its old magic. There is not a flaw in the manner except toward the end where Maugham succumbs to sentiment. Fred:

'Eric was worth ten of her. He meant all the world to me. I loathe the thought of her. I only want to get away. I want to forget. How could she trample on that lone noble heart!' Dr Saunders raised his eyebrows. Language of that sort chilled his sympathy. 'Perhaps she's very unhappy,' he suggested mildly.

'I thought you were a cynic. You're a sentimentalist.'

'Have you only just discovered it?'

Sincerity in a work of art is always dangerous and Maugham, uncharacteristically, lets it mar a key scene because, by showing that boy cared more for boy than girl, he almost gives away at least one game. But recovery was swift and he was never to make that mistake again. As he observed in *Cakes and Ale*:

I have noticed that when I am most serious people are apt to laugh at me, and indeed when after a lapse of time I have read passages that I wrote from the fullness of my heart I have been tempted to laugh at myself. It must be that there is something naturally absurd in a sincere emotion, though why there should be I cannot imagine, unless it is that man, the ephemeral inhabitant of an insignificant planet, with all his pain and all his striving is a jest in an eternal mind.

What then of *Cakes and Ale*? The story is told in the first person by the sardonic Ashenden, a middle-aged novelist (Maugham was fifty-six when the book was published in 1930). The manner fits the story, which is not told but acted out. What telling we are told is simply Maugham the master essayist, heir of Hazlitt, comment-

ing on the literary world of his day – life, too. In this short novel
he combines his strengths – the discursive essay 'peppered' this
time with apposite literary allusions to which is added the high
craftsmanship of the plays. The dialogue scenes are better than
those of any of his contemporaries while the amused comments on
literary ambition and reputation make altogether enjoyable that
small, now exotic, world.

Plot: a great man of letters, Edward Driffield (modelled on
Thomas Hardy), is dead and the second wife wants someone to
write a hagiography of this enigmatic rustic figure whose first wife
had been a barmaid; she had also been a 'nymphomaniac' and she
had left the great man for an old lover. The literary operator of the
day, Alroy Kear (Maugham's portrait spoiled the rest of poor
Hugh Walpole's life), takes on the job. Then Kear realises that
Ashenden knew Driffield and his first wife, Rosie. When Ashenden
was a boy, they had all lived at the Kentish port, Blackstable. The
first line of the book:

> I have noticed that when someone asks for you on the
> telephone and, finding you out, leaves a message . . . as it's
> important, the matter is more often important to him than to
> you. When it comes to making you a present or doing you a
> favour most people are able to hold their impatience within
> reasonable bounds.

Maugham is on a roll, and the roll continues with great wit and
energy to the last page. He has fun with Kear, with Driffield, with
himself, with Literature. Ashenden purrs his admiration for Kear:
'I could think of no one of my contemporaries who had achieved
so considerable a position on so little talent.' He commends Kear's
largeness of character. On the difficult business of how to treat
those who were once equals but are now failed and of no further
use at all, Kear 'when he had got all he could from people . . .
dropped them.' But Maugham is not finished:

> Most of us when we do a caddish thing harbour resentment
> against the person we have done it to, but Roy's heart, always

in the right place, never permitted him such pettiness. He could use a man very shabbily without afterward bearing him the slightest ill-will.

This is as good as Jane Austen.

Will Ashenden help out even though it is clear that second wife and Kear are out to demonise the first wife, Rosie, and that nothing that Ashenden can tell them about her will change the game plan? Amused, Ashenden agrees to help out. He records his memories of growing up in Blackstable, of the Driffields who are considered very low class indeed: Ashenden's clergyman uncle forbids the boy to see them, but he does. Rosie is a creature of air and fire. She is easy, and loving, and unquestioning. Does she or does she not go to bed with her numerous admirers in the village and later in London where Ashenden, a medical student, sees them again (they had fled Blackstable without paying their bills)?

In London Driffield's fame slowly grows until he becomes the Grand Old Man of Literature. Ashenden's secret – for the purposes of the narrative – is that he, too, had an affair in London with Rosie and when he taxed her with all the others, she was serene and said that that was the way she was and that was that. As writer and moralist Maugham has now travelled from the youthful blurter-out of the truth about woman's potential passion for sex to an acceptance that it is a very good thing indeed and what is wrong with promiscuity if, as they say, no one is hurt? In the end Rosie leaves Driffield for an old love; goes to New York, where, presumably, she and old love are long since dead.

As the narrative proceeds, Maugham has a good deal of fun with the literary world of the day, where, let us note, not one academic can be found (hence its irrelevance?). On the subject of 'longevity is genius', he thinks old extinct volcanoes are apt to be praised as reviewers need fear their competition no longer:

But this is to take a low view of human nature and I would not for the world lay myself open to a charge of cheap cynicism. After mature consideration I have come to the conclusion that the real reason for the applause that comforts the declining years of the author who exceeds the common span is that intelligent people after thirty read nothing at all.

This auctorial self-consciousness now hurls old Maugham into the mainstream of our *fin-de-siècle* writing where texts gaze upon themselves with dark rapture. 'As they grow older the books they read in their youth are lit with its glamour and with every year that passes they ascribe greater merit to the author that wrote them.' Well, that was then; now most intelligent readers under thirty read nothing at all that's not assigned.

'I read in the *Evening Standard* an article by Mr Evelyn Waugh in the course of which he remarked that to write novels in the first person was a contemptible practice . . . I wish he had explained why . . .' Maugham makes the modest point that with 'advancing years the novelist grows less and less inclined to describe more than his own experience has given him. The first-person singular is a very useful device for this limited purpose.'

In *Looking Back*, Maugham 'explains' his uncharacteristic portrait of a good and loving woman who gave of herself (sympathy, please, no tea) as being based on an actual woman/affair. Plainly, it is not. But this charade is harmless. What he has done is far better: he makes a brand-new character, Rosie, who appears to be a bad woman, but her 'badness' is really goodness. Once again, nothing is what it seems. To the end this half-English, half-French writer was a dutiful and often worthy heir to his great forebears Hazlitt and Montaigne.

Posterity? That oubliette from which no reputation returns. Maugham:

> I think that one or two of my comedies may retain for some time a kind of pale life, for they are written in the tradition of English comedy . . . that began with the Restoration dramatists . . . I think a few of my best short stories will find their way into anthologies for a good many years to come if only because some of them deal with circumstances and places to which the passage of time and the growth of civilization will

give a romantic glamour. This is slender baggage, two or three plays and a dozen short stories . . .

But then it is no more than Hemingway, say, will be able to place in the overhead rack of the economy section of that chartered flight to nowhere, Twentieth Century Fiction.

I would salvage the short stories and some of the travel pieces, but I'd throw out the now-too-etiolated plays and add to Maugham's luggage *Cakes and Ale*, a small perfect novel, and, sentimentally, *The Narrow Corner*. Finally, Maugham will be remembered not so much for his own work as for his influence on movies and television. There are now hundreds of versions of Maugham's plays, movies, short stories available on cassettes, presumably forever. If he is indeed half-trashy, then one must acknowledge that the other half is of value; that is, *classicus*, 'belonging to the highest class of citizens,' or indeed of any category; hence, our word 'classic' – as in Classics *and* Commercials. Emphasis added.

*The New York Review of Books*
1 February 1990

97

# 6
# FORD'S WAY

When the old New Criticism separated Author from Text, the person and place of Author became irrelevant to any rigorous scrutiny of parthenogenetic Text. Since that split occurred more than a half century ago, Text has given way to Theory. Today, with neither significant Text nor lively Author, powerful school-teachers issue charters to be studied by adepts within the plywood of Academe, where involuntary readers search for validating signs and significations among the entrails of the latest Theory, ether-ised, as it were, upon a *tabula rasa*. Lately those American school-teachers who practise Literary Theory have taken to referring to themselves as avant-garde. (At least that was the phrase that I think I heard. The telephone connection was faulty. When I asked what was the garde they were avant to, there was only transatlantic stammering.) In any case, like early Christians we live now in the Piscine Age, with Scorpio rising.

Back in the days of the Scales, there were critics who used to describe what they had read in order to attract and illuminate those common readers who had volunteered to join what was agreed by all to be civilization as written down. The lord of the Scales at mid-century was Edmund Wilson: a true American, he believed in progress. In time, with effort and sufficient goodwill, he believed that the 'half-serious reader' would become serious, and after first disembarking at the Finland station he would book a room at Axel's Castle, and there know the sublime. But none of this happened. Railroads were superseded by airlines (signifi-cantly, in Europe, the train is coming back) and Axel's Castle is now a part of the B. Dalton chain of motels. As a source of interest for the serious, film has replaced the novel as the novel replaced the poem in the last century, soon to be, for us, but one.

The half-serious reader of yesteryear is now the film-buff. The 'educated' – that is, functionally literate public – looks at television a great deal and reads many magazines and newspapers. They read few novels and though a few of these few are read by hundreds of thousands of passionately non-serious readers, that is still a small number in a country where something like three hundred million people buzz in and out. If a new novel is highly praised it might be consumed by five thousand readers. Edna St Vincent Millay's verse used to be read in greater quantities.

Exactly forty years ago I wrote that the novel had lost the general public for good. Since this was unacceptable news to the ambitious pen-person, my simple rather obvious statement became: he says the novel is dead. My words were then made an occasion for the display of astonishing new talent, testifying to the rare rude health of Lawrence's bright book of life. Well, the truth has never helped anyone who wanted to write fiction, and perhaps it is just as well that once Author was driven from the Grove, the Text in its turn should be deconstructed and abandoned as well in favour of Theory.

Such is the overview from Parnassus. Up close, here on the ground, pen-persons still charge about hawking their wares, and American schoolteachers still delight in appropriating for them-selves the dignity and authority of the great makers of literature. But even as they prance about, English departments are losing would-be adepts even faster than Christian churches are losing priests, and the celebration of Pulitzer Eve and Booker Day are as nothing compared to the evangelical hordes that celebrate the celluloid Host at Cannes. Nevertheless, here, on the ground where we all must live until we, too, are simply history – that ultimate act of imagination – novels are still being written for the many by the – no, not few, the many. In England there are more novelists than novel-readers. But even in deliciously perverse backward little England the separation of Text from Author has had a most unexpected effect. The Text as object of interest has little or no interest for readers, while the Author as subject has come into his terrible own. Faced with reading *Across the River and into the Trees*, even the idlest of half-serious readers will turn to a biography of Hemingway. The phenomenon of the past twenty years has been the replacement of Text by Author's life, usually the work of a word processor, manipulated by a journalist or beautiful-letters writer.

In England, after the Guelph-Pooters and that con-man for all seasons, Churchill, Bloomsbury is the most popular continuing saga for half-serious readers. Who will breast *The Waves* when Mrs Woolf's diaries and letters are all now at hand like a life-preserver? What real reader does not know every detail of the private lives of the Bloomsbury writers and painters even better than those of his own acquaintance? I once knew, alas, not well, a sensitive high-strung English woman – nerves, indeed, stretched perilously taut – who said that if ever again, even by accident, she were to come across the name Carrington in print, she would kill herself. She . . . Mine eyes dazzle.

In freedom's land the lives of our midcentury poets are studied with all the pity and awe that each sought as he proceeded along his dolorous way to a supremely calculated death through falling from a high place – metaphor! – into a berry patch, or through placing – even more triumphant *closing* metaphor! – a plastic bag over the head in order to suffocate. Who needs *anyone's* poems when we have before us, with footnotes, so many lives gallantly given for the graduate schools?

Today's bookstores are crowded with the lives of writers whose books one would not dream of reading. Where the latest serious novel may sell a few thousand copies, a life of any truly messy author will sell the way novels once did. Look through the pages of this eminently serious journal and you will find that books about writers will outnumber books by writers. Fortunately, every now and then, one of these books may have a missionary function. Such is the case of Alan Judd, who has nicely produced for us *Ford Madox Ford*, whose previous compendious biographer liked neither man nor work, if one has read correctly Arthur Mizener's *The Saddest Story*.

Mr Judd is himself a lively writer with an attractive conversational style. He never bores. He likes Ford the man as perceived through that perfect confusion known as history (a.k.a. the survivors' revenge). He is shrewd about the novel in general and those novels by Ford in particular, which is pleasing to one who would place Ford among this century's half-dozen major novelists in English. In order to avoid disorder, the names of the other five will not – repeat *not* – be released until January 1, 2000 A.D. at noon. Yet even as one writes the word 'major' the whole game seems hardly worth playing. If Ford is no longer interesting to the few who read voluntarily, no critic's praise is going to be of much use beyond providing a small signpost at a largely abandoned crossroads, whose only travelled lane leads to Academe, which is nowhere in the yellow wood.

Anyway, over there, through the woods, you may find the best of historical novels, which is to say a novel that takes place in history (a category almost as valid if not as dignified as the one that takes place each summer at Bread Loaf), *The Fifth Queen*, whose subject is not so much the story of the eighth Henry's fifth wife as of Tudor England, and the beginning of the modern world that Ford still lived in. We occupy far different quarters in time, and no one has yet fixed the date when we ceased to be modern and became merely contemporary; yet somewhere close to the dateline is Ford's *The Good Soldier*, a book he called his Great Auk's egg; into this he put everything that he knew about the novel, whose art is entirely dependent on what is left out. Finally, he wrote the three – or four? – volumes known as *Parade's End*, and for those who continue to find satisfaction in, say, Flaubert's *Sentimental Education* or Proust's even longer deeper river, Ford has provided easily the best set of English variations on the theme of time and what it does to love and appetite and all the rest, including that now quaint concept, honour. Along with those three masterpieces,

Ford wrote some seventy other books. 'I never knew him when he was not writing a book,' said Katherine Anne Porter. But in a world where books were read voluntarily, this was the normal condition of the born writer; today, however, when one looks on all those books that bear Ford's name, even the most eccentric fan becomes intimidated and cannot finish, say, *The Rash Act*, which Judd admires.

So why isn't Ford on every syllabus? Why is Judd as defensive in tone as his predecessor Arthur Mizener was offensive? Why do the remaining 'voluntaries' not seem to know Ford's best work? Judd provides some reasons. As he is English and so, administratively at least, is his subject, there is a bit of confusion here about class and category, always big trouble in these now sunny northern isles. Class, category – even nationality. Ford's father, Franz Hueffer, was born in Münster – musical Hun with money, who had married into the Rossetti circle, oily lot; was connected with the Garnetts – a small anchor there. Even so, an English writer who was born Huffer or Hueffer, December 17, 1873? Difficult. Ford went to top-drawer-but-three schools in England; was blond, Germanic, blue-eyed; fortunately, as Judd nicely notes, 'He was always tall', which may have been some slight compensation for a Hunnish name during the Thirty Years German War now ending, as I write, in a shower of ecus. In due course, the name was changed from Hueffer to Ford. But nothing helped class its owner. As all good writers are, by their work, socially de-classed, he was not unique. But something about him *was* off-putting. Hemingway didn't like his smell. David Garnett confessed to a physical distaste for Ford . . . 'too mobile lips'. Ford was also pretty fat from maturity on; he smoked and drank far too much and he was besotted by women. This last would do him no good at all in a certain set of very peculiar islands where women are only appreciated by novelists like Henry James, who lusted for men, while in the great republic to the west women figure only as interlocutors of some agonized Man, awash with testosterone, as he tries to do and be what a man must do and be in spite of all ball-cutting women except for, maybe, the rare bore-proof Italian Contessa who can be relied on to ask, at intervals, like a metronome, 'Tell me again, Papa, what it was you did that was so manly and so brave and so true in *La Guerra Grande.*'

Until recently, when writing in England became a respectable hereditary occupation, to be a writer at all in a bourgeois society was to banish oneself to the margin. But Ford was born to be, proudly, an artist. The young Hueffers 'grew up conscious of themselves as heirs to a culture that transcended national boundaries'. Hence, Ford could easily and naturally befriend an icy Pole with a Berlitz problem, responding to the dictum of his beloved grandfather, the painter Ford Madox Brown, who maintained that to work hard for a genius greater than one's own is the highest virtue. Yet good as Ford was to others, he seemed to set everyone's teeth on edge. From youth 'he had been an exponent of the Grand Manner'; he spoke of Art not cricket. He was 'oracular without repartee or cruelty'; finally, 'he never signposted his irony . . . and so it was often missed'. That is one clue to his unpopularity. The British can recognise irony only when it is dispensed with an old auntie-ish twinkle, like that of E. M. Forster, while Americans have yet to discover there is such a thing. Once we do, the national motto will produce gargantuan laughter from sea to shining sea. *E pluribus unum* indeed!

Judd is very funny about one of Ford's rambles. Apparently Shakespeare had an ancestor called Hill; so did Ford. So, he mused, perhaps he was a descendant of Shakespeare, the sort of remark that could demoralise an American faculty room, impervious to his freighted tagline: '*Someone* has to be.'

Ford's unnatural liking for women and their company did him no good with the English. The fact that he was hopeless in his relations with women did him no harm with women in those days before Eve's shovel reclaimed the Garden. Stella Bowen: 'He had a genius for creating confusion.' As a conscientious biographer Judd is obliged to tell us about Ford's wives and mistresses, the sort of thing one tends to skip in biographies unless, as in the case of an American modernist poet, there is nothing else to write about save prescription drugs and prizes and tenure. Judd makes Ford's private life sound as interesting as it is possible to make that sort of thing. Early marriage to Elsie; affair with her sister Mary; then on to dashing syphilitic Violet Hunt, the Morgan Le Fay of Edwardian biographies, who once ravished the youthful lizard-lovely body of W. Somerset Maugham, thus ensuring his life-long allegiance to Sodom. Then there comes the Australian Miss Stella Bowen, who kept a written record, usually a fatal business for a loved one, but Ford comes out well in her accounts: then on to Jean Rhys followed by a twilight love with what sounds like a nice American, who survived (survives?). By Elsie, there were two daughters: one became a nun and never saw Ford again; the other did not become a nun and never saw him again. What to make of this? Nothing at all. Just a life.

I must confess to lifelong boredom with the main purpose of literary biography: the Life as opposed to the Work, which is, after all, all. I have also never had the slightest interest in knowing on whom a writer has based the character of Jeff, say, and should Jeff's affair with Jane be just like a real-life one with Gladys, I feel gravity tugging at the volume in my hand. It makes not the slightest difference whether or not one knows a writer's raw material because it is *what* he does with the stuff of his life that matters, and *how* he does it is to be found in the surviving words not in long since made beds. George Painter's enjoyable recreation of Proust's world is a distinguished work in its own right, but it sheds not a gleam of light on Proust's great fiction. Was Madame Verdurin the Duchesse de Montmorency *ci-devant* Blumenthal? Yes, no, maybe, in part – so what? Although the game is fun to play for its own sake, it is not the sort of game that an English teacher ought to encourage his students to play. It is enough that they learn how to read and understand the fiction *tout court*; to perceive what it is on the page that makes, as the Master said with unusual hard preciseness, *Interest*.

One does not want to discourage the great mills that now churn out literary biography along with bio- and necro-porn. I think that a certain amount of author's private life is useful in establishing who he was; and if certain figures influenced him greatly, then one might just as well describe them, as Judd does Marwood, Ford's 'model' for the doomed gentleman character of his best work. Beyond that, there is only pointless strain if one seeks to find the originals for characters that are themselves autonomous upon the page and should need no historical antecedent to give them life. This is also applicable, most poignantly, to history itself. But that lesson is for another day.

What interests one in Ford's case? Bloomsbury has turned out to be the epic novel of the twentieth century (will Cousin Maynard take Lytton's Duncan away from him while in the wings a ballerina warms up at the barre?) But contra Bloomsbury there is another epic narrative, lightly described in Miranda Seymour's *A Ring of Conspirators*. This subversive ring was centred in and around Romney Marsh. Personally, I find the ring more congenial and interesting than overblown Bloomsbury and it is within the ring that Ford came into his own as a young writer, established at Peat Farm. Nearby, Henry James, Joseph Conrad and Stephen Crane, who did so much better in prose what Hemingway was later to be credited for. Also the popular enchanter, H. G. Wells.

Judd's story gets very interesting indeed when he describes the unlikely collaboration of Ford and Conrad, which did the former permanent harm in the eyes of bookchatland while benefiting, if nothing else, the Pole's English. Mindful of grandfather's injunction to help genius, Ford at twenty-four made himself available to the forty-one-year-old Conrad. The results of their joint efforts (*The Inheritors, Romance, The Nature of a Crime*) are not memorable, but the fact that a young man with his own work to do should help a down-at-heels foreigner suggests altruism, a quality as hated by the generality as it is rare. Practically, Conrad was the gainer, though gratitude was not in his nature – but then Conrad was a rare sort of coincidence and had he not invented himself, no one else would have wanted to except, perhaps, Ford. But then Ford had a dowsing-rod for genius and hardly ever made a mistake from the pre-war (No.1) Ezra Pound to the pre-war (No.2) Robert Lowell. Later as an entrepreneur ('There entered then into me the itch of trying to meddle in English literary affairs'), he edited the *English Review* (1908-09) and, later still, the *Transatlantic Review* (1924-5). Most of the great figures of the Old Modernism owed him a good deal, and repaid him predictably with malice.

If nothing else, Ford gained an audience in Conrad. Each thought the novel could be high art, whose author's non-presence was an irradiating holy ghost: 'What is to be aimed at in a style is something so unobtrusive and so quiet – and so beautiful if possible – that the reader should not know he is reading, and be conscious only that he is living in the life of the book . . . a book so quiet in tone, so clearly and so unobtrusively worded, that it should give the effect of a long monologue spoken by a lover at a little distance from his mistress's ear – a book about the invisible relationships between man and man', and so on. There is hardly any novelist who would not more or less subscribe to this prescription.

Ford is stern if not rigid about the intrusion of self. Of *Tess of the D'Urbervilles*, 'Hardy was not content mercilessly to render but intervened and pleaded.' Better, simply, to show. In this Ford was like the other conspirators. Crane's power was in his apparent absence from his seen-heard narrative. Writer Crane is everything and nothing, like the weather, while James's theory of point of view has now a Sinai-esque power to it (few Jacobites ever seem to notice the author's brazen 'I' on the first page of *The Ambassadors*; of course the Master was dictating by then). For Ford, 'it is, for instance, an obvious and unchanging fact that if an author intrudes his comments into the middle of a story he will endanger the illusion conveyed by that story – but a generation of readers may come along who would prefer witnessing the capers of the author [Richard Poirier's 'performing self'] to being carried away by stories and that generation of readers may coincide with a generation of writers tired of self-obliteration . . . then you will have a movement toward diffuseness, backboneless sentences, digressions and inchoateness'. He had seen ahead to our own time while officiating at the birth in English of Modernism, giving Joyce, during the accouchement, the inspired interim title for *Finnegans Wake*, *Work in Progress*, parts of which Ford published. In the 1920s and '30s, Ford saw himself as a link between the garde of the past, Meredith, Hardy, James, and the avant-garde, Joyce, Pound, Lawrence, whose hangers-on, like Hemingway, wanted to abolish the past and be themselves the only morning of the only world to matter. Ford's insistence on the power of the predecessors made him look old-fashioned and pompous to those who painted their workrooms red in order to remind themselves to be modern. But whatever theory Ford as practitioner might hold, he never lost his passion for the making and delivery of literature to voluntary readers: 'If a boy tells me he does not like Virgil, I tell him to find something he does like and to read it with attention.'

Judd thinks Ford's poems much underrated. He wrote them, according to Robert Lowell, 'with his left hand – casually and even contemptuously'. Judd has included several very long swatches not only to show us what Ford could do in that line but to fill in the narrative gaps. There are nice lines here and there but the effect, finally, is that of Frost on a bad day; yet as Pound reminds us, 'that style of poetry we have come to take for granted but when (Ford) started it he was virtually alone'. Pound acknowledged his own debt to Ford, as did Lowell, Tate, William Carlos Williams . . . The poetry, like the prose, unfurls rather like monologue with many dashes and ellipses. In life, we are told, Ford's voice was superbly pitched for intimate narrative, and so it is in the best of his work. The only flaw is the awful copiousness, and the unblot-tedness: '. . . he would often sit and play patience, working it out, word for word, and then simply do it. He revised very little and disliked even proofreading.' Plainly, a swift-drying egg-tempera master ill-suited for slow oils. Since the best writers have nothing to say, only to add, Ford said it all at once and so was not left with those second thoughts – inspired blots – that ultimately add the highest interest.

As is so often the case, Ford's life went on until it stopped. Judd is a pleasant tour guide, with an easy colloquial style that occasionally goes beyond mere prose to something menacing and new: 'Quite what passed between she and Mary, like what passed between Mary and Ford, we do not know.' This is superb, and reminiscent, if I may drop for an instant the reviewer's anonymous mask, of the butler's line from *Duluth*, 'Whom shall I say is calling she?' There are mistakes – it is George Davis, not Davies, who, at *Harper's Bazaar*, published so many good writers. There are delights: Judd's description of Henry James, from Ford's point of view, captures with rare distinction the Master's cosy cruelty. But then Ford's simpleness excited the malice of the intricate. Witness Conrad's tribute to *The Fifth Queen*: 'The swansong of historical romance and, frankly, I am glad to have heard it.'

Judd accompanies the good soldier to America, to teaching (at Oberlin); then back to France and death at sixty-one. He notes again and again Ford's faculty for irritating people, and much is made of his lying, which seems to have been nothing more than a dressing-up and rearrangement of data which in their original form lacked – what shall I say? colour? interest? Most people, writers or not, do this. Certainly, Ford never lied deliberately in order to harm others, as did Truman Capote, or to make himself appear brave and strong and true as did Hemingway, whose own lying finally became a sort of art-form by the time he got round to settling his betters' hash in *A Moveable Feast*. Ford's essential difference from the others was the fact that he was all along what he had imagined himself to be, that latterday unicorn, a gentleman. He enlisted in the Army when he was over-age. He saw action, and stayed overseas when he could have gone home. For some reason the voluntariness of his enlistment – like so much else – upsets American book-chatters, particularly Arthur Mizener, who only finds fault with the (by military standards) elderly Ford's clumsiness as a soldier. After all, he was there, and he did not need to be there, unlike the ambulance drivers, say, who were under no military orders to die when told to.

In the wars of Venus, Ford did not traduce publicly his various mates; he kept a Tietjens silence no matter how goaded. In literary matters he lacked 'envy to an almost dangerous degree . . .' He believed above all in the importance of art – specifically the art of the novel, which puts him well outside contemporary taste, not to mention Theory. Finally, Ford thought there was such a thing as honour, a set of values by which a life and a work could be measured. In the Piscine age the word honour has no meaning at all for Americans, and who would be so cruel as to ask a Brit of today what honour is as opposed to was?

*The Times Literary Supplement*
22–28 June 1990

# 7

# OSCAR WILDE:
# ON THE SKIDS AGAIN

Must one have a heart of stone to read *The Ballad of Reading Gaol* without laughing? (In life, practically no one ever gets to kill the thing he hates, much less loves.) And did not *De Profundis* plumb for all time the shallows of the most-reported love affair of the past hundred years, rivalling even that of Wallis and David, its every nuance (O Bosie!) known to all, while trembling rosy lips yet form, over and over again, those doom-laden syllables *The Cadogan Hotel*? Oscar Wilde. Yet again. Why?

In *Four Dubliners* (1987), Richard Ellmann published essays on Yeats, Joyce, Wilde, and Beckett. 'These four', he admits, 'make a strange consortium. Yet resemblances of which they were unaware begin to appear.' Certainly no one could detect these resemblances better than the late Professor Ellmann, who devoted much of a distinguished career to Joyce and Yeats. He tells us that at eighteen Yeats heard Wilde lecture, while Joyce, at twenty, met Yeats and called him too old. In 1928 young Beckett met Joyce and they became friends . . . So much for the traffic; somewhat more to the point, 'Wilde and Yeats reviewed each other's work with mutual regard, and sometimes exploited the same themes. Joyce memorialized Wilde as an heroic victim, and repeatedly quoted or referred to him in his writings later. Beckett was saturated in all their works. . . . Displaced, witty, complex, savage they companion each other.' I wonder.

Since Ellmann had already written magisterial works on two of the four, symmetry and sympathy plainly drew him to a third; hence, this latest biography of Wilde, this last biography by Ellmann, our time's best academic biographer. Although Ellmann was unusually intelligent, a quality seldom found in academe or, indeed, on Parnassus itself, Wilde does not quite suit his schema or his talent. Aside from the fact that the four Dubliners, as he acknowledges, 'were chary of acknowledging their connection', I suspect that the controlling adjective here is 'academic'. To an academic of Ellmann's generation, explication is all.

The problem with Wilde is that he does not need explication or interpretation. He needs only to be read, or listened to. He plays no word games other than that most mechanical of verbal tricks: the paradox. When he rises to the sublime in poetry or prose there is so much purple all over the place that one longs for the clean astringencies of Swinburne.

On those occasions when Wilde is true master, the inventor of a perfect play about nothing and everything, we don't need to have the jokes explained. One simply laughs and wonders why no one else has ever been able to sustain for so long so flawlessly elegant a verbal riff. I would not like to rise in the academic world with a dissertation on Wilde's masterpiece and I suspect (but do not know) that hardly anyone has tried, particularly now that ever-easy Beckett's clamorous silences await, so temptingly, tenure seekers.

All in all, Wilde provides little occasion for Ellmann's formidable critical apparatus. Where Ellmann showed us new ways of looking at Yeats and, above all, at Joyce, he can do nothing more with Wilde than fit him into a historical context and tell, yet again, the profane story so well known to those who read. Is this worthwhile? I am not so sure. Ellmann does straighten out earlier versions of the gospel – or bad news, I suppose one should say. He rises to the essential prurience; and it is interesting to know that at thirty-one, after a lifetime of vigorous heterosexuality which had given him not only two children but syphilis, Wilde was seduced by Robert Ross, then aged seventeen, at Oxford. It is also interesting to know that Wilde, unlike Byron, Charlemagne, and Lassie, was not into buggery, preferring either oral sex or the Dover-sole kiss *cum* intercrural friction. What a one-time Warden of All Souls did for Lawrence, Ellmann now does for Wilde. Future generations will be in his – their – debt.

Future generations. Now let us be relevant, the essential task of the irrelevant (O Oscar!): *Will there be future generations?* The British press of the Aidsy Eighties thinks not. According to the *Daily Mail*, the last man on earth died in 1986, clutching to his dehydrated bosom a portrait of Margaret Thatcher. According to the *New York Post* (an Australian newspaper whose editors are able to do simple sums), the human race will be dead by century's end due to rabid homos and drug-takers (mostly black and Hispanic and viciously opposed to prayer in America's chaste bookless schools). Therefore, it is now necessary to trot out an Oscar Wilde suitable for our anxious plague-ridden times. In the four decades since the Second World War, Wilde had gradually become more and more a victim-hero of a hypocritical society whose most deeply cherished superstitions about sex were to be violently shaken, first, by the war, where the principal secret of the warrior male lodge was experienced by millions on a global scale and, second, by Dr Alfred C. Kinsey, who reported that more than one third of the triumphant Butch Republic's male population had participated in the tribal mysteries. The revolution in consciousness attributed to the Beatles and other confusions of the 1960s actually took place in the 1940s: war and Kinsey, penicillin and the pill. As a result, Oscar Wilde ceased to be regarded as a criminal; he had been nothing worse than maladjusted to a society that was not worth adjusting to. Wilde himself became a symbol of mental if not of physical health: Ellmann pinpoints the when and how of the syphilis that killed him when every orifice, suddenly, hugely, voided in a Paris hotel room. The cumulative effect of Ellmann's Wilde may suit altogether too well the Aidsy Eighties.

Currently, our rulers are tightening the screws; too much sexual freedom is bad for production and, even worse, for consumption. Sex is now worse than mere sin; it is murderous. In the selfish pursuit of happiness another may die. One understands those paranoids who think that AIDS was deliberately cooked up in a laboratory, for the idea of plague is endlessly useful, transforming society-persecutor into society-protector: urine samples here, blood tests there.

Although Ellmann certainly did not set out to recast Wilde for our dismal age, he was, like the rest of us, a part of the way we live now, and his Wilde is more cautionary-tale than martyr-story. There is the obligatory Freudianism. *Cherchez la mère* is indulged in, legitimately, I suppose. Jane Wilde, self-dubbed Speranza Francesca, was, if not larger than life, a good deal larger than average. A Protestant, Lady Wilde kept a literary salon rather than saloon in Dublin, favoured an independent Ireland, wrote thundering verse worthy of her son (anent child-nurture: 'Alas! The Fates are cruel. / Behold Speranza making gruel!') She loved sensation-making and came into her own at a treason trial in Dublin, where she was gavelled down by the judge as she tried to make herself, rather than the defendant, the fount of sedition. Later, she endured the trial for seduction, of her husband, Sir William, an oculist. Trials were, rather ominously, her ice cream. Son deeply admired mother and vice versa. But Ellmann controls himself: 'However accommodating it is to see a maternal smothering of masculinity as having contributed to [Oscar's] homosexuality there is reason to be skeptical.'

Although Ellmann has not worked out that homosexual is an adjective describing an act not a noun descriptive of a human being, he has been able to assemble data which he then tests against fashionable theory; in this case he finds theory wanting. Oscar was a brilliant creature neither more nor less 'masculine' than anyone else. What he learned from his mother was not how to be a woman but the importance of being a Show-off and a Poet and a questioner of whatever *quo* was currently *status*. He also inherited her talent for bad poetry. In due course, he re-created himself as a celebrity (a terrible word that has been used in our sense since the mid-1800s), and he was well known long before he had actually done anything at all of note. The Anglo-Irish gift of the gab, combined with an actor's timing, made him noticeable at

Oxford and unescapable in London's drawing-rooms during the 1880s. He invented a brand-new voice for himself (the Irish brogue, no matter how Merrion Squared, was dispensed with), and Beerbohm reports on his 'mezzo voice, uttering itself in leisurely fashion, with every variety of tone'. He also took to gorgeous costumes that set off his large ungainly figure to splendid disadvantage. With the death of Sir William, he possessed a small inheritance, expensive tastes and no focused ambition other than poetry, a common disease of that day; also, as Yeats put it, 'the enjoyment of his own spontaneity'.

What is most interesting in Ellmann's account is the intellectual progress of Wilde. He is particularly good on Wilde's French connection, much of it unknown to me, though I once asked André Gide several searching questions about his friend, and Gide answered me at length. That was in 1948. I have now forgotten both questions and answers. But until I read Ellmann I did not know how well and for how long the two had known each other and what an impression Wilde ('Creation began when you were born. It will end on the day you die'.) had made on Gide's tormented passage through that strait gate that leads the few to life.

As a result of a collection of fairy tales, *The Happy Prince* (a revelation to at least one American child forty years later), Wilde became famous for writing as well as for showing-off, and Paris stirred, as it sometimes will, for an Anglo (the Celtic distinction is unknown there). With the publication of the dialogue 'The Decay of Lying', Wilde took note of a change of direction in literature, and the French were both startled and delighted that the cultural wind was coming from the wrong side of the Channel. Ellmann writes:

In England decadence had always been tinged with self-mockery. By 1890, symbolism, not decadence, had the cry, as Wilde acknowledged in the preface to *Dorian Gray*. 'All art is at once surface and symbol. Those who go beneath the surface do so at their peril. Those who read the symbol do so at their peril.' These aphorisms were a bow to Stéphane Mallarmé, whom he had visited in February 1891, when he was writing the preface.

Wilde then proceeded to conquer Parisian literary life in much the same way that he had the drawing-rooms of London and the lecture halls of the United States. Incidentally, Ellmann's list of the number of places where Wilde spoke is positively presidential. In hundreds of cities and towns he lectured on the Beautiful, with numerous household hints. In his two chats 'The House Beautiful' and 'The Decorative Arts', he foreshadowed today's how-to-do-it books. He was a sensation. My twelve-year-old grandfather (during Reconstruction, Southern boys were bred early and often) recalled Wilde's performance (July 15, 1882) at the Opera House in Vicksburg, Mississippi: 'He wore', and the old man's voice trembled, 'a *girdle*, and he held a flower in his hand.' Happily, my grandfather never knew that two weeks later Wilde was received by General Grant. (As I write these lines, I wonder *how* did he know that Wilde was wearing a girdle?)

The siege of Paris was swift, the victory total. Symbolism did not need to lay siege to Wilde; he surrendered to the modernist movement, now the world's oldest *vague*, whose long roar shows no sign of withdrawing. Wilde also appropriated Mallarmé's unfinished *Hérodiade* for his own *Salomé*, written in French for Bernhardt; but the play was admired. It is interesting just how learned the writers of the last century were: the educational system Greeked and Latined them; other languages came easily to them, cultures, too. Today's writers know very little about anything. But then those who teach cannot be taught.

During the enchantment of Paris, Wilde himself was, significantly, overwhelmed by Huysmans' *A Rebours*, still a touchstone as late as the 1940s. The young Proust was impressive to Wilde because of his 'enthusiasm for English literature, especially for Ruskin (whom he translated) and George Eliot . . .' But when Proust invited him to dinner, Wilde arrived before Proust: 'I looked at the drawing room and at the end of it were your parents, my courage failed me.' Wilde departed, after the thoughtful observation to M. and Mme Proust: 'How ugly your house is.'

With the local cat-king, Edmund de Goncourt, Wilde was no less tutorial. In a newspaper piece, Goncourt had got all wrong Wilde's remarks about Swinburne, while Wilde himself was sneered at as 'this individual of doubtful sex, with a ham actor's language, and tall stories'. Wilde chose to ignore the personal attack in a letter that set straight the gossip: 'In Swinburne's work we meet for the first time the cry of flesh tormented by desire and memory, joy and remorse, fecundity and sterility. The English public, as usual hypocritical, prudish, and philistine, has not known how to find the art in the work of art: it has searched for the man in it.' *Tiens!* as Henry James liked to write in his notebook. The biographer has license to go a-hunting for the man; the critic not; the reader – why not just read what's written?

Wilde the playwright is duly recorded, duly celebrated. Ellmann has some nice greenroom gossip for those who like that sort of thing. It is interesting to know that when Beerbohm Tree addressed a 'brilliant lady' on stage he did so with his back to the audience (a Bernhardt trick, too). But then when he had an epigram to launch, he would turn to face the audience, to their ravishment. For those who like such things, there is also a very great deal about Wilde's love affair with a boring boy-beauty called Bosie. At this late date it is no longer a story worth retelling, and if Ellmann had added anything new to it I did not notice. The trial. Prison. Exile. The usual. I suspect that one of the reasons we create fiction is to make sex exciting; the fictional meeting between Vautrin and Lucien de Rubempré at the coach house in Balzac's *Illusions Perdues* is one of the most erotic ever recorded. But details of the real Oscar and Bosie in bed together or in combination with bits and pieces of England's adenoidal trade, more gifted at blackmail than ganymedery, create for the reader neither tumescence nor moistness; rather, one's thoughts turn sombrely to laundry and to the brutal horror of life in a world without dry cleaning.

Ellmann's literary criticism is better than his telling of the oft-told tale. He is particularly good on *Dorian Gray*, a book truly subversive of the society that produced it – and its author. He is interesting on Wilde's conversion to a kind of socialism. Of Wilde's essay 'The Soul of Man Under Socialism', Ellmann tells us that it 'is based on the paradox that we must not waste energy in sympathizing with those who suffer needlessly, and that only socialism can free us to cultivate our personalities. Charity is no use – the poor are . . . right to steal rather than to take alms.' On the other hand, Wilde was wary of authoritarianism, so often socialism's common-law helpmeet. In the end, Wilde veered off into a kind of anarchy; and defined the enemy thus:

> There are three sorts of despots. There is the despot who tyrannizes over the body. There is the despot who tyrannizes over the soul. There is the despot who tyrannizes over the soul *and* body alike. The first is called the Prince. The second is called the Pope. The third is called the People.

Joyce was impressed by this and borrowed it for *Ulysses*. Inadvertently (I suspect), Richard Ellmann does make it clear that for all the disorder of Wilde's life he was never, in the Wordsworthian sense, 'neglectful of the universal heart'.

Yeats thought Wilde a man of action, like Byron, who had got waylaid by literature. When this was repeated to Wilde, he made an offhand remark about the boredom of Parliament. But Yeats did sense in Wilde the energy of the actor: of one who acts, rather than of one who simply, bemusedly *is* – the artist. But whatever Wilde might or might not have done and been, he was an extremely good man and his desire to subvert a supremely bad society was virtuous. Cardinal Newman, writing of their common day, said, 'The age is so very sluggish that it will not hear you unless you bawl – you must first tread on its toes, and then apologise.' But behaviour suitable for an ecclesiastical busybody is all wrong for Oscar Wilde, whose only mistake was to apologise for his good work and life.

*The Times Literary Supplement*
2–8 October 1987

# 8

# HOW I DO WHAT
# I DO IF NOT WHY

I

In the beginning, there was the spoken word. The first narrations concerned the doings of gods and kings, and these stories were passed on from generation to generation, usually as verse in order to make memorizing easier. Then, mysteriously, in the fifth century B.C. all the narratives were written down, and literature began. From Greece to Persia to India to China, there was a great controversy. Could a narrative be possessed that had been committed to writing rather than to memory? Traditionalists said no; modernists said yes. The traditionalists lost. Now, twenty-five hundred years later, there is a similar crisis. Modernists believe that any form of narration and of learning can be transmitted through audiovisual means rather than through the, now, traditional written word. In this controversy I am, for once, a conservative to the point of furious reaction.

In any case, we are now obliged to ask radical questions. What is the point to writing things down other than to give directions on how to operate a machine? Why tell stories about gods and kings or, even, men and women?

Very early, the idea of fame – eternal fame – afflicted our race. But fame for the individual was less intense at the beginning than for one's tribe. Thucydides is often read as a sort of biographer of Pericles when, indeed, he was writing the biography, to misuse the word, of their city, Athens. It is the idea of the city that the writer wants us to understand, not the domestic affairs of Pericles, which he mentions only as civic illustrations. Love had not yet been discovered as opposed to lust. Marriage was not yet a subject except for comedy (Sophocles did not care who got custody of the children, unless Medea killed them; or they were baked in a pie). For more than two millennia, from Homer to Aeschylus to Dante to Shakespeare to Tolstoy, the great line of our literature has concerned itself with gods, heroes, kings, in conflict with one another and with inexorable fate. Simultaneously, all around each story, whether it be that of Prometheus or of a Plantagenet prince, there is a people who need fire from heaven or land beyond the sea. Of arms and the man I sing, means just that. Of the people then and now, of the hero then and his image now, as created or re-created by the poet. From the beginning, the bard, the poet, the writer was a most high priest to his people, the custodian of their common memory, the interpreter of their history, the voice of their current yearnings.

All this stopped in the last two centuries when the rulers decided to teach the workers to read and write so that they could handle machinery. Traditionalists thought this a dangerous experiment. If the common people knew too much might they not overthrow their masters? But the modernists, like John Stuart Mill, won. And, in due course, the people – proudly literate – overthrew their masters. We got rid of the English while the French and the Russians – ardent readers – shredded their ancient monarchies. In fact, the French – who read and theorize the most – became so addicted to political experiment that in the two centuries since America's rather drab revolution they have exuberantly produced one Directory, one Consulate, two empires, three restorations of the monarchy, and five republics. That's what happens when you take writing too seriously. Happily, Americans have never liked reading all that much. Politically ignorant, we keep sputtering along in our old Model T, looking wistfully every four years for a good mechanic.

Along with political change – the result of general literacy and the printing press – the nature of narrative began to fragment. High literature concerned itself, most democratically, with the doings of common folk. Although a George Eliot or a Hardy could make art out of these simple domestic tales, in most hands crude mirrors of life tend to be duller than Dumas, say, and, paradoxically, less popular. Today's serious novel is apt to be a carefully written teacherly text about people who teach school and write teacherly texts for dwindling classes. Today's popular novel, carelessly, recklessly composed on – or by – a machine, paradoxically has taken over the heroes and kings and gods, and places them in modern designer clothes amongst consumer dreams beyond the dreams of Scheherazade.

This is a strange reversal. The best writers tend to write, in a highly minimal way, of the simple and the dull, while the worst give us whirlwind tours of the house – I mean home – of Atreus, ripping every skeleton from its closet, and throwing back every Porthault sheet. The fact that this kind of bad writing is popular is not because the reading public – an endangered minority – cherishes bad writing for its own sake but because the good writers fail to interest them. As a result, everything is now so totally out of whack that the high academic bureaucrats have dropped literature, with some relief, and replaced it with literary theory, something that one needs no talent to whip up. As a result, in twenty years, enrolment in American English departments has been cut by more than half. Writers and writing no longer matter much anywhere in freedom's land. Mistuh Emerson, he dead. Our writers are just entertainers, and not all that entertaining either. We have lost the traditional explainer, examiner, prophet.

So what am I up to? If nothing else, I continue, endlessly, to explain, to examine, to prophesy, particularly in the six novels (*Burr; Lincoln; 1876; Empire; Hollywood; Washington, D.C.*) where I deal with the history of the United States from the beginning to now. The fact that there is still a public eager to find out who we are and what we did ought to encourage others to join me but, by and large, the universities have made that impossible. They have established an hegemony over every aspect of literature – except the ability to make any. They have also come to believe that a serious novelist deals only with what he knows and since our educational system is what it is he is not apt to know much about anything; and since our class system is uncommonly rigid he is not going to have much chance to find out about any world other than the one he was born into – and the school he went to. Certainly, he will never, like his predecessors, be able to deal with his nation's rulers. They prefer the shadows. Mary McCarthy recently listed all the things that cannot be put into a serious novel – from sunsets to a hanging to a Cabinet meeting. Also, to be fair, though our political life is entirely devoid of politics, it is so vivid with personalities and the stuff of bad fiction that one can hardly expect the novelist to compete with the journalist.

One of the absolutes of bookchat land is that the historical novel is neither history nor a novel. On the other hand, a literal record of a contemporary murder is, triumphantly, a novel. This is what I call 'the Capote confusion', his monument. Actually, there is no such thing as The Novel as opposed to novels. No one can say what a novel ought to be. But history is something else. Although I try to make the agreed-upon facts as accurate as possible, I always use the phrase 'agreed upon' because what we know of a figure as recent, say, as Theodore Roosevelt is not only not the whole truth – an impossibility anyway – but the so-called facts are often contradicted by other facts. So one must select; and it is in selection that literature begins. After all, with *whose* facts do you agree? Also, in a novel, as opposed to a literal history, one can introduce made-up characters who can speculate on the motives of the real people. How real are the real people? Do I have them say what they really said, or am I, like Shakespeare, reinventing them? For those of you ablaze with curiosity regarding the difference between Shakespeare and me, I'll give you an example.

There is in Washington, DC, my native city and often subject, a South Korean newspaper called the *Washington Times*. This paper is owned by the Moonies and its political line is, baroquely, fascist. Now let's watch one of their employees in action. The first scene of a recent book of mine, *Empire*, takes place in England, at a country house that has been rented for the summer of 1898 by Henry Adams and Senator Don Cameron for the use of their friend John Hay, our Ambassador. All those present at a lunch that I describe were actually there, including Henry James, an old friend of Hay and of Adams, who was living in nearby Rye. Confronted with such a scene, the hostile reviewer – who writes only of what *he* knows – often shouts name-dropper. But how is it possible to tell the story of John Hay without mentioning the fact that as Lincoln's secretary, he got to meet Lincoln? The South Korean reviewer does the ritual attack on me: I hate my native land because I deplore the National Security State. Because I deplore our imperial adventures, I am an *isolationist*. He tells us:

> 'Henry James and Henry Adams figure in *Empire*, neither of them believably, alas . . . for their main function is to serve as spokesmen for Mr Vidal's isolationism. "You speak of the laws of history and I am no lawyer," says the Vidalized James. "But I confess to misgivings. How can we, who honestly cannot govern ourselves, take up the task of governing others? Are we to govern the Philippines from Tammany Hall?" Neither in style nor in substance does this mini-editorial sound even remotely like the Master.'

That is very magisterial indeed. Plainly, a James scholar. But let's look at what the Master actually wrote apropos the Spanish-American war. In a letter, he remarks on his 'deep embarrassment of thought – of imagination. I have hated, I have almost loathed it.' James also spoke most sardonically of 'the exportation of Tammany and King Caucus' to the newly acquired Philippines, 'remote countries run by bosses'. My South Korean critic did not quote easily the harshest of the 'Vidalized' Henry James's remarks: 'The acquisition of an empire civilized the English. That may not be a law but it is a fact. . . . But what civilized them might very well demoralize us even further.' That's about as anti-imperial – or 'isolationist' – as you can get. Now did the real Henry James ever say so un-American a thing? Yes, he did, when he confided to his nephew Harry: 'Expansion has so made the English what they are – for good or for ill, but on the whole for good – that one doesn't quite feel one's way to say for one's country "No – I'll have none of it." Empire has educated the English. Will it only demoralize us?' Now you see how I have 'my' James say, in substance, precisely what the original said. I do condense and rearrange, something a biographer must never do but a novelist must do. If the James of *Empire* is not credible then he himself would not be credible to a jingo on a Washington newspaper, who also tells us that no young woman – like my invented Caroline – could have taken over a Washington newspaper and made a success of it. But less then twenty years later one Eleanor Patterson, whom I knew very well, did just that and published the earlier *Washington Times-Herald.* As for America's perennially venal press, the *Washington Times* reviewer will be stunned to hear Henry James, in real life, blame the newspapers for the despicable war with Spain because of 'the horrible way in which they envenomize all dangers and reverberate all lies'. Like Mark Twain and William Dean Howells he was, incredibly, an 'isolationist' with a contempt for the popular press. So, as you can see, I do not invent my literary ancestors. If anything, they invented me.

I have mentioned agreed-upon facts as the stuff of history. But if it is impossible to take seriously the press of one's own time, why should the historian treat old newspaper cuttings as unimpeachable primary sources? For instance, I am now writing about Warren Harding. One of the few quotations of Harding that I have known all my life was what he said after his unlikely nomination for president, 'We drew to a pair of deuces, and filled.' This strikes absolutely the right note for the agreed-upon Harding that our canting society requires: a sleazy, poker-playing, hard-drinking, womanising nonentity put in office by cynical Republican bosses. Yet the journalist Mark Sullivan was with Harding before, during, and after the 1920 convention. In *Our Times* he quotes the poker phrase; then, in a footnote, he says this sort of phrase was not characteristic of Harding, who had a considerable sense of his own dignity. Apparently, Sullivan, who could have asked Harding at any time during the next three years if he had made this remark, never did. Instead he tells us that maybe Harding said it when he was 'off balance' from excitement. 'Or he may never have said it – it may have been some reporter's conception of what he ought to say.' There we have it. In effect, the press invents us all; and the later biographer or historian can only select from the mass of crude fictions and part-truths those 'facts' that his contemporaries are willing to agree upon.

Where many English department hustlers now favour literary theory over literature, the workaday bureaucrats of the History departments are solemnly aware that *their* agreed-upon facts must constitute – at least in the short term – a view of the republic that will please their trustees. Since all great Americans are uniquely great, even saints, those who record the lives of these saints are hagiographers. This is quite a big solemn business, not unlike the bureaucracy of some huge advertising firm, handling a hallowed account like Ivory Soap. A major bureaucrat is Comar Vann Woodward, Sterling Professor of History Emeritus at Yale. A Southerner, he noticed, many years ago, that blacks were people. This Newtonian revelation brought him tenure; and landed him many important accounts.

Like so many academic bureaucrats the Sterling Professor is highly protective of his turf; he does not want the untenured loose in the field. Sadly, he noted in the *New York Review of Books*, regarding my novel *Lincoln*, that the 'book was extravagantly praised by both novelists and historians – a few of the latter at least. Some of the foremost Lincoln scholars do not share these views. After listing numerous historical blunders and errors of the novel, Richard N. Current, a leading Lincoln biographer, declares that "Vidal is wrong on big as well as little matters. He grossly distorts Lincoln's character and role in history."' Woodward gives no examples of these distortions. He does tell us that 'Roy P. Basler, editor of *The Collected Works of Abraham Lincoln*, estimates that "more than half of the book could never have happened as told by Vidal."' Apparently, Woodward believes that it is sufficient merely to assert. He does not demonstrate, doubtless because he is innocent of the text in question; so he cites, vaguely, other assertions.

Vladimir Nabokov used to say that when anyone criticised his art, he was indifferent. That was their problem. But if anyone attacked his scholarship, he reached for his dictionary. After reading Woodward, I took the trouble to read the two very curious little essays that he cites. What case do they make? Is half the book all wrong; and Lincoln himself grossly distorted? Although I do my own research, unlike so many professors whose hagiographies are usually the work of those indentured servants, the graduate students, when it comes to checking a finished manuscript, I turn to Academe. In this case Professor David Herbert Donald of Harvard, who has written a great deal about the period which the Sterling Professor, as far as I recall, has not written about at all. Once the book was written, I employed a professional researcher to correct dates, names, and even agreed-upon facts.

Professor Richard N. Current fusses, not irrelevantly, about the propriety of fictionalising actual political figures. I also fuss about this. But he has fallen prey to the scholar-squirrels' delusion that there is a final Truth revealed only to the tenured few in their footnote maze; in this he is simply naive. All we have is a mass of more or less agreed-upon facts about the illustrious dead, and each generation tends to rearrange those facts according to what the times require. Current's text seethes with resentment, and I can see why. 'Indeed, Vidal claims to be a better historian than any of the academic writers on Lincoln ("hagiographers" he calls them).' Current's source for my unseemly boasting is, God help us, the Larry King radio show, which lasts several hours from midnight on, and no one is under oath for what he says during – in my case – two hours. On the other hand, Larry King, as a source, is about as primary as you can get.

Now it is true that I have been amazed that there has never been a first-rate biography of Lincoln, as opposed to many very good and – yes, scholarly – studies of various aspects of his career. I think one reason for this lack is that too often the bureaucrats of Academe have taken over the writing of history and most of them neither write well nor, worse, understand the nature of the men they are required to make saints of. In the past, history was the province of literary masters – of Gibbon, Macaulay, Burke, Locke, Carlyle and, in our time and nation, Academe's *bête noire*, Edmund Wilson. In principle, it would be better if English teachers did not write novels and history teachers did not write history. After all, teaching is a great and essential profession, marvellously ill-practised in our country as was recently demonstrated when half of today's college freshmen could not locate, on an unmarked map of the world, the United States. Obviously, there are fine academic historians (to whom I am indebted) but the Donalds, McPhersons, and Foners are greatly outnumbered by – the others.

Then, zeroing in on my chat with Larry King, Current writes that '. . . by denying there is any real basis for Vidal's intimation that Lincoln had syphilis, [Stephen] Oates "shows," according to Vidal, "that, . . . Mr Oates is not as good a historian as Mr Vidal."' First, I like Current's slippery 'any real basis' for Lincoln's syphilis. No, there is no existing Wassermann report or its equivalent. But there is the well-known testimony of William Herndon, Lincoln's law partner, that Lincoln told him that he had contracted syphilis in his youth and that it had 'hung to him'. This is a primary source not to be dismissed lightly; yet Mr Oates was quoted in the press as saying that there was never *any* evidence that Lincoln had had syphilis, ignoring Lincoln's own words to Herndon. It was *Newsweek*, not I, who said that Mr Vidal is a better historian than Mr Oates. I have no opinion in the matter as I've never read Oates except on the subject of me, where he is bold and inaccurate.

Current finds my trust in Herndon naive; and quotes Professor Donald on Herndon as being important largely because of 'the errors that he spread'. But Donald was referring to Herndon's haphazard researches into Lincoln's family and early life, conducted after Lincoln's death. I am not aware that Donald or anyone – except a professional hagiographer – could doubt Herndon when he says that Lincoln himself told him something. For the record, Donald's actual words: 'Herndon stands in the backward glance of history, mythmaker and truthteller.'

Current has literary longings; he frets over my prose. I spell 'jewelry' and 'practice' in the English manner and speak of a house *in* Fourteenth Street instead of *on* Fourteenth Street. It was not until H. L. Mencken, in 1919, that an attempt was made to separate the American language from the English; and even then many writers ignored and still ignore the Sage of Baltimore. Since *Burr* and *1876* were written in the first person, as if by an American early in the last century, I used those locutions that were then common to agreed-upon American speech. For consistency's sake, I continued them in *Lincoln*. As for myself, neither in prose nor in life would I say that someone lived on Fourteenth Street, though in the age of Reagan I have detected quite a few people living on rather than in streets. I also note that two novels I've been rereading follow my usage: *The Great Gatsby* (1925), *The Last Puritan* (1936). Current wins only one small victory: I use the word *trolley* in 1864 although the word did not surface until the 1890s. But his other objections are not only trivial but wrong. He says Charles Sumner was struck with a 'cane' not, as I say, a 'stick'; then ar. I now the words are interchangeable, at least in Senator Sumner's circles. He also trots out the tired quibble over the origin of 'hooker'. For the purposes of a Civil War novel it is enough to give General Hooker the credit because the whores in Marble Alley, back of what is now the Washington Post Office, were commonly known as Hooker's Division. According to Partridge's *Dictionary of Slang*, the only British meaning we have for the word at that time is a watch-stealer or pickpocket.

Current then fires off a series of statements that I have written such and such. And such and such is not true. This is dizzy even by contemporary American university standards. For instance, 'Ulysses S. Grant had not failed in "the saddlery business."' That he had failed is an offhand remark I attribute (without footnote) to a contemporary. The truth? At thirty-seven Grant had failed at every civilian job he had put his hand to, obliging him to become a clerk in his father's firm, Grant & Perkins, which 'sold harnesses and other leather goods . . . providing new straps for old saddles' (William McFeely's *Grant*), and the business was run not by failure Grant but by his younger brother Orvil. Current is also outraged by a reference to Lincoln's bowels, whose 'frequency', he tells us, 'cannot be documented'. But, of course, they can. 'Truth-teller' Herndon tells us that Lincoln was chronically constipated and depended on a laxative called blue-mass. Since saints do not have bowels, Current finds all this sacrilegious; hence 'wrong'.

Now there is no reason why Current, master of our language though he is, should understand how a novel – even one that incorporates actual events and dialogue – is made. The historian-scholar, of course, plays God. He has his footnotes, his citations, his press-clippings, his fellow scholar-squirrels to quote from. If he lacks literary talent, he will simply serve up the agreed-upon facts as if they were the Truth, and should he have a political slant – and any American schoolteacher is bound to, and most predictable it is – the result will emerge as a plaster saint, like that dead effigy of Jefferson by Dumas Malone and his legion of graduate students.

Although a novel *can* be told as if the author is God, often a novel is told from the point of view of one or more characters. For those of us inclined to the Jamesian stricture, a given scene ought to be observed by a single character, who can only know what he knows, which is often less than the reader. For someone with no special knowledge of – or as yet interest in – Grant, the fact that harnesses and *other* leather goods were sold along with saddles by the failure Grant is a matter of no interest. The true scholar-squirrel, of course, must itemise everything sold in the shop. This is the real difference between a novel and a biography. But though I tend in these books more to history than to the invented, I am still obliged to dramatise my story through someone's consciousness. But when it comes to a great mysterious figure like Lincoln, I do not enter his mind. I only show him as those around him saw him at specific times. This rules out hindsight, which is all that an historian, by definition, has; and which people in real life, or in its imitation the novel, can never have.

Current is a master of the one-line unproved assertion. Here are some of what he calls my false 'contentions'. 'As early as April 1861 Lincoln was thinking of emancipation as possibly justifiable as "a military necesssity."' I looked up the scene in the novel and found that it was not Lincoln but the abolitionist Sumner who was thinking along those lines; Lincoln himself was noncommittal. Then 'Vidal pictures Lincoln as an ignoramus in regard to public finance. He makes him so stupid as to think Secretary of the Treasury Chase personally signed every greenback, and so uninformed as to have "no idea what the greenbacks actually represented."' This is nicely – deliberately? – garbled. It is not Chase whom Lincoln thinks signs the greenbacks but the treasurer, Lucius Crittenden; this provided a famous scene in Carl Sandburg's hagiography, on which I do an ironical variation.

Current tells us that I go along with the 'innuendo' that Stanton 'masterminded the assassination'. If he had actually read the whole book, he would have been able to follow almost every turn to Booth's assassination plot, in which Stanton figures not at all; had he got to the end of the book, he would have heard Hay make fun of those who believed that Stanton had any connection with the murder of the man to whom he owed everything. Next I 'intimate' that there was a second plot afoot, involving 'Radical Republicans in Congress'. There was indeed a second plot, to be found in Pinkerton's Secret Service files. But no one knows who masterminded it.

Next, I propose the following outrage; that 'Lincoln excluded Union-held areas from the Emancipation Proclamation' as a favour to 'pro-Union slaveholders'. Yet it is a fact that seven counties in and around Norfolk, Virginia, and several Louisiana parishes were allowed to maintain slavery while slavery was banned in the rest of the south. Why did Lincoln do this? He needed Unionist votes in Congress, and one belonged to a Louisiana Congressman. After all, Lincoln was never an abolitionist; he was a Unionist, and as he most famously said, if he could preserve the Union only by maintaining slavery, he would do so. Apparently, saints don't make deals.

* * *

By and large, Current's complaints range from the trivial to the pointless. Does he find me wrong on anything of consequence? Yes, he does. And I think it is the whole point to his weird enterprise. Current tells us that 'there is no convincing evidence' for Vidal's contention that 'as late as April 1865 [Lincoln] was still planning to colonise freed slaves outside the United States'. This is a delicate point in the 1980s, when no national saint can be suspected of racism. I turned to one of my authorities for this statement; and realised that I may have relied on suspect scholarship. Here is the passage I used:

> Lincoln to the last seemed to have a lingering preference for another kind of amendment, another kind of plan. He still clung to his old ideas of postponing final emancipation, compensating slaveholders, and colonising freedmen. Or so it would appear. As late as March of 1865, if the somewhat dubious Ben Butler is to be believed, Lincoln summoned him to the White House to discuss with him the feasibility of removing the colored population of the United States.

This is from a book called *The Lincoln Nobody Knows* (p. 230) by Richard N. Current. So either Current is as wrong about this as he is about me, or he is right and between March and April 15, 1865, when Lincoln departed this vale of tears, the President changed his mind on the colonising of slaves. If he did, there is no record known to me – or, I suspect, to anyone else.

What is going on here is a deliberate revision by Current not only of Lincoln but of himself in order to serve the saint in the 1980s as opposed to the saint at earlier times when blacks were still coloured, having only just stopped being Negroes. In coloured and Negro days the saint might have wanted them out of the country, as he did. But in the age of Martin Luther King even the most covertly racist of school boards must agree that a saint like Abraham Lincoln could never have wanted a single black person to leave freedom's land much less bravery's home. So all the hagiographers are redoing their plaster images, and anyone who draws attention to the discrepancy between their own past crudities and their current falsities is a very bad person indeed, and not a scholar, and probably a communist as well.

Roy P. Basler, Woodward's other 'authority', is given to frantic hyperbole. He declares Carl Sandburg's *Lincoln* a 'monumental achievement'. Well, it's a monument all right – to a plaster saint, of the sort that these two professional hagiographers are paid to keep dusted. Basler finds my *Lincoln* the 'phoniest historical novel I have ever had the pleasure of reading'. Well, there may be *one* phony bit, the Crittenden signature story, which I got from Basler's monumental biographer, Sandburg. Basler should have at least liked that. Also, 'more than half the book could never have happened as told'. Unfortunately, he doesn't say which half. If I knew, we could than cut it free from the phony half and publish the result as Basler's Vidal's *Lincoln*.

Like Current, Basler gets all tangled up in misread or misunderstood trivia. He goes on at great length that it was not the Reverend James Smith whom Lincoln appointed consul in Scotland but his son Hugh. Well, the son, Hugh, was appointed consul on June 10, 1861; then died; and the father was appointed, later, in his place. Basler says that Mary Todd's scene with General Ord's wife 'is histrionically exaggerated out of all proportion to the recorded facts'. But it conforms with those recorded facts given by Justin G. and Linda Levitt Turner's standard *Mary Todd Lincoln: Her Life and Letters*. He is also most protective of the saint. For instance, every saint is a kind and indulgent yet gently stern father, devoted to his children who worship him. But Lincoln's oldest son, Robert, did not much like his father.

Basler gets all trembly as he writes:

> When Vidal has Robert Lincoln say to Hay about his father, 'He hates his past. He hates having been a scrub. . . . He wanted me to be what he couldn't be,' I find no excuse. Robert did admit that he and his father had never been close after he was grown, and he may have felt neglected, but for him to speak thus is beyond comprehension.

But he did speak thus, to Senator Thomas Pryor Gore of Oklahoma, my grandfather, who often talked to me about Robert's bleak attitude toward his father, who, having sent his son to Exeter and Harvard in order to move him up in the world, then found that he had a son with whom he had not much in common. I myself attended Exeter four score years after Robert, and memories of Lincoln were still vivid; and well described not long ago in the alumni bulletin: how Lincoln spoke at the Academy shortly after Cooper Union, and enthralled the boys. But not Robert.

Basler is also protective of the only recently beatified, by Academe, Walt Whitman. (This miracle was accomplished by making Walt Whitman homoerotic rather than homosexual.) 'Consider', he rails, 'the three pages [actually one and a half] that he devotes to a fictional interview with Secretary of the Treasury, Salmon P. Chase, looking for a job.' Basler correctly notes that a Mr Trowbridge presented a letter to Chase from Emerson, asking that Whitman be given a job. I have Whitman delivering the letter. Basler is stern. 'Anyone who knows about Whitman would recognise that presenting the letter in person . . . is wholly false to Whitman's character at this time of his life, and his conversation with Chase is entirely what Vidal might have said, but not Whitman.' If Whitman had thought a meeting with Chase would have got him a job he would have done so because, as he wrote of himself then, 'I was pulling eminent wires in those days.'

As for Whitman's dialogue with Chase, I quite fancied it. He describes the decorations of the Capitol and how 'not in one's flightiest dreams has there been so much marble and china, gold and bronze, so many painted gods and goddesses'. Whitman compares the Capitol – favourably – but fatally for the teetotaller Chase – to Taylor's saloon in New York. I took this particular passage from Whitman's *Democratic Vistas*, as anyone immersed in the Whitman style – or mine for that matter – would know. Literary criticism is not, perhaps, Basler's strong suit. Actually, I needed the encounter to fill in my portrait of Chase, who, exactly as I described, detested Whitman as the author of a 'very bad book', which he had not read; then, being an autograph collector,

Chase kept the Emerson letter; then, being a jittery man on the subject of public rectitude, he turned the letter over to the Treasury archive. This is not too bad for a page and a half – of agreed-upon facts, used to illuminate the character not of Whitman but of Chase.

Basler like Current is eager to bring the saint into the mainstream of today's political superstition. Both are appalled whenever I mention his scheme for colonising the ex-slaves. Both deny that he ever had anything but love and admiration for blacks, who were, he believed, in every way his equals, once slavery was past. 'The one thing I most resented', writes Basler, 'is the perpetuation of "Lincoln's unshaken belief that the colored race was inferior to the white . . ." I have never found any such categorical avowal in anything Lincoln wrote or was reported to have said.' The slippery adjective here is 'categorical'. Yet Basler himself wrote in *The Lincoln Legend* (pp. 210–211), '[Lincoln] never contemplated with any degree of satisfaction the prospect of a free negro race living in the same country with a free white race.' Not even I have dared go so far as to suggest that I have ever had any way of knowing what Lincoln may or may not have *contemplated*! In any case, Basler, like Current, is revising himself.

It is my radical view that Americans are now sufficiently mature to be shown a Lincoln as close to the original as it is possible for us so much later in time to get. Since the race war goes on as fiercely as ever in this country, I think candour about blacks and

Actually, Lincoln's views of blacks were common to his time and place but, as he was an uncommon man, he tried to transcend them, as he did in a speech in Peoria, in 1854: 'My first impulse', he said rather daringly for that year, 'would be to free all slaves and send them to Liberia.' He then lists all the objections that others would later make to him. He finally throws in the towel when he asks: 'Free them and make them politically and socially our equals? Our own feelings would not admit of it, and if mine would, we well know that those of the great mass of whites will not.'

whites and racism is necessary. It was part of Lincoln's greatness that, unlike those absolute abolitionists, the Radical Republicans, he foresaw the long ugly confrontation, and tried to spare future generations by geographically separating the races. The fact that his plan was not only impractical but inadvertently cruel is beside the point. He wanted to *do* something; and he never let go the subject, unless of course he had a vision in the last two weeks of his life, known only to Current, who has chosen not to share it.

Recently, an excellent academic historian, Theodore S. Hamerow, published a book called *Reflections on History and Historians*. It was reviewed in *The New York Times* by an English history don, Neil McKendrick. Here is what two professionals have to say of the average American history teacher. As presented by Hamerow, he is 'cynical'. I quote now from McKendrick: 'He is also mean-minded, provincial and envious. We hear verdict after verdict condemning, in the words of one academic, "the wretched pedantry, the meanness of motive, the petty rancors of rivalry, the stultifying provincialism."' But then 'most professors of history do little research and less publishing and there are statistical tables to prove it. What little is produced is seen as 'coerced productivity,' mainly a parade of second-hand learning and third-rate opinions." Thus, the high professional academics view their run-of-the-mill colleagues.

Recently in *The New York Times* Herbert Mitgang took me to task, indirectly, when he wrote: 'Several revisionist academics have advanced the incredible theory that Lincoln really wanted the Civil War, with its 600,000 casualties, in order to eclipse the Founding Fathers and insure his own place in the pantheon of great presidents.' Now there is no single motive driving anyone but, yes, that is pretty much what I came to believe, as Lincoln himself got more and more mystical about the Union, and less and less logical in his defence of it, and more and more appalled at all the blood and at those changes in his country, which, he confessed – with pride? – were 'fundamental and astounding'. The Lincoln portrayed by me is based on a speech he made in 1838 at the

Young Men's Lyceum in Springfield. He began by praising the Founding Fathers and their republic; then he went on:

> This field of glory is harvested, and the crop is already appropriated. But new reapers will arise, and they too will seek a field. It is to deny what the history of the world tells us is true to suppose that men of ambitions and talents will not continue to spring up amongst us. And when they do, they will as naturally seek the gratification of their ruling passions as others have done before them. The question, then, is can that gratification be found in supporting and maintaining an edifice that has been erected by others? Most certainly it cannot.

Thus Lincoln warns us against Lincoln.

> Towering genius disdains a beaten path. It seeks regions unexplored. . . . It denies that it is glory enough to serve under any chief. It scorns to tread in the path of any predecessor however illustrious. It thirsts and burns for distinction; and, if possible, it will have it, whether at the expense of emancipating slaves or enslaving free men.

Nothing that Shakespeare ever invented was to equal Lincoln's invention of himself and, in the process, us. What the Trojan War was to the Greeks, the Civil War is to us. What the wily Ulysses was to the Greeks, the wily Lincoln is to us – not plaster saint but towering genius, our nation's haunted and haunting re-creator.


2


It's savoury scholar-squirrel stew time again! Or, to be precise, one scholar-squirrel and one plump publicist-pigeon for the pot. So, as the pot boils and I chop this pile of footnotes fine, let me explain to both pigeon and the no doubt bemused readers of these pages why it was that *The New York Times*, the Typhoid Mary of

American journalism, should have wanted to discredit, one week before airing, the television dramatisation of my book on Abraham Lincoln. The publicist (a caption-*and*-text writer for two Civil War picture books that he shrewdly guesses I've never looked at) tells us that 'The *Times* did not assign me to "bloody" the mini-series . . . but to measure its faithfulness to history', etc. This begs the question. Why, if the *Times* were so uncharacteristically concerned with faithfulness to fact of any kind, should they select him, a non-historian, whose current job, he told me, disarmingly, is that of publicist for the admirable Mario Cuomo? I suspect that he was chosen because a publicist will give an editor exactly what he wants. In any case, my own long history with *The New York Times* does, in a curious way, illuminate not only this peculiar dispute but the rather more interesting nature of history itself.

In 1946 my first novel was published. A war novel, it was praised by the daily book reviewer of the *Times*, one Orville Prescott, whose power to 'make or break' a book was then unique; and now unimaginable. I was made. Then, in 1948, two books were published within weeks of each other. First, *The City and the Pillar* by me; then *Sexual Behavior in the Human Male* by Dr Alfred C. Kinsey, *et al.* In my novel, I found the love affair between two ordinary American youths to be a matter-of-fact and normal business. Dr Kinsey then confirmed, statistically, that more than a third of the American male population had performed, at least once, a vile and abominable act against nature. Since the generation of American males that he was studying had just won the last great war that our sissy republic ever was to win (as R. M. Nixon would say, I mean 'sissy' in the very best sense of that word), it was unthinkable that . . . The polemic began; and goes on.

At the time, Orville Prescott told my publisher, Nicholas Wreden of E. P. Dutton, that he would never again read much less review a book by me. The *Times* then refused to advertise either my book or the Kinsey report. True to Prescott's word, my next five novels were not reviewed in the daily *Times* or, indeed, in *Time* or *Newsweek*. In freedom's land what ought not to be is not and must be blacked out. I was unmade. For ten years I did television, theatre, movies; then returned to the novel.

The war goes on, though with less spirit than in the old days when the Sunday editor of the *Times*, Lester Markel, canvassed five writers, among them my friend Richard Rovere, to see if one would 'bloody' *The Best Man*, a play that their autonomous daily reviewer had liked. Finally, Douglass Cater wrote a mildly dissenting piece, which was duly published. Simultaneously, a writer was assigned to 'bloody' my campaign for Congress in New York's Twenty-ninth District, a polity usually unnoticed by *The New York Times*; and then . . . and then. . . . Anyway, we need not believe the publicist when he says that he was not engaged to 'bloody' the television *Lincoln*. Of course he was; and I fell into the trap.

The publicist wrote to tell me that he was writing about the television *Lincoln* and the problems of dramatised history. Since I had nothing to do with the production, I thought that the *Times* might be playing it straight. Plainly, I had lost my cunning. I was interviewed on the telephone. He asked me if I read historical novels. I said, almost never. I'm obliged to read history. A few moments later he said, 'As you never read history . . .' I realised then that I'd been had yet again by the foxy old *New York Times*. I remarked upon the mysteriousness of history. Quoted Henry Adams's famous summing up on the 'why' and the 'what'. The publicist got the quotation right but attributed it to Thoreau. The headline of the *New York Times* story:

## A FILTERED PORTRAIT OF LINCOLN
## COMES TO THE SMALL SCREEN.

Filtered is meant to indicate some sort of bias. A second headline was set up in type reminiscent of the *National Enquirer*:

THE PRODUCERS OF THE MINISERIES
ADAPTED IT FROM GORE VIDAL'S NOVEL,
A WORK ALREADY FAULTED BY HISTORIANS.

That was the best – and pretty good, too – that the *Times* could do to scare off viewers. The publicist's story was dim. There was no mention of those historians who had praised *Lincoln*. The caption writer found many things 'troubling'; none of any consequence, except Lincoln's attitude towards blacks.

The publicist tells us that 'Lincoln hardly made' a shady bargain with Salmon P. Chase 'to win his support for his 1864 reelection campaign, by offering him in return the job of chief justice'. I don't recollect the phrase *shady bargain* in either book or drama. But if the publicist does not understand Lincoln's devious game with Chase then he doesn't understand politics in general or Lincoln in particular. Although Lincoln had ended Chase's dream of being the Republican nominee that year, Chase could still have made trouble. Chase was also one of the few men in public life whom Lincoln genuinely disliked. In the summer of 1864, Chase, who had resigned as Lincoln's Secretary of the Treasury, was making overtures to the Democratic Party: 'This . . . might mean much', he wrote, 'if the Democrats would only cut loose from slavery and go for freedom . . . *If they would do that, I would cheerfully go for any man they might nominate.*' Aware of Chase's conniving, Lincoln confided to his secretary, John Hay, 'What Chase ought to do is to help his successor through his installation . . . ; go home without making any fight and wait for a good thing hereafter, such as a vacancy on the Supreme Bench or some such matter.'*

Lincoln played a lovely game with Chase; he even got him to stump Indiana and Ohio for him. He hinted to Chase's friends that Chase was under serious consideration for the chief justice-ship, which my publicist-critic thinks impossible because the Chief Justice was still alive. Unknown to the caption writer, the Chief Justice, Roger B. Taney, was eighty-seven years old that summer and poorly. The new president was bound to make the appointment. So there was a lot of manoeuvring, by the dark of the moon, on Lincoln's part to put Chase, in his daughter's phrase, 'on the shelf'. In exchange for not rocking the boat (supporting McClellan, say), Chase became chief justice after Taney's death, which was

---

* See Robert B. Warden, *An Account of the Private Life and Public Services of Salmon Portland Chase* (1874), p.627; Tyler Dennett, ed., *Lincoln and the Civil War in the Diaries and Letters of John Hay* (1939), p.203.

after the election. Was Chase chosen because he was the best man for the job? No he was not. Politics is bargains and their shadiness depends entirely on which side of the street you happen to be standing.

The publicist's confusions about Lincoln and slavery and what I am supposed to have written are simply hortatory. He seems to think that I think that Lincoln was 'desperately seeking a way to renege on Emancipation while at the same time spearheading the Thirteenth Amendment that abolished slavery'. This is OK for *The New York Times* but not for a responsible paper. Neither I nor the dramatisers ever suggested that he wanted to renege, desperately or not, on Emancipation. It will also come as news to any Lincoln scholars that the saint 'spearheaded' the Thirteenth Amendment. He favoured it. The spear-carriers were abolitionists, Radical Republicans. But Lincoln and the blacks is the crux of all this nonsense, and I shall address the question in due course.

From the tone of Professor Richard N. Current's letter I fear that I may have hurt his feelings. In a covering letter to the editors of *The New York Review of Books*, he refers to my 'personal attack' on him. As Current is as unknown to me as Lincoln was to him in his book *The Lincoln Nobody Knows*, I could hardly have been personal. I thought my tone in the last exchange sweetly reasonable if necessarily disciplinary. I am sorry he finds 'hysterical' my 'diatribe'. What I was obliged to do in his case was to take, one by one, his flat assertions that such-and-such as written by me (often it wasn't) was untrue; and so great does he feel his emeritus weight that that was that.

Finally, about halfway through, I gave up answering him. Now he is at it again. He tells us that I have 'pretended' to be a scholar-squirrel; I give the impression (false, it would seem) that I have visited libraries and looked at old newspapers, etc. Now, in the case of *Lincoln*, I have relied heavily on the diaries of John Hay and Salmon P. Chase since I observe Lincoln from the viewpoint of each. Current seems to think that I could not possibly have read these diaries despite internal evidence to the contrary. As for old newspapers, I used a reporter's shorthand version of the Gettysburg Address, which differs somewhat from the official text. But, by and large, I have always relied heavily on the work of *scholars* in my reflections on American history and, in a way, I have become their ideal reader because I have no professional axe to grind, no tenure to seek, no prizes or fellowships to win.

How does a scholar differ from a scholar-squirrel? The squirrel is a careerist who mindlessly gathers little facts for professional reasons. I don't in the least mind this sort of welfare for the 'educated' middle class. They must live, too. But when they start working in concert to revise history to suit new political necessities, I reach for my ancient Winchester.

Current tells us that '[Vidal] implied that he was a greater Lincoln authority than Stephen B. Oates or any other academic historian except David Herbert Donald.' As I pointed out in the last exchange, it was *Newsweek* that found me to be (in reference to Lincoln's alleged syphilis) a better historian than Mr Oates, whom I have never read. I do not 'imply' (Current has a guardhouse lawyer's way with weasel-words) that I am a better historian than anyone. This is the sort of thing that obsesses academic careerists. Scholar-squirrels spend their lives trying to be noted and listed and graded and seeded because such rankings determine their careers. Those of us engaged in literature and, perhaps, in history as well don't think in such terms. We also don't go on Pulitzer Prize committees to give a friend a prize which, in due course, when he is on the committee, he will give us for our squirrellings.

Current feels that I 'grossly distort' Lincoln by showing him 'as ignorant of economics, disregardful of the Constitution, and unconcerned with the rights of blacks'. Even a casual reading of *Lincoln* shows that I spend quite a lot of time demonstrating the President's concern with the rights of blacks, and where and how they should be exercised. Disregardful of the Constitution? No other president until recent years has shown so perfect a disregard for that document in the guise of 'military necessity'. The Chief Justice himself thought the President so disregardful that he hurled the Constitution at his head. Lincoln just ducked; and the corpus of one Mr Merryman of Baltimore was not delivered up for trial, as the Chief Justice had ordered. I should like Current to demonstrate (elsewhere, please) Lincoln's mastery of economics. Meanwhile, I highly recommend *Lincoln's Preparation for Greatness* (1965), by Paul Simon (yes, the Illinois senator), where he records Lincoln's activities in the state House of Representatives. During four terms, Lincoln and eight other school-of-Clay legislators, known as 'the long Nine', nearly bankrupted the state with a 'Big Improvements' bill that took Illinois forty-five years to pay off. The story about Lincoln's confusions over who signed the greenbacks occurs in Sandburg; and is in the public domain.* I'm sorry if Current finds my last 'screed' somewhat 'maundering', but there are a limited number of ways of saying 'false' without actually using the word.

Current, lord of language, wants Lincoln to be Will Rogers, all folksy and homey. But Lincoln's own language resounds with what Current calls 'Briticisms'. Lincoln's prose was drenched in Shakespeare. Of course, H. L. Mencken was not the first to try to separate American English from English. But in our country, he has been the prime instigator. Finally, prose is all a matter of ear. A word like *screed*, for instance, is now used only by the semiliterate when they want to sound highfalutin, usually in the course of a powerful letter to the editor.

I shall go no further into the word *hooker* other than to observe that a word, in different contexts, picks up additional meanings. A copperhead is a snake is a traitor is a Democrat, depending on the year the word is used and the user. One authority gives a New York origin for *hooker*. In Washington, in the Civil War, General Hooker's name added new resonance. Another authority says the word comes from the verb *to hook*, as the whores in London hooked arms with potential customers as a means of introduction.

Current affects not to understand what I mean by 'agreed-upon facts' as the stuff of history. He would like the reader to think that

* Carl Sandburg, *Abraham Lincoln: The War Years* (1939), Volume I.

I invent something and get someone to agree to it. The point to my long disquisition on *The New York Times* is to show that one cannot trust *any* primary source. If the *Times* says that I said Thoreau wrote something that Henry Adams actually wrote, my 'error' becomes a fact because the *Times* is a primary source for scholar-squirrels – scholars, too. To take at face value any newspaper story is to be dangerously innocent. But one can't challenge everything that has ever been printed. So, through weariness and ignorance, there is a general consensus, which then becomes what I call an 'agreed-upon' fact. We all decide not to worry it. Yet in two standard biographies of John Hay, though the writers agree upon the year of his birth, each gives a different natal month. I have also found that whenever I do make a mistake in writing about history, it is usually because I have followed an acknowledged authority who turns out to be wrong.

On Emancipation and the exemption of certain areas for political reasons: Lincoln maintained slavery in the slave states within the Union and freed those in the Confederacy. Current is more than usually confused here. He thinks Lincoln maintained slavery in 'liberated' or 'restored' sections of Louisiana because the Union controlled these counties and no political necessity was involved. Like so many hagiographers, Current refuses to face the fact that before Lincoln became a saint he was a superb politician. He did nothing without political calculation. He was also a master of telling different people different things, causing no end of trouble for later worshippers who can't deal with all the contradictions. Emancipation was as much a political as a military necessity for Lincoln. For instance, when Lincoln appointed the pro-slavery Edward Stanly governor of occupied North Carolina, it was with the understanding that Lincoln would *not* interfere with slavery in the southern states. When the Emancipation Proclamation was issued, according to one professor of history:

> Stanly went to Washington intending to resign. After several talks with Lincoln, however, Stanly was satisfied. He returned to his job, but first he called at the office of James C. Welling,

editor of the *National Intelligencer*. Welling wrote in his diary: 'Mr Stanly said that the President had stated to him that the proclamation had become a civil necessity to prevent the Radicals from openly embarrassing the government in the conduct of the war.'

So Lincoln speaks with forked tongue in this passage (p.227) from Richard N. Current's *The Lincoln Nobody Knows* (1958). Personally, I'd not have let this agreed-upon fact sail so easily by. Wouldn't Stanly lie to Welling, to explain his behaviour? Or might Welling have misunderstood what Stanly said Lincoln said? Or, unthinkable thought, could Lincoln have lied to Stanly? Current accepts too readily a story highly discreditable to the Great Emancipator he would now have us worship in all his seamless integrity.

Here comes Grant again. One thing about Current, he knows not defeat. I 'asserted that Ulysses S. Grant "had gone into the saddlery business, where he had attractively failed."' The 'assertion' in the novel was John Hay's, in an idle moment, about a man he knew nothing much of in 1862. Triumphantly, Current now writes, 'The point is that Grant had never gone into the saddlery, harness, or leather-goods business and therefore could not have failed at it. He was only an employee.' This is the sort of thing that gives mindless pedantry a bad name. Even in Current's super-American English, it is possible to fail at a job by being fired or being carried if your father owns the place. 'At thirty-seven Grant had to go back [home] and admit that he was still a failure: the boy who could not bargain for a horse had become a man who could not bring in a crop of potatoes or collect a batch of bills. It was humiliating.'* After a year as a clerk, under the managership of his younger brother, Grant was saved by the war and, as he himself wrote, 'I never went into our leather store after the meeting [where he got his command] to put up a package or do other business.'

But note the Current technique throughout this supremely

* William S. McFeely, *Grant; A Biography* (1981), p.64.

unimportant business. He zeroes in on an idle remark by someone who knows nothing about Grant other than his failure in civilian life, most recently in leather goods. The man who said it is a character living in history, not looking back on it. Current seems to think that I should supply the indifferent Hay with the full and absolute knowledge of Grant's affairs that a scholar-squirrel could find out but a contemporary stranger could hardly have known. Owing to Current's uneasy grasp of any kind of English he seems to think that to fail at a business means you must own the business and go broke. That's one meaning. But you can also fail by losing your job or by being tolerated as a hopeless employee by your family. Current wonders why I don't answer more of his charges. They are almost all of them as specious as this.

One of the signs of obsession is an inability to tell the difference between what matters and what does not. The obsessed give everything the same weight. Current juggles words this way and that to try to 'prove' what is often pointless and unprovable. There *is* an issue here but he can't focus on it. The issue is Lincoln and the blacks. The United States was then and is now a profoundly racist society that pretends not to be, and so requires the likes of Current to disguise the American reality from the people while menacing the society's critics, most successfully, it should be noted, within the academy where the squirrels predominate. I shall indulge Current on two minor points and then get to what matters.

Lincoln's bowels. This occupies a few lines in my book. It is necessary to mention the subject because one of Booth's conspirators tried to poison Lincoln's laxative, which was made up at Thompson's drugstore; whether or not prescription clerk David Herold actually poisoned the medicine is not agreed upon.* Current thinks that constipation is a central theme to the book, the Emancipator as Martin Luther. Herndon tells us: 'Mr Lincoln had an evacuation, a passage, about once a week, ate blue mass. Were you to read his early speeches thoroughly and well, you could see his, then, coarse nature, his materialism, etc.' That's all. Since

---

* Louis J. Weichmann, *A True History of the Assassination* (New York, 1977), p.44.

Herndon shared an office with Lincoln for seventeen years there is no reason for this subject not to have been mentioned. After all, many of Lincoln's famed funny stories concerned the outhouse. Current should read them. Also, Current might have given some thought to the sentence after constipation – Lincoln's early 'coarse nature, his materialism'; this is provocative.

But Current is now prey to obsession: 'Vidal would have us believe that every time Lincoln defecated he reported it to Herndon.' I would not have anyone believe such a thing since Herndon in my book makes no mention of Lincoln's bowels, a subject of interest only to the putative poisoners. I fear Current is now sailing right round the bend. He claims that I said on NBC's *Today* show (he seems to be watching rather too much TV) that Lincoln definitely gave Mary Todd syphilis and that she had died of paresis that had affected the brain. He quotes me as saying that one is not 'under oath' on television so that one can presumably tell lies. When I say I'm not under oath, I mean that I'm free to speculate on matters that cannot be proven. I would not write that Lincoln gave his wife syphilis, but I can certainly, in conversation, give an opinion. Since my book stops in 1865 and Mary Todd didn't die until 1882, I never tried to 'prove' the subject. But years ago a doctor friend in Chicago told me that an autopsy had been performed on Mrs Lincoln (but only on the head, an odd procedure even then) and that the brain was found to have physically deteriorated, ruling out mere neurosis, the usual explanation for her behaviour. I didn't write about this and have never followed it up. If Current can tear himself away from the Larry King show, he might have a go at it.

As for Lincoln's syphilis, I use the words Herndon himself used: 'About the year 1835–36 Mr Lincoln went to Beardstown and during a devilish passion had connection with a girl and caught the disease [syphilis]. Lincoln told me this. . . . About the year 1836–37 Lincoln moved to Springfield. . . . At this time I suppose that the disease hung to him and, not wishing to trust our physicians, he wrote a note to Doctor Drake.' Since there is no reason for Herndon to lie about this, I suppose we should all agree upon it as a fact. But since no saint has ever had syphilis, Herndon is a liar and so the consensus finds against him. I don't much admire this sort of thing. Current, historian and master of the American language, now reveals another facet to a protean nature that nobody knows: Current, diagnostician:

> If Vidal had the slightest concern for truth, he could easily have learned from such a reference as *The Merck Manual of Diagnosis and Therapy* that Mrs Lincoln's symptoms and those of a paretic do not correspond.

This is a brave leap in the dark and, once again, Current, the Mr Magoo of the History Department, lands on his face. From the *Merck Manual*:

> General paresis or demential paralytica generally affects patients in their 40s and 50s. The onset is usually insidious and manifested by behavior changes. It also may be present with convulsions or epileptic attacks and there may be aphasia or a transient hemiparesis. Changes in the patient include irritability, difficulty in concentration, memory deterioration, and defective judgment. Headaches and insomnia are associated with fatigue and lethargy. The patient's appearance becomes shabby, unkempt, and dirty; emotional instability leads to frequent weeping and temper tantrums; neurasthenia, depression, and delusions of grandeur with lack of insight may be present.

This exactly describes Mrs Lincoln's behaviour as reported by contemporaries and by such sympathetic biographers as Ruth Painter Randall and the Turners.* I am in Current's debt for leading me to this smoking, as it were, gun. But where, I wonder, is the autopsy report? Could Robert Lincoln have destroyed all copies? Has Walter Reed collected it in its great presidential net?

* * *

* Ruth Painter Randall, *Mary Lincoln: Biography of a Marriage* (1953); Justin G. Turner and Linda Levitt Turner, eds., *Mary Todd Lincoln: Her Life and Letters* (1972).

Current admits to changing his mind about Lincoln in the course of many years of squirrelling. But although he no longer holds to his views on Lincoln and the blacks as presented in *The Lincoln Nobody Knows* (a book, he'll be relieved to know, I never took very seriously, largely because of the megalomaniacal title in which he has inserted himself), he does find, as do I, disconcerting the way that Lincoln lovers (no hater would be allowed tenure anywhere in bravery's home) keep changing the image to conform to new policies. When the civil rights movement took off in the sixties, uppity blacks toyed with the notion that Lincoln was a honkie (Julius Lester, in *Look Out, Whitey!*, etc.). Immediately the agreed-upon facts of earlier times (colonise the freed slaves, reimburse the slave owners, etc.) had to be papered over and a new set of agreed-upon facts was hurried into place, so that LaWanda Cox could deliver a new verdict: 'There is no mistaking the fact that by 1865 Lincoln's concern for the future of the freed people was directed to their condition and rights at home, rather than abroad.'*

This is the new line, and I have no particular quarrel with it. But certain hagiographers are now pretending that Lincoln was *never* serious about colonisation, which is a falsification of the record. In Lincoln's second annual message to Congress (December 1, 1862) he said: 'I cannot make it better known than it is, that I strongly favor colonization.' Certainly for the first two years of his administration Lincoln was mad on the subject. Gradually, he *seems* to have let the notion go because of the logistical impossibility of shipping out three or four million people who were less than enthusiastic about a long sea voyage to the respective wilds of Haiti, Panama, Liberia.

Current says that he 'did not . . . state it as my opinion . . . that Lincoln remained a colonizationist'. That was wise, because no one knows. I don't give my personal view either, though I did note (but did not write) that usually when Lincoln started in on the necessity of reimbursing the slave owners, colonisation was seldom

* LaWanda Cox, *Lincoln and Black Freedom: A Study in Presidential Leadership* (1981), p.23.

far behind: the two seemed twinned in his head. The revisionists now admired by Current maintain that the only evidence that Lincoln at the end was still pondering colonisation is Ben Butler's testimony that the President mentioned it to him some time after February 3, 1865. I found most intriguing Mark E. Neely, Jr's case that Lincoln could not have talked to Butler at the time that Butler says he did, because Butler had written Secretary of War Stanton a letter assuring him that he had stayed in New York until March 23, in conformance with War Department policy that forbade officers from visiting the capital without permission.* This is a scholarly not squirrelly finding. But if one is to factor out Butler as a crucial witness because he is a liar, why believe the letter to Stanton? If Dan Sickles and other general officers slipped into town without permission, why not the irrepressible Butler? My point is that when one decides a source is apt to be untrue (Herndon, Butler, *The New York Times*), how does one choose what to believe – if anything – from the discredited source?

I understand the politics behind the current (no pun) revisionists but I think they rather overdo it. One dizzy squirrel claims that after 1862, Lincoln discarded the idea of colonisation with indecent haste. Yet on July 1, 1864, John Hay writes, 'I am glad the President has sloughed off that idea of colonization.'† For obvious reasons, the revisionists never quote the next sentence. 'I have always thought it a hideous & barbarous humbug & the thievery of Pomeroy and Kock have about converted him to the same belief.' This sounds a lot more tentative than the revisionists would like us to believe. Perhaps they will now have to establish that Hay is untrustworthy.

In any event, when the black separatist movement starts up in the next decade, new revisionists will supersede the present lot, and Butler's probity will be rehabilitated and Lincoln the coloniser re-established.

\* \* \*

* Mark E. Neely, Jr, 'Abraham Lincoln and Black Colonization: Benjamin Butler's Spurious Testimony', *Civil War History*, Vol. XXV (March 1979), pp.77–83.
† *Diaries and Letters of John Hay*, p.203.

On the dust jacket, between the title *Lincoln* and my name, there is a one-inch-high caveat: *A Novel*. I tell the story of Lincoln's presidency from the imagined points of view of his wife, of E. B. Washburne, John Hay, Salmon P. Chase, and, marginally, David Herold, one of the conspirators. I never enter Lincoln's mind and, unlike the historian or biographer, I do not make magisterial judgements or quibble with others in the field. The five points of view were dictated, in the case of Hay and Chase, because they kept diaries, skimpily I fear, and many of their letters are available. What I aimed to achieve was balance. Hay admired Lincoln, Chase hated him, Mary Todd loved him, and so on. Each sees him in a different way, under different circumstances.

I am also reflecting upon the nature of fact as observed in fiction, and, indeed, fiction in fact. That is why the scholar-squirrels fascinate me much more than the scholars because they are like barometers, ever responsive to any change in the national weather. This bad period in American history has been, paradoxically, a good period for American history writing. There have never been so many intelligent biographies (yes, they are often written in academe but not by the squirrels) and interesting historians. But pure history, if such a thing could be, is flawed because 'history will never reveal to us what connections there are, and at what times, between . . .' For the novelist it is the imagining of connections that brings life to what was. Finally, 'History', as Tolstoy also observed, 'would be an excellent thing if only it were true.' Perhaps, in the end, truth is best imagined, particularly if it is firmly grounded in the disagreed- as well as agreed-upon facts.

My side of these exchanges is now complete. Let others argue elsewhere.

*The New York Review of Books*
18 August 1988

# Part II: Political

# 1

# H. L. MENCKEN
# THE JOURNALIST

I

After politics, journalism has always been the preferred career of
the ambitious but lazy second-rater. American exceptions to
mediocrity's leaden mean: from column A, there was Franklin D.
Roosevelt; from column B, H. L. Mencken.

Although Henry Louis Mencken was a magazine editor (*The
Smart Set, American Mercury*), a literary critic, an expositor of
Nietzsche, and a school-of Samuel Johnson compiler of *The American Language*, he never ceased to be a journalist for the *Sunpapers* in
his hometown of Baltimore, where he was born in 1880 and where
he died in 1956. From 1906 to 1948, he was connected with the
Baltimore *Sun*, as a columnist, feature writer, editor. He was the
most influential journalist of his day; he was also the wittiest.

As a working journalist, Mencken's lifelong subject was nothing
less than Freedom's land and Bravery's home, the United States
where flourished such gorgeous clowns as Calvin Coolidge, and
'The Great Croon of Croons,' Franklin D. Roosevelt, the not-so-
great Great Commoner, William Jennings Bryan, and many, many
others. But if only God could have invented such a cast, it was
Mencken who proved to be God's most attentive and appreciative
drama critic. It was Mencken who described the show. He revelled
in absurdity; found no bonnet entirely bee-less. He loved the
national bores for their own sweet sake.

As he contemplated the meagre lives of our dull presidents, he wrote: 'There comes a day of public ceremonial, and a chance to make a speech . . . A million voters with IQs below 60 have their ears glued to the radio. It takes four days' hard work to concoct a speech without a sensible word in it. Next a dam must be opened somewhere. Four dry Senators get drunk and make a painful scene. The Presidential automobile runs over a dog. It rains'.

American journalism's golden (a kinder adjective than 'yellow') age coincided with Mencken's career; that is, from century's turn to mid-century's television. During this period, there was still a public educational system and although Mencken often laughs at the boobs out there, the average person could probably get through a newspaper without numb lips. Today, half the American population no longer reads newspapers: plainly, they are the clever half.

For Mencken, the old-time journalist, or 'newsie,' was a combination of François Villon and Shane. He was 'wildcattish.' He was free-lance, a knight for hire. In 1927, Mencken was already looking back nostalgically to the time when a journalist 'used to make as much as a bartender or a police sergeant', now 'he makes as much as the average doctor or lawyer, and his wife, if he has one, maybe has social ambitions.' Today, of course, the 'journalist' is often paid movie-star prices for movie-star appearances on television or along the lecture circuit, and he needs no wife to inspire him to a cozy lunch à deux with Nancy Reagan or Barbara Bush.

Mencken did acknowledge that, even then, some journalists liked to mingle with the wealthy and the powerful but, for him, there was always a greater fascination in those lower depths where dwell bartenders and police sergeants.

Mencken's ideal popular paper for that vast public which 'gets all its news by listening' (today one would change 'listening' to 'staring' – at television), would be 'printed throughout, as First Readers are printed, in words of one syllable. It should avoid every idea that is beyond the understanding of a boy of ten' on the ground that 'all ideas are beyond them. They can grasp only events.' But they will heed only those events that are presented as drama with one side clearly right and the other clearly wrong.

They can no more imagine neutrality than they can imagine the fourth dimension.' Thus, Mencken anticipates not only the television news programme but the television political campaign with its combative thirty-second spot commercials and sound-bites. Movies were already showing the way, and Mencken acknowledged the wisdom of the early movie magnates whose simpleminded screened *agons* had made them rich. Unfortunately, once rich, they pined for culture, against which Mencken sternly warns with his famous injunction: 'No one in this world, so far as I know – and I have researched the records for years, and employed agents to help me – has ever lost money by underestimating the intelligence of the great masses of the plain people. Nor has anyone ever lost public office thereby.'

Today, Mencken's boisterous style and deadpan hyperboles are very difficult even for 'educated' Americans to deal with, and Sanskrit to the generality. Although every American has a sense of humour – it is his birthright and encoded somewhere in the Constitution – few Americans have ever been able to cope with wit or irony and even the simplest jokes often cause unease, especially today when every phrase must be examined for covert sexism, racism, ageism.

American character (which does and does not exist) fascinated Mencken, who observed, in 1918, that the universal image of Uncle Sam the money-grubber was mistaken. 'The character that actually marks off the American is not money-hunger at all; it is what might be called, at the risk of misunderstanding, social aspiration.' For the American, money plays only a part in moving upward 'to break down some barrier of caste, to secure the acceptance of his betters.' 'Unlike Europe, no one has a station,' [so far as he knows, of course: Class is a national dirty secret] 'unless he makes it for himself.' Of course Mencken lived in simpler times. For the American of 1918 'There is always something just behind him and tantalizing him, menacing him and causing him to sweat.'

Mencken quotes Wendell Phillips: 'More than any other people, we Americans are afraid of one another.' Mencken acknowledges this truth, and he puts it down to the desire to conform, which means howling with the rest of the mindless pack as it careens from nowhere to nowhere in pursuit of such instant-enemies of the week as Gaddafi, Noriega, Saddam, put in place by our packmeisters, successively, like that mechanical rabbit used to keep racing dogs on course. For this sense of collective security, the individual must sacrifice himself in order 'to belong to something larger and safer than he is,' and he can 'work off steam within prudent limits. Beyond lie the national taboos. Beyond lies true independence and the heavy penalties that go therewith.'

A century earlier, that shrewd passerby, Tocqueville, also noted the force of the majority on the individual to conform. But Mencken was obliged to live a lifetime in such a society and so, unlike the French penologist, he can present data from inside the slammer: 'The taboos that I have mentioned are extraordinarily harsh and numerous. They stand around nearly every subject that is genuinely important to man: they hedge in free opinion and experimentation on all sides. Consider, for example, the matter of religion. It is debated freely and furiously in almost every country in the world save the United States,' but here the critic is silenced. 'The result is that all religions are equally safeguarded against criticism, and that all of them lose vitality. We protect the status quo, and so make steady war upon revision and improvement.'

In August 1925, Mencken meditated on how Europeans view Americans, and how they noted 'our growing impatience with the free play of ideas, our increasing tendency to reduce all virtues to the single one of conformity, our relentless and all pervading standardization . . . Europe doesn't fear our military or economic prowess, rather it is Henry Ford that gives them the shivers . . . By Americanization it means Fordization – and not only in industry but also in politics, art and even religion.' Nor is this simply the spontaneous power of public opinion; it is the deliberate power of the state brought into play. 'No other nation of today is so rigorously policed. The lust to standardize and regulate extends to the most trivial minutia of private life.'

At the time that Mencken wrote this alcohol had been prohibited by law to the American people, as well as almost every form of sex, disturbing reading matter, and so on. Mencken also adverts to the Scopes trial of that year, whose verdict forbade the teaching of Darwin's theory of evolution in the schools of Christian Tennessee. This trial convinced thoughtful Europeans that Americanism was 'a conspiracy of dull and unimaginative men, fortuitously made powerful, against all the ideas and ideals that seem sound to their betters,' leading the Europeans to suspect 'that a nation cherishing such notions and feelings, and with the money and the men to enforce them, deserved to be watched very carefully.'

2

As a first-generation American, Mencken liked playing the vaude-ville German, with a passion for beer, Brahms, German culture. 'My grandfather made a mistake when he came to America, and I have always lived in the wrong country.' Like so many *echt*-Americans, Mencken deeply resented the British. Not only did he share in the tribal dislike of Teuton for Anglo but he resented the ease with which the Brits manipulated American politics in their favour at the time of the two world wars. During the first world war, Mencken's pro-Germanism got him banned from the *Sun*. But despite Mencken's somewhat stagy dislike of Brits, socialism, radicals, the 'Anglo-maniacal' Woodrow Wilson, and the reformers Franklin and Eleanor Roosevelt, he tended to make very good *patriotic* sense of American politics.

Mencken notes that from the start of the republic, 'Setting aside religion, [politics] was literally the only concern of the people. All men of ability and ambition turned to it for self-expression.' This is wondrously wise and an echo of Pericles's comment that the man who thinks politics not his business has no business. In the 18th and early 19th centuries, politics drew 'the best literary talent into its service – Franklin, Jefferson and Lincoln may well stand as examples – it left the cultivation of belles lettres to women and

157

second-rate men.' Now, of course, the second-rate have taken over politics. As for beautiful letters . . .

Mencken's alarm at our system's degradation was in no way based upon a starry-eyed notion of the revered but always circumvented Constitution. Although that long-ignored primer says that only Congress may declare war, President Bush has only recently confided to us that 'we have fought 204 wars of which only five were declared,' so put that in your peace-pipe and smoke it! Mencken would not have been startled. For him, 'All government, in its essence, is organized exploitation, and in virtually all of its existing forms it is the implacable enemy of every industrious and well-disposed man.' This must have got a good chuckle from the Baltimore burgher over his breakfast of chipped beef and scrapple.

Mencken continues. Government 'invades his liberty and collars his money in order to protect him, but in actuality, it always makes a stiff profit on the exchange. This profit represents the income of the professional politicians, nine-tenths of whom are professional rogues.' That was then. The rogues are smoother now and often endearing on television. They are also no longer paid for by such chickenfeed as kickbacks on city contracts. Rather, they are the proud employees of the bankers and the military industrial procurers who have bought them their offices, both square and oval. But though we are worse off than in Mencken's day, he was at least able to give one cheer for the Constitution, or at least for the idea of such a document, as a kind of stoplight: 'So far you may go, but no further. No matter what excuse or provocation, you may not invade certain rights, or pass certain kinds of laws.'

Inevitably, Mencken's journalism is filled with stories of how our enumerated rights are constantly being evaded or struck down because it is the reflexive tactic of the politicians 'to invade the Constitution stealthily, and then wait to see what happens. If nothing happens they go on more boldly; if there is a protest they reply hotly that the Constitution is worn out and absurd, and that progress is impossible under the dead hand. This is the time to watch them especially.'

Mencken also notes that in the first decade of this century there was 'a sudden change . . . Holes began to be punched in the Bill of Rights, and new laws of strange and often fantastic shape began to slip through them. The hysteria of the late war completed the process. The espionage act enlarged the holes to great fissures. Citizens began to be pursued into their houses, arrested without warrants, and jailed without any form of trial. The ancient writ of habeas corpus was suspended: the Bill of Rights was boldly thrown overboard.'

Although the extent of the decadence of the democratic process at our end of the century was unknown if not unsuspected to Mencken at his, he knew enough of history and its engine, entropy, that 'no government, of its own motion, will increase its own weakness, for that would mean to acquiesce in its own destruction . . . governments, whatever their pretensions otherwise, try to preserve themselves by holding the individual down . . . Government itself, indeed, may be reasonably defined as a conspiracy against him. Its one permanent aim, whatever its form, is to hobble him sufficiently to maintain itself.' As a self-styled 'Presbyterian Tory' (with Manichean tendencies), Mencken regarded attempts at reform as doomed while the thought of any Utopian system bettering things caused him deep distress because to create Utopia you would have to enslave more and more people in order to better – while worsening – their lot.

Curiously enough, of all those good and bad Americans who shuddered at the sudden sharp wind from the east known as Communism, Mencken, as early as 1930, figured that there was no way that communism could ever set up shop within our alabaster cities, much less take sickle to our fruited plains. Mencken's reasoning is exquisitely sound: 'That Americans, in the mass, have anything properly described as keen wits is surely far from self-evident. On the contrary, it seems likely that, if anything, they lie below the civilised norm.' Incidentally, for several decades I have been trying to convince Europe that Americans are not innately stupid but merely ignorant and that with a proper educational system, et cetera. But the more one reads Mencken, the more one eyes, suspiciously, the knuckles of his countrymen, looking to see callouses from too constant a contact with the greensward.

Mencken believes Americans to be more gullible than most people, dwelling as we do in 'the home of freak economic schemes' (often, alas, contagious) and 'the happy hunting ground of the most blatant and absurd sort of charlatans in politics.' From this intimate knowledge of the American 'mind,' Mencken thought that Americans, as lovers of 'the bizarre and the irrational would embrace communism with joy, just as multitudes of them, in a previous age, embraced free silver. But, as everyone knows, they will have none of it.' Mencken concedes the attraction of Utopias to the foreign-born and educated Americans but 'two-thirds of the native-born Communists that I have encountered are so plainly *mashuggah* that it would be flattery to call them stupid.'

Mencken gives two reasons for the failure of communism/socialism to take root in the United States. The first is that Americans have long since been vaccinated by the likes of Bryan and Roosevelt (TR) against this sort of virus: in effect, the folks had been there before and they are aware of so 'gross' a social and economic solution. Mencken's second reason strikes me as not only true but inspired. Americans were more sensitive to 'the concrete debacle in Russia' because 'they probably felt themselves, in a subtle and unconscious way, to be nearer to the Russians than any Europeans. Russia was not like Europe, but it was strangely like America. In the same way the Russians were like Americans. They, too, were naturally religious and confiding; they, too, were below the civilized average in intelligence; and they, too, believed in democracy, and were trying to give it a trial.

For Mencken, communist literature was 'as childish as the literature of Christian Science' while communism itself 'will prob-ably disappear altogether when the Russian experiment comes to a climax, and Bolshevism either converts itself into a sickly imitation of capitalism or blows up with a bang. The former seems more likely.' This is pretty good for 1930.

As Mencken thought all government bad, it follows that he was a Jeffersonian who believed that the least we had of a bad thing the better. As 'an incurable Tory in politics,' he was congenitally anti-liberal, though 'I always give heed to them politely, for they are at least free men.' Surprisingly, he has respectful words for Emma Goldman and Alexander Berkman, victims of Federal persecution (it is not taught in our schools that once upon a time, at the behest of the Secretary of Labor, foreign-born Americans could be deported, without due process). Mencken finds the two radicals 'extremely intelligent – [and] once their aberrant political ideals are set aside they are seen to be very sharp wits. They think clearly, unsentimentally and even a bit brilliantly. They write simple, glowing and excellent English.' Mencken confesses that he cannot understand how they can believe so childishly in the proletariat, but 'the fact that a human brain of high amperage, othewise highly efficient, may have a hole in it is surely not a secret. All of us, in our several ways, are illogical, irrational, almost insane.' Mencken's tolerance for the bees aswarm in the bonnets of others was very great if the swarm be honest and its honey pure.

The state as hostile tropism is Mencken's central philosophic notion as a journalist. Whether the state is used to deport or imprison people for their ideas or the colour of their skin (as in the case of the Nisei) or simply to harass citizens who drink whisky, he was that malevolent state's hard critic. He illuminates our marvelous bill of rights, no sooner promulgated than struck with the first of those sets of alien and sedition acts that continue, in one form or another, to this day. He is very funny about the Noble Experiment to prohibit alcohol (1919–33) which made the United States the world's joke-nation, a title still unceded.

As for America's once triumphant mass-production of the automobile, he notes that this achievement promptly became a pretext for the persecution of the citizenry by creating 'a body of laws which fills two courtrooms to suffocation every day (in Baltimore), and keeps three judges leaping and tugging like fire-engine horses. The situation is made more intoxicating by the fact that nine-tenths of the criminals are persons who would not otherwise fall into their toils – that the traffic regulations tap whole new categories of victims . . . The ideal of the *polizei*, at all times and everywhere, is to get their hands upon every citizen at least once a day.' Today the tobacco smoker is at risk. Tomorrow, who knows who will fall victim to the state's endless sense of fun?

3

Like all good writers, Mencken is a dramatist, at his best when he shows us the ship of state in motion on high seas while his character studies of the crew of this ship of fools still give delight though every last one now lies full fathom five. Ding dong dell.

As a reporter Mencken covered many political conventions from 1904 to 1948. As a Baltimore *Sun* columnist, he wrote about national politics whenever the spirit moved or, indeed, shoved him. In 1925, he was amused, as always, by the collapse yet again of the Liberals and their journals: '*The Nation* gradually abandons Liberalism for libertarianism. *The New Republic* hangs on, but is obviously not as vigorous and confident as it used to be.' Mencken delights in 'Dr Coolidge,' Liberalism's natural enemy. But then 'A politician has no actual principles. He is in favour of whatever seems to him to be popular at the moment.' Even so, Coolidge 'believes naturally in Law Enforcement – by lawful means if possible: if not, by any means at hand, lawful or lawless . . . he actually got his first considerable office . . . by posturing as a fascist of the most advanced type.' This was in 1919 when governor Coolidge of Massachusetts broke the Boston police strike and became famous.

But Coolidge is only an engaging character actor in a drama whose star throughout is William Jennings Bryan (Democratic candidate for president 1896, 1900, 1908 – spokesman or person for Free Silver and the common person – or man). Bryan had become famous and popular and dangerous to the status quo when he put together a huge coalition of poor farmers and poorer labourers and, in their interest, spoke against the rich and their gold standard. Bryan gave the country's ownership its first big scare since the rebellion of Daniel Shays. Alas, Mencken was not at the convention in '96 when with a single speech ('You shall not crucify mankind upon a cross of gold!'), Bryan got the nomination at the age of thirty-six and as his friend and ally, my grandfather, used to say, 'He never learned anything else ever again in his life.'

As much as Mencken despised Bryan, the demagogue, he is moderately touched by Bryan's appearance at the 1904 convention 'in his familiar alpaca coat and his old white string tie,' looking 'weak and haggard' (he was suffering from pneumonia) until he started to speak and brought down the house, yet again. Four years later he would be the doomed nominee: four years after that, Wilson made him his secretary of state, a post he resigned when he saw that the Administration was moving toward war, an act of principle that Mencken rather meanly does not credit in a man he calls 'the magnificent job-seeker.'

At the end, Mencken was present in Dayton, Tennessee for the Scopes trial where the old man seemed 'maleficent' to Mencken when he spoke for superstition and the literal interpretation of the Bible. Bryan and the Bible won the day, but Bryan himself was dead a few weeks later, killed, my grandmother always said, by an ungovernable passion for 'chicken and rice and gravy'.

For Mencken, Bryan is the *id* – to use Freudian jargon – of American politics: the ignorant, religious, underclass leader whose fateful and dramatic climax came in the trial to determine whether or not we are descended from monkeys. Herbert Hoover is the *ego*; he also represents the British interest, forever trying to draw the great stupid republic into their wars and combinations. Calvin Coolidge is a near-fascist clown, whose career is 'as appalling and as fascinating as a two-headed boy.' Warren G. Harding is the master of a glorious near-English in which 'the relations between word and meaning have long since escaped him'; Harding's style 'reminds me of a string of wet sponges; it reminds me of tattered washing on the line: it reminds me of stale bean soup, of college yells, of dogs barking idiotically through endless nights. It is so bad that a sort of grandeur creeps into it.' Mencken's descriptions of these wondrous clowns are still a delight because, though the originals are long since erased from the collective 'memory' of the United States of Amnesia, the types persist. 'I am not,' Mencken observes demurely at one point, when blood is on the walls, 'a constructive critic.'

For Mencken 'the best of [politicians] seem to be almost as bad the worst. As private citizens they are often highly intelligent and realistic men, and admirable in every way.' But because of the superstitious mass, they are not allowed to make sense. 'When they accomplish anything, it is usually by accident.' Even of his sometimes hero, Al Smith, he deplored his speeches but then, 'like all habitual orators, he plainly likes to make speeches, no matter how dull the subject or hot the hall.'

Mencken is quite aware that behind the diverting spectacle of our politics stands the ownership of the country, Business. He understands the general preference of the Business-boss for the Lawyer-employee in politics. Partly it is because 'A lawyer practising his craft under Anglo-Saxon jurisprudence becomes a pedant almost inevitably. The system he follows is expressly designed to shut out common sense,' which is just as well because 'Big Business, in America, is almost wholly devoid of anything even poetically describable as public spirit. It is frankly on the make . . . Big Business was in favour of Prohibition, believing that a sober workman would make a better slave than one with a few drinks in him. It was in favor of all the gross robberies and extortions that went on in the [First] war,' and profited by the curtailment of civil liberties and so on. Coolidge was their man; so was Herbert Hoover, 'the perfect self-seeker . . . His principles are so vague that even his intimates seem unable to put them into words . . . He knows who his masters are, and he will serve them.'

Mencken is also aware that there is a small but constant resistance to the 'masters,' but he gives the resistance little aid or comfort. Essentially, he is on the side of Business if not Business-men because 'business is the natural art of the American people.' He pities those with 'believing minds' who would follow this or that demagogue, and he lived long enough to attend the 1948 convention of the Progressive Party where Henry Wallace picked up the banner marked Nay; but Mencken was put off not so much by the poignant, plaintive 'nay' as he was by the colouring of the letters, red.

Even so, the Tory Mencken understood the roots of radicalism. Although 'it is assumed that men become radicals because they are naturally criminal, or because they have been bribed by Russian gold', what actually moves them 'is simply the conviction that the Government they suffer under is unbearably and incurably corrupt . . . The notion that a radical is one who hates his country is naive and usually idiotic. He is, more likely, one who likes his country more than the rest of us, and is thus more disturbed than the rest of us when he sees it debauched. He is not a bad citizen turning to crime; he is a good citizen driven to despair.' But Mencken himself is no radical because 'I believe that all government is evil, and that trying to improve it is largely a waste of time. But that is certainly not the common American view . . . When they see an evil they try to remedy it – by peaceful means if possible, and if not, then by force.' Yet, paradoxically, Mencken can also write that 'history . . . is the upward struggle of man, out of darkness and into light,' presumably a struggle with ooze alone.

Eventually, Franklin Delano Roosevelt would appear to be the answer to the radicals' dream and Mencken regarded him, at the beginning, with a cold but not disapproving eye as FDR metamorphosed from a John the Baptist for Al Smith to the Christ himself, or the national *super-ego*. With some pleasure, Mencken described the Democratic convention that nominated FDR for vice-president, largely because he bore the name of a famous Republican president. Also, he was chosen to 'perfume the ticket.' As 'leader of the anti-Tammany Democrats in New York,' he could be counted on 'to exorcise the Tammany split from the party.' Finally, 'he is a civilised man and safely wet.'

When FDR's turn came at Chicago 1932, Mencken wrote, 'I can recall no candidate of like importance who ever had so few fanatics whooping for him.' But Mencken allowed that FDR was good on radio, and he smiled a lot. By the 1940 convention, Mencken was hostile not only to the New Deal but to the approaching war. To Mencken 1940 looked like a re-run of 1916 when Wilson had campaigned as 'the man who kept us out of war.' Politics being nothing if not imitative of what has worked before, he glumly observed that 'Roosevelt himself has promised categorically, on at least a dozen occasions, to keep out of the war, and with the most pious and eye-rolling solemnity' even though 'his foreign policy . . . has been unbrokenly devious, dishonest and dishonorable. Claiming all the immunities of a neutral, he has misled the country into countless acts of war, and there is scarcely an article of international law that he has not violated.' But Roosevelt won the election. And the war came.

Roosevelt's opponent in the election of 1940 was Wendell Willkie, an eloquent 'barefoot boy,' as they called him, 'from Wall Street,' with a Hoosier accent and considerable demagogic skills, Just before he was nominated, I shook his limp hand, and he glared at me with blind eyes in a white sweating face and croaked, 'Ah'd be a lah-er if ah sed ah diduhn wanna be Prez Nigh Stays.' The only occasion where I gazed as Mencken gazed upon the same political spectacle was the Republican convention at Philadelphia where Willkie was nominated. This was in June, 1940, and I was guide to my blind grandfather, former Senator T. P. Gore. A Democrat, TPG was not about to miss any convention that might be fun. On a hot evening, we rode to the convention hall in a streetcar with former vice-president Charles G. Dawes, a bright, crickety little man, wearing a white straw hat. At the hall, the heat was dreadful. Young women gave out palmetto fans with 'Fan for Van' written on them; thus, the great moose of Michigan, Senator Arthur H. Vandenberg, majestically hurled himself into the ring. Senator Robert A. Taft was also a candidate. He was even then, known as 'Mr Conservative.' Twelve years later, when he was denied the nomination in favour of D. D. Eisenhower, he let slip a terrible truth that no Republican can be nominated for president without the permission of the Chase Manhattan Bank.

We sat in the bleachers to stage left of the podium where stood the former president, Herbert Hoover, face like a rosy marshmallow. Carefully, I described the scene for my blind grandfather; he had entered political history not only as the first senator from the new state of Oklahoma but as the orator who had started the longest demonstration ever recorded at any convention (for Bryan, at Denver, 1908). TPG was one of the few speakers that Mencken could endure, noting that in 1928, when he 'rose to second the nomination of his old friend, Senator Reed, there was humour in his brief speech, and also a very impressive earnestness. He won the crowd instantly and got a great round of applause. No other rhetorician came near his mark . . .'

Hoover 'stood before the mike like a schoolboy reciting a piece, and seldom varied his intonation or made a gesture.' Mencken brings it all alive to me a half-century later though he finds Hoover paler than I did but then I had never seen the President before – or since. I was deeply impressed by Hoover's rigid gravitas. But my grandfather, whose wit and politics were not unlike Mencken's, after listening to the ovation for the ex-president, said, 'Hoover's the only man here who doesn't know that he's finished.'

As the galleries chanted, 'We want Willkie,' I became addicted to the convention as then practised, and it is ironic that in 1968, thanks to some television 'debates' with a rightwing publicist, I should have helped preside over the transformation of the party conventions from the comings-together of the nation's tribes to a series of low-rated TV specials. No one can now say, with Mencken, 'Me, I like [conventions] because they amuse me. I never get tired of the show . . . so unimaginably exhilarating and preposterous that one lives a gorgeous year in an hour.'

4

Currently, any use of the word 'race' in the United States is considered an *a priori* proof of the user's racism. Abstract nouns are now subject to close scrutiny to make sure that the noun's deployer is not a racist or sexist or ageist or bigot. Meanwhile, any word or phrase that might cause distress must undergo erasure while euphemism (the E – or is it the U or Eu-word?) is the order of the day as 'body bag' suddenly becomes, in Pentagonese, 'human remains pouch' since 'pouch' is a resolutely cheery word, suggesting cute marsupials Down Under while 'bag' is a downer, as in 'bag lady.' Munich, appeasement, Hitler. A babble of words that no one understands now fills the airwaves, and language loses all meaning as we sink slowly, mindlessly, into herstory rather than history because most rapists are men, aren't they?

Mencken is a nice antidote. Politically, he is often right but seldom correct by today's stern standards. In a cheery way, he dislikes most minorities and if he ever had a good word to say about the majority of his countrymen, I have yet to come across it. Recently, when his letters were published, it was discovered that He Did Not Like the Jews, and that he had said unpleasant things about them not only as individuals but In General, plainly the sign of a Hitler-Holocaust enthusiast. So shocked was everyone that even the *New York Review of Books'* unofficial de-anti-Semitiser, Garry Wills (he salvaged Dickens, barely), has yet to come to his aid, with An Explanation. But in Mencken's private correspondence, he also snarls at black Americans, Orientals, Britons, women and WASPS, particularly the clay-eating Appalachians whom he regarded as sub-human. But private irritability is of no consequence when compared to what really matters, public action.

Far from being an anti-Semite, Mencken was one of the first journalists to denounce the persecution of the Jews in Germany at a time when the New York *Times*, say, was notoriously reticent. On November 27, 1938, Mencken writes (Baltimore *Sun*), 'It is to be hoped that the poor Jews now being robbed and mauled in Germany will not take too seriously the plans of various politicians to rescue them.' He then reviews the various schemes to 'rescue' the Jews from the Nazis who had not yet announced their own final solution.

To the British proposal that the Jews be admitted to British Guiana, Teutonophile Mencken thinks that the *Ostjuden might* hack it in British Guiana but not the German Jews as 'they constitute an undoubtedly superior group ... Try to imagine a German-

Jewish lawyer or insurance man, or merchant, or schoolmaster [in] a place where the climate is that of a Turkish Bath . . .' Tanganyika he thought marginally better but still pretty bad, at least 'as good as the worst parts of Mexico.' He then suggests that Canada could 'absorb 100,000 or even 200,000 with ease, and they would be useful acquisitions, especially in the western prairie populations, which are dominated today by a low-grade of farmers, without any adequate counterbalance of a competent middle class.' Today Mencken could not write this because the farmers Anti-Defamation League of Saskatchewan would be offended, and his column banned in Canada. 'Australia, now almost as exclusive as Sing Sing, which it somewhat resembles in population, could use quite as many [Jews] as Canada and New Zealand.' The Australian government would, today, file a protest; and Mencken's column would be banned.

Then Mencken gets down to business: 'The American plan for helping the refugees is less openly brutal than the British plan, but almost as insulting to them, and even more futile.' After many official and unofficial condemnations of Germany, including 'the Hon. Mr Roosevelt's' declaration that 'he could scarcely believe that such things could occur in a Twentieth Century civilization,' the President is still not willing to relax the immigration laws or do anything 'that might cause him political inconvenience.' Mencken finds such 'pecksniffery . . . gross and disgusting . . . and I hope that American Jews will not be fetched by it.' Mencken also notes how the 'Aframerican press' found amazing Roosevelt's solicitousness for German Jews, so unlike his complaisance to the ongoing crimes against black Americans.

Mencken concludes: 'There is only one way to help the refugees, and that is to find places for them in a country in which they can really live. Why shouldn't the United States take in a couple of hundred thousand of them, or even all of them?' He notes two popular objections. One, there is already a lot of unemployment in the United States, to which he responds that it is unlikely the Jewish immigrants will either loaf or be incompetent. Two, there is anti-Semitism of the sort then being fanned by the Ku Klux

Klan but, as he observes, 'not many Jews are likely to go to Mississippi or Arkansas.'

I am certain that those who wish to will be able to find anti-Semitism in Mencken's proposal to admit all Jewish refugees. Certainly he *generalizes* about Jews. (How does he know that they don't *all* want to go to Mississippi?) But then perhaps the whole message is code; certainly the remark about Jewish 'efficiency' is a classic blood libel.

As of 1934, Mencken was moderately impressed by Eretz Israel and agreeably condescending to the Arabs, who 'breed like flies but die in the same way.' Mencken was generally approving of the European Jewish settlers, though he predictably cast a cold eye on the collectivist farms and kibbutzim. Of one of them, he wrote, presciently, 'It was founded in 1921, and is still in the first flush of its success. Will it last? Probably not. As soon as its present kindergartners grow up they will begin to marry outside, and then there will be quarrels over shares, and it will no doubt go the way of Brook Farm, Aman and all the other predecessors.' Mencken thought that there was only a 50–50 chance of the Jewish plantation in Palestine enduring. 'On the one hand [Eretz Israel] is being planted intelligently and shows every sign of developing in a healthy manner. But on the other hand there are the Arabs – and across the Jordan there is a vast reservoir of them, all hungry, all full of enlightened self-interest. Let some catastrophe in world politics take the British cops away, and the Jews who now fatten on so many lovely farms will have to fight desperately for their property and their lives.' The catastrophe came right on schedule in the form of Hitler and of such professional Jewish terrorists as Begin and Shamir.

One of the few groups that Americans are fairly free to denounce, after the Arabs, are the Japanese. Mencken was most alert to 'the yellow peril.' (I use quotes to forestall the usual letters accusing me of hating all orientals along with Mencken, when neither did nor does.) In 1939, Mencken was thinking seriously about Japan. As there is no public memory in the United States, let me remind the reader that since the Japanese victory over Russia in 1904, the

United States had been preparing for a war with Japan in order to establish who would be *numero uno* not only in the Pacific but in Asia.

By 1939, Japan was busy conquering China, having acquired Korea and Manchuria, and the Nippon imperial eye was set on the southeast Asian oil fields, at that time in the hands of two 'local' Asiatic powers, the British and the Dutch.

As a 'racist,' Mencken blithely generalized about race, a real no-no in to-day's world where each and every one of the five billion people on our common crowded planet is a treasured and unique creation, sharing nothing at all with anyone else except, maybe, the Big Fella in the Sky. But generalize he did, something no longer allowed in freedom's land. Mencken writes: 'The Japanese, judged by Western eyes, are an extremely homely people, and no doubt the fact has a good deal to do with their general unpopularity.' Mencken thought that they look both 'sinister and ludicrous,' not an encouraging or likable combination. 'They look, taking one with another, like Boy Scouts with buck teeth, wearing horn-rimmed spectacles . . . I have never met a Caucasian who professed any affection for the Japs, though there are not a few white fans for the scenery,' etc. Already guilty of Racist Generalizing, Mencken proceeds, sickeningly, to grade *all* Japanese: 'They are a people of very considerable talents, and will have to be reckoned with in the future history of the human race. They have long since got past the stage of sitting respectfully at the feet of the West . . . In all the fields of human endeavor save theology, politics and swine justice they are showing the way to their ofay mentors. They have made important durable contributions to knowledge in each and every one of the exact sciences, and they have taken such a lead in trade and industry that the only way left to beat them is to murder them.' But even this solution, particularly favoured by England, won't be easy because they have 'a considerable knack for war.'

As 'nearly all white men dislike the Japs and like the Chinese,' Mencken tried to give an accurate impression of our soon-to-be great adversary and, as I gaze out over the Hollywood hills towards Japanese Universal Pictures, our eventual conquerors. But accuracy in reporting on Pacific matters is always difficult because the American press have always given us a view of the Japanese that 'is seldom accurate and not always honest,' to say the least. As of 1939, China and Chiang Kai-shek were, as always, on the brink of victory but, somehow, Japan always won and, as Mencken remarked, 'The Japs, in truth, had as sound a mandate to clean up China as the United States have had to clean up Cuba.' Or Mexico, Nicaragua, Salvador, Panama, Grenada, not to mention Korea, Cambodia, Iran and Iraq.

Three years later, the Japs, heavily provoked, sank the American fleet at Pearl Harbor and the great race war was on with Round One (with guns) going to the white race (1945) and Round Two (with computers) going to the yellow race (1990). Mencken was particularly good – that is, prophetic – on American skulduggeries south of the border where he often visited and duly noted our eerie inability to do anything honest or even intelligent whether in Cuba or Haiti or in dealing with Nicaragua's Sandino.

Like Puck, Mencken found most mortals fools. He showed us odd glimpses of the vacuous Duke of Windsor and his Baltimore lady as well as of Rudolph Valentino whom he once entertained in what must have been an unusually alcoholic session for a young Italian. Mencken commiserated with the assault by the press on the lad's manhood and he shed a public tear at the beauty's demise not long after.

In literary matters, Mencken was a shield to the-meat-and-potatoes of naturalism-realism, a sounder diet than one of, shall we say, frozen fish? He was a champion of Dreiser; a foe of censorship. He was good on Conrad but at sea with James and insensitive to Wharton. He knew cooking and provided a sound recipe for 'shore soup,' the crab-based glory of the eastern shore of Maryland. He was passionate about music. Disliked jazz but admired 'Aframerican' musicians. Interested in architecture, he was appalled by the ugliness of American cities except for San Francisco where 'There is nothing European about the way life is lived; the color is all Asiatic' because it is so happily cut off from 'the rest of the dun and dour Republic.' He described the average person's way of life in New York as that of a 'sardine in a can' while the grass in the so-called parks 'looks like embalmed sauerkraut.' He hated chiropractors. He was amazed, as an editor, to find that graduates of West Point write the best English. He took a bitter pride in 'the love of ugliness [that] is apparently inherent in the American people. They cherish and venerate the unspeakable.'

Matthew Arnold wrote that a 'style is the saying in the best way what you have to say. The what you have to say depends on your age.' Mencken certainly said what he had to say about the age that he had been assigned to. When asked why, if he can find nothing to 'revere' in the United States, he lived there, he replied, 'Why do men go to zoos?'

Religion as generally practised by the Americans of his day, he saw as a Great Wall of China designed to keep civilization out while barbarism might flourish within the gates. He himself was a resolute breacher of the Great Wall, and to the extent that some civilization has got through, he is one of the few Americans that we can thank. Plainly, so clear and hard a writer would not be allowed in the mainstream press of today, and those who think that they would like him back would be the first to censor and censure him.

As for Mencken himself, he wrote his own epitaph in 1921 for *Smart Set*: 'If, after I depart this vale, you ever remember me and have thought to please my ghost, forgive some sinner and wink your eye at some homely girl.' I realize that he has viciously used the G-word and, even worse, the long-since banned H-word. But there he is. And here we are, lucky we.

Originally published as the
Foreword to *The Impossible H. L. Mencken:
a Selection of his
Best Newspaper Stories*,
edited by Marion Elizabeth Rodgers,
Doubleday/Anchor Books.

# 2

# THE NATIONAL
# SECURITY STATE

Every now and then, usually while shaving, I realise that I have
lived through nearly one third of the history of the United States,
which proves not how old I am but how young the Republic is.
The American empire, which started officially in 1898 with our
acquisition of the Philippines, came to a peak in the year 1945,
while I was still part of that army which had won us the political
and economic mastery of two hemispheres. If anyone had said to
me then that the whole thing would be lost in my lifetime, I would
have said it is not possible to lose so much so quickly without an
atomic catastrophe, at least. But lose it we have.

Yet, in hindsight, I can see that our ending was implicit in our
beginning. When Japan surrendered, the United States was faced
with a choice: either disarm, as we had done in the past, and enjoy
the prosperity that comes from releasing so much wealth and
energy to the private sector, or maintain ourselves on a full military
basis, which would mean a tight control not only over our allies
and such conquered provinces as West Germany, Italy, and Japan
but over the economic – which is to say the political – lives of the
American people. As Charles E. Wilson, a businessman and
politician of the day, said as early as 1944, 'Instead of looking to
disarmament and unpreparedness as a safeguard against war, a
thoroughly discredited doctrine, let us try the opposite: full pre-
paredness according to a continuing plan.'

The accidental president, Harry Truman, bought this notion.

Although Truman campaigned in 1948 as an heir to Roosevelt's New Deal, he had a 'continuing plan'. Henry Wallace was on to it, as early as: 'Yesterday, March 12, 1947, marked a turning point in American history, [for] it is not a Greek crisis that we face, it is an American crisis. Yesterday, President Truman . . . proposed, in effect, America police Russia's every border. There is no regime too reactionary for us provided it stands in Russia's expansionist path. There is no country too remote to serve as the scene of a contest which may widen until it becomes a world war.' But how to impose this? The Republican leadership did not like the state to be the master of the country's economic life while, of the Democrats, only a few geopoliticians, like Dean Acheson, found thrilling the prospect of a military state, to be justified in the name of a holy war against something called communism in general and Russia in particular. The fact that the Soviet Union was no military or economic threat to us was immaterial. It must be made to appear threatening so that the continuing plan could be set in motion in order to create that National Security State in which we have been living for the past forty years.*

What is the National Security State? Well, it began, officially, with the National Security Act of 1947; it was then implemented in January 1950 when the National Security Council produced a blueprint for a new kind of country, unlike anything that the United States had ever known before. This document, known as NSC-68 for short, and declassified only in 1975, committed – and still, fitfully, commits – us to the following programme. First, never negotiate, ever, with Russia. This could not last forever; but the obligatory bad faith of US-USSR meetings still serves the continuing plan. Second, develop the hydrogen bomb so that when the Russians finally develop an atomic bomb we will still not have to deal with that enemy without which the National Security State

---

* For those interested in the details, I recommend H. R. Shapiro's *Democracy in America*, the only political history of the United States from British shires to present deficits. Needless to say, this masterly work, fourteen years in the making, is published privately by Manhattan Communication, 496 LaGuardia Place, Suite 406, New York, NY 10012. The present volume is only half the whole and lacks scholarly apparatus (index, bibliography) but not scholarship.

175

cannot exist. Third, rapidly build up conventional forces. Fourth, put through a large increase in taxes to pay for all of this. Fifth, mobilise the entire American society to fight the awful spectre of communism. Sixth, set up a strong alliance system, directed by the United States (this became NATO). Seventh, make the people of Russia our allies, through propaganda and CIA derring-do, in this holy adventure – hence the justification for all sorts of secret services that are in no way responsible to the Congress that funds them, and so in violation of the old Constitution.

Needless to say, the blueprint, the continuing plan, was not openly discussed at the time. But, one by one, the major political players of the two parties came around. Senator Arthur Vandenburg, Republican, told Truman that if he really wanted all those weapons and all those high taxes to pay for them, he had better 'scare hell out of the American people'. Truman obliged, with a series of speeches beginning October 23, 1947, about the Red Menace endangering France and Italy; he also instituted loyalty oaths for federal employees; and his attorney general (December 4, 1947) published a list of dissident organisations. The climate of fear has been maintained, more or less zealously, by Truman's successors, with the brief exception of Dwight Eisenhower, who in a belated fit of conscience at the end of his presidency warned us against the military-industrial complex that had, by then, established permanent control over the state.

The cynicism of this *coup d'état* was breathtaking. Officially we were doing nothing but trying to preserve freedom for ourselves and our allies from a ruthless enemy that was everywhere monolithic and all-powerful. Actually, the real enemy were those National Security Statesmen who had so dextrously hijacked the country, establishing military conscription in peacetime, overthrowing governments that did not please them, and finally keeping all but the very rich docile and jittery by imposing income taxes that theoretically went as high as 90 per cent. That is quite an achievement in a country at peace.

We can date from January 1950 the strict governmental control of our economy and the gradual erosion of our liberties, all in order to benefit the economic interest of what is never, to put it tactfully, a very large group – defence spending is money but not labour-intensive. Fortunately, all bad things must come to an end. Our huge indebtedness has made the maintenance of the empire a nightmare; and the day Japan stops buying our Treasury bonds, the troops and the missiles will all come home to a highly restless population.

Now that I have defined the gloomy prospect, what solutions do I have? I shall make five proposals. First, limit presidential election campaigns to eight weeks. That is what most civilised countries do, and all democratic ones are obliged to do. Allow no paid political ads. We might then entice that half of the electorate which never votes to vote.

Second, the budget. The press and the politicians constantly falsify the revenues and the disbursements of the federal government. How? By wrongly counting Social Security contributions and expenditures as a part of the federal budget. Social Security is an independent, slightly profitable income-transferring trust fund, which should be factored out of federal revenue and federal spending. Why do the press and the politicians conspire to give us this distorted view of the budget? Because neither they nor their owners want the public to know how much of its tax money goes for a war that does not exist. As a result, Federal Reserve chairman Alan Greenspan could say in March 1989, and with a straight face, that there are only two options for a serious attack on the deficit. One is to raise taxes. The other is to reduce the entitlement programmes like Social Security and Medicare. He did not mention the defence budget. He did not acknowledge that the so-called entitlements come from a special fund. But then, he is a disciple of Ayn Rand.

In actual fact, close to 90 per cent of the disbursement of the federal government go for what is laughingly known as 'defence'. This is how. In 1986 the gross revenue of the government was $794 billion. Of that amount, $294 billion were Social Security contributions, which should be subtracted from the money available to the National Security State. That leaves $500 billion. Of the $500 billion, $286 billion go to defence; $12 billion for foreign arms to our client states; $8 billion to $9 billion to energy, which means, largely, nuclear weapons; $27 billion for veterans' benefits, the sad and constant reminder of the empire's recklessness; and, finally, $142 billion for interest on loans that were spent, over the past forty years, to keep the National Security State at war, hot or cold. So, of 1986's $500 billion revenue, $475 billion was spent on National Security business. Of that amount, we will never know how much was 'kicked back' through political action committees and so-called soft money to subsidise candidates and elections. Other federal spending, incidentally, came to $177 billion in 1986 (guarding presidential candidates, cleaning the White House), which was about the size of the deficit, since only $358 billion was collected in taxes.

It is obvious that if we are to avoid an economic collapse, defence spending must be drastically reduced. But it is hard to reduce a budget that the people are never told about. The first politician who realises why those politicians who appear to run against the government always win, could not only win himself but be in a position to rid us of the National Security State – which is what people truly hate. 'Internal Improvements' was the slogan of Henry Clay's popular movement. A neo-Clayite could sweep the country if he wanted seriously to restore the internal plant of the country rather than invade Honduras or bob expensively about the Persian Gulf or overthrow a duly elected government in Nicaragua while running drugs (admittedly, the CIA's only margin of profit).

Third, as part of our general retrenchment, we should withdraw from NATO. Western Europe is richer and more populous than America. If it cannot defend itself from an enemy who seems to be falling apart even faster than we are, then there is nothing that we, proud invaders of Grenada, can effectively do. I would stop all military aid to the Middle East. This would oblige the hardliners in Israel to make peace with the Palestinians. We have supported Israel for forty years. No other minority in the history of the United States has ever extorted so much Treasury money for its

Holy Land as the Israeli lobby, and it has done this by making common cause with the National Security State. Each supports the other. I would have us cease to pay for either.

Fourth, we read each day about the horrors of drug abuse, the murder of policemen, the involvement of our own government in drug-running, and so on. We are all aware that organised crime has never been richer nor the society more demoralised. What is the solution? I would repeal every prohibition against the sale and use of drugs, because it is these prohibitions that have caused the national corruption, not to mention most of the addiction. Since the American memory has a span of about three days, I will remind you that in 1919 alcohol was prohibited in the United States. In 1933 Prohibition was repealed because not only had organised crime expanded enormously but so had alcoholism. What did not work then does not work now. But we never learn, which is part of our national charm. Repeal would mean that there is no money for anyone in selling drugs. That's the end of the playground pusher. That's the end of organised crime, which had already diversified and is doing very nicely in banking, films, and dry-cleaning. Eventually, repeal will mean the end of mass drug addiction. As there will always be alcoholics, there will always be drug addicts, but not to today's extent. It will be safe to walk the streets because the poor will not rob you to pay for their habit.*

Fifth, in 1986 I described how the American empire ended the day the money power shifted from New York to Tokyo and we became, for the first time in seventy-one years, a debtor nation. Since then, we have become the largest debtor country in history. I suggested a number of things that might be done, some of which I've again mentioned. But, above all, I see our economic survival inextricably bound up with that of our neighbour in the Northern Hemisphere, the Soviet Union. Some sort of alliance must be made between us so that together we will be able to compete with Japan and, in due course, China. As the two klutzes of the north, each

* I called for the legalisation of drugs pretty much in these same words on the op-ed page of *The New York Times*, September 26, 1970.

unable to build a car that anyone wants to drive, we deserve each other. In a speech at Gorbachev's anti-nuclear forum in Moscow, I quoted a Japanese minister of trade who said that Japan would still be number one in the next century. Then, tactlessly, he said that the United States will be Japan's farm and Western Europe its boutique. A Russian got up and asked, 'What did he say about us?' I said that they were not mentioned but, if they did not get their act together, they would end up as ski instructors. It is my impression that the Russians are eager to be Americans, but, thanks to the brainwashing of the National Security State's continuing plan, Americans have a built-in horror of the Evil Empire, which the press and the politicians have kept going for forty years. The Press, which should know better, is of no help. The Iran-*Contra* hearings were a sudden dramatic confrontation between the real government of the United States, as represented by Ollie North, *et al.*, and the cosmetic government. Ollie told us as much. But no one got the point.

Happily, our National Security State is in the red, in more ways than one. Time for a change?

*The Nation*
4 June 1988

# 3

# OLLIE

Lieutenant Colonel Oliver L. North (USMC) has now metastas-
ised in the national psyche rather the way that Tom Sawyer did
more than a century ago. Like Tom, Ollie is essentially fictional;
like Tom, Ollie is an American archetype: the con-man as Peck's
Bad Boy. It is hardly possible for any of us not to succumb, if only
momentarily, to Ollie's boyish charm, as he hurries back and forth
across our television sets, on his way, or so one gathers from the
twinkle in his eye, to some top-secret *Contra* massage parlour.
Actually my own favourite image of him is from the past: he has
come, a mere boy, in uniform – direct from the battlefield – to put
the case for the Vietnam War on a right-wing television programme. The enraptured host is actually salivating at so much
gung-ho martial spirit. Although I was, as always, briefly stricken,
one detail bothered me. Why did he keep his garrison cap on? In
the Army we took them off indoors. Could it be that Ollie was
deliberately playing a part even then? Could it be that he was not
absolutely entirely sincere? Perish, as they say, the thought. He is
a Marine.

Much is made by the present administration of the Marines to
whom, in my day, we used to go tell it to. Since a number of rogues
in high places are former Marines, we are daily reminded of the
corps's bravery and of its motto, *Semper fidelis* (always faithful),
faithful particularly to those in high places. Now the real Marines
are indeed brave, that is, the enlisted men. On the other hand, I

betray no secret when I say that those of us who served in the Army in the Pacific during the Second World War regarded Marine officers as, by and large, a bunch of dangerous boneheads, exuberantly careless with the lives of their men. Certainly they managed to decimate my generation with their legendary frontal assaults, and if the recent off-the-wall ramblings of their retiring commander (General P. X. Kelly) are typical, their collective IQ has not risen in the last forty years. So let us never forget that Ollie is not really a Marine at home in Montezuma's hall; he is a *Marine officer*, and should be kept on a tight leash along with gutsy Don Regan and pastryman Bud McFarlane.

In the coming days, Ollie will be the nation's number one daytime television star. There will be incredible suspense. Will he be *fidelis* to the president who let him off the leash to commit so many astonishing crimes? Will he be the strong silent sort like G. Gordon Liddy, who held his tongue so that he could later find it, most profitably, on the lecture circuit? Or will Ollie just go ahead and shred Ron and Nancy and Galanos and all those who drove him to crime? Tune in. This is high drama. It is also simply appalling in its implications.

Thirty years ago I wrote that should the United States ever have a dictator, it would not be a spellbinding autocrat like Douglas MacArthur; rather it would be someone really nice and folksy like Arthur Godfrey, a popular radio-TV pitchman of the era. In due course, big money, out to make even bigger bucks, cold-bloodedly hired an Arthur Godfrey to act the part of president. And we went along with him – or at least half of that bemused 50 per cent of the electorate which bothers to vote in presidential elections did. Luckily, age and incompetence have saved us from a dictatorship, and the actor himself will soon be gone. But, for a moment, it was a very close thing indeed: a president deliberately tried to over-throw the Constitution and place himself outside those laws he had sworn faithfully to execute. In retrospect, all this will seem pretty funny. Of course, Ollie will do time; he will also discover God yet again, be born a third time, and have a book written for him. He will be a celebrity for ever and will enjoy the friendship of Pat

Boone. On the other hand, we, the TV audience (and that is really all that we are – passive viewers and active consumers), will be living on in a republic that no longer works, its political system burnt out and its resources wasted during the reign of an actor whom we allowed so unwisely to step off the screen and into the White House.

Perhaps the most startling aspect of this whole affair has been the fact that no one seems particularly troubled. Congress is thrilled by the attention but its members refuse to lift the lid on anything important like, let us say, the CIA. But then the CIA is now totally unaccountable to anyone and Congress dares not ask such questions as: Were arms flown by the agency to the *Contras* in Nicaragua? And were those planes then filled with cocaine for the return journey? Of course, only a communist would ask such a question. Meanwhile, Marines are casually sacrificed in Lebanon by a government with no morality and an officer corps with no sense; the President compulsively tells lies on television as he has done throughout his entire political career and no one minds because he has such a nice smile.

The last best hope of earth, two trillion dollars in debt, is spinning out of control, and all we can do is stare at a flickering cathode-ray tube as Ollie 'answers' questions on TV while the press, resolutely irrelevant as ever, asks politicians if they have committed adultery. From V-J Day 1945 to this has been, my fellow countrymen, a perfect nightmare.

NB: The true significance of Ollie was missed by all at the time, including me. There are two governments of the United States: the more or less secret National Security State (National Security Council, Pentagon, CIA, etc) and the cosmetic 'constitutional' government of Congress, the judiciary and the never-ending, issueless presidential election. In the constant presence of a benign crisis manager from Langley, Ollie tried to tell the Senate that he worked for the real government to which they were irrelevant, while Reagan's easygoing vagueness in the matter derived from the president's dual function. Although he is the chief irrelevancy, he is also, if he chooses to be, a player in the actual government. He was very much at play in Nicaragua and Iran; but the cosmetic Congress dares not put a finger on him.

Several days after my piece in *Newsweek* appeared, the White House correspondent for *Time* magazine rang me. I've known him slightly for a long time. He is called Hugh Sidey; and he has yet to meet a president he could not worship. He had been at Camp David with President and Mrs Reagan, and the President had said, 'with a twinkle in his eye', how inaccurate Vidal is (good to know that he reads *Newsweek*). Apparently in my book about Lincoln, I show Lincoln watching the dawn from his office. But, said Reagan, you can't see the sun rise from the office. Sidey had been going through the book with a researcher: there was (how do they say at *Time?*) an edge of panic in his voice. We can't find the scene, he said. Because, I said, there is no such scene in the book: Lincoln did not get up as early as Reagan. I also reminded him – and the President – that Lincoln's office was at the south-east end of the second floor of the White House, with a fine view of the Potomac as well as of sunrises and sunsets. The present office, which has no view, was only built in 1904. Sidey reported in the next issue of *Time* the President's aria about how wrong I was 'because I had Lincoln seeing something he couldn't have seen from the White House'. The very stuff of history.

*Newsweek*
13 July 1987

# 4

# CUE THE GREEN
# GOD, TED

There has not been a political debate in the United States since
the one that ended with the Japanese attack on Pearl Harbor.
From September 1939 to December 7, 1941, the ruling class of the
United States was split between those who would join the Allies in
their war against Hitler and those who would stay out. For three
years there was fierce argument in Congress, the press, the schools.
At my school, Exeter, there was a sharp division between the
isolationists, known as America Firsters, and the interventionists.
True to the populist tradition in which I was brought up, I was
isolationist. Then, or as Lincoln once so bleakly put it, *and the war
came*; and I enlisted in the Army, age 17.

Since the victory of 1945, the United States, as befits the leader
of something called 'the free world', has fought open and unsuccessful wars in Korea and Vietnam; and relatively covert wars in
Cambodia, Laos, the Caribbean, Central America, Africa, Chile,
the Middle East, etc. In almost every case, our overwhelming
commitment to freedom, democracy and human rights has
required us to support those régimes that would deny freedom,
democracy and human rights to their own people. We justify our
affection for fascist (or, to be cozy, authoritarian) régimes because
each and every one of them is a misty-eyed convert to our national
religion, which is anti-communism. Then, once our dictator is in
place, we echo Andy Hardy: Hey, kids, let's put on an election!

And so, in the presence of cold-eyed avatars of Tammany and Daley, our general does.

To their credit, our rulers don't often bore us with tortured rationalisations or theological nit-picking. They don't have to. Since we have no political parties and no opposition media, there is always a semblance of 'consensus' for these wars. Congress funds the Pentagon, which then responds to the National Security State's directives to overthrow an Arbenz here or a Sihanouk there or – why not? – devastate a neutral country like Laos to show how tall we can stand in all our marvellously incredible credibility. Voices of dissent are either blacked out or marginalised, while known apostates of the national religion are either demonised or trivialised. Meanwhile, no one has noticed that the National Security State, in its zeal to bring the national religion to all nations, has now deprived us of our original holy text – our Old Testament – the Constitution.

Every war that we have fought since 1945 has been by executive (or National Security Council) order. Since only Congress may declare war, these wars have all been in violation of the Constitution. To the House of Representatives was assigned, uniquely, the power of the purse. But, in thrall to those religious wars that we forever fight, our debts are now so great that Congress dares not prepare a proper budget. So the power of the purse has been replaced by a ridiculous formula, involving a blind arbitrary cutting of the budget should Federal waste exceed a certain arbitrary figure. Although the most militant of our national religionists enjoy calling themselves conservatives, they have not managed to conserve either the letter or the spirit of the Old Testament.

For some time knowledgeable foreigners have found it difficult to talk about much of anything to Americans because we appear to know so little about much of anything. History of any kind is a closed book to us. Geography is no longer taught in most public schools. Foreign languages make everyone's head ache – anyway, *they* all know English. As for politics, that's simple: it's either *us* (what the silver-tongued felon Spiro Agnew, or his wordsmith

186

William Safire, so memorably dubbed 'the greatest nation in the country') or *them* – foreigners who envy us our vast choice of detergents, our freedom to repeat as loudly as we want the national prayers, our alabaster cities to which, we tell ourselves, they can't wait to emigrate. On the other hand, the average American, when it comes to his own welfare, is very shrewd indeed. He knows that we are in an economic decline and that our quality of life, though better that that of Russia (all that really matters, our priests hum softly) is noticeably lousy. But the reasons for our decline are never made clear because the corporate ownership of the country has absolute control of the pulpit – 'the media' – as well as of the schoolroom.

David Hume's celebrated *Of the First Principles of Government* (1758) has never been more to the point than now:

> Nothing appears more surprising to those, who consider human affairs with a philosophical eye than the easiness with which the many are governed by the few, and the implicit submission with which men resign their own sentiments and passions to those of their rulers. When we inquire by what means this wonder is effected, we shall find that, as Force is always on the side of the governed, the governors have nothing to support them but opinion. It is, therefore, on opinion only that government is founded, and this maxim extends to the most despotic and most military governments as well as to the most free and most popular.

The corporate grip on opinion in the United States is one of the wonders of the Western world. No First World country has ever managed to eliminate so entirely from its media all objectivity – much less dissent. Of course, it is possible for any citizen with time to spare, and a canny eye, to work out what is actually going on, but for the many there is no time, and the network news is the only news even though it may not be news at all but only a series of flashing fictions intended, like the avowed commercials, to keep docile huddled masses, keep avid for products addled consumers.

I seldom watch television. But when I do set out to twirl the dial, it is usually on Sunday, when our corporate rulers address us from their cathode pulpit. Seedy Washington journalists, sharp-eyed government officials who could not dispose of a brand-new car in Spokane, think-tank employees, etiolated from too long residence 'neath flat rocks, and always, always, Henry Kissinger, whose destruction of so many Asians and their once-charming real estate won him a prize for peace from the ironists of northern Europe. The level of the chat on those programmes is about as low as it is possible to get without actually serving the viewers gin. The opinion expressed ranges from conservative to reactionary to joyous neofascist. There is even, in William Safire, an uncloseted anti-Gentile.

I was once placed between two waxworks on a programme where one of the pair was solemnly identified as a 'liberal'; appropriately, he seemed to have been dead for some time, while the conservative had all the vivacity of someone on speed. For half an hour it is the custom of this duo to 'crossfire' clichés of the sort that would have got them laughed out of the Golden Branch Debating Society at Exeter. On air, I identified the conservative as a liberal and vice versa. The conservative fell into the trap. 'No, no!' he hyperventilated. 'I'm the conservative!' (What on earth they think these two words mean no one will ever know.) It was the liberal who got the point; from beyond, as it were, the tomb he moaned, 'He's putting us on.'

I have been involved in television since the early 1950s, when it ceased to be a novelty and became the principal agent for the simultaneous marketing of consumer goods and of National Security State opinion. Although I thought I knew quite a bit about the ins and outs of the medium, I now know a lot more, thanks to Ben H. Bagdikian's *The Media Monopoly* and *Manufacturing Consent*, a study of 'the political economy of the mass media', by Edward S. Herman and Noam Chomsky. These two studies demonstrate exactly how the few manipulate opinion. To begin with: the average American household keeps the set throbbing seven hours a day. This means the average American has watched 350,000 commercials by age 17. Since most opinion is now controlled by twenty-nine corporations – due to be at least one fewer if Time-Warner or Paramount-Time or, most chilling of all, Nation-Time comes to pass – one can then identify those twenty-nine CEOs as a sort of politburo or college of cardinals, in strict charge of what the people should and should not know. They also select the Presidents and the Congresses or, to be precise, they determine what the politicians may talk about at election time – that famed agenda that never includes the interesting detail that, in peacetime, more than two-thirds of the Federal revenue goes to war. Although AIDS can be discussed as a means of hitting out at unpopular minorities, the true epidemic can never be discussed: the fact that every fourth American now alive will die of cancer. This catastrophe is well kept from the public by the tobacco companies, the nuclear power companies (with their bungled waste disposal) and other industries that poison the earth so that corporate America may enjoy the freedom to make money without the slightest accountability to those they are killing.

The invention of the talk show on television was, at first, a most promising development. Admittedly, no one very radical would ever be allowed on, but a fair range of opinion could be heard, particularly as the Vietnam war began to go bad. On the original *Today* show, Hugh Downs and I would talk off and on for an hour as news, weather, commercials floated lazily on. But Hazel Bishop, an obscure lipstick company, changed all that. The firm began running commercials not linked to specific programmes and it was soon determined that the thirty-second commercial duplicates exactly the attention span of the average viewer. Therefore, no in-depth interview can last for more than seven minutes; three minutes is considered optimum. Recently, I found myself confronting the amiable Pat Sajak. I was all set to do what I think of as my inventing-the-wheel-in-seven-minutes (why what's wrong is wrong and what to do) when my energy level crashed. I did say that if you wanted to know what the ownership of the country wants you to know, tune in to *Nightline* and listen to Ted Koppel and his guests. The effect of this bit of information must have been surreal. Since no voices other than those of the national consensus are heard, how could a viewer know that there are any other viewpoints?

I was made aware of the iron rules in 1968, when William F. Buckley Jr and I had our first live chat on ABC at the Republican Convention in Miami Beach. I was billed as the conservative; he as the pro-crypto – or was it the other way around? Anyway, we were hired to play the opinion game in order to divert the audience from the issues. Buckley Junior's idea of a truly deep in-depth political discussion is precisely that of corporate America's. First, the Democrat must say that the election of a Republican will lead to a depression. Then the Republican will joyously say, Ah Hah, but the Democrats always lead us into war! After a few minutes of this, *my* attention span snapped. I said that there was no difference at all between the two parties because the same corporations paid for both, usually with taxpayers' money, tithed, as it were, from the faithful and then given to 'defence,' which in turn passes it on to those candidates who will defend the faith. With that bit of news for the national audience, I revealed myself not only as an apostate to the national religion; I came close to revealing what I really am: a dedicated anti-anticommunist, a category far more vile to the true believer than a mere communist. Although my encounters with Buckley Junior got ABC its highest ratings, I was seen no more at election time. Last year, Peter Jennings proposed to ABC that, for old times' sake, it might be a good idea to have me on. 'No,' he was told, 'He'll just be outrageous.'

In 1972 the future Supreme Court Justice Lewis Powell wrote to the US Chamber of Commerce proposing that they 'buy the top academic reputations in the country to add credibility to corporate studies and give business a stronger voice on the campuses'. One wonders, stronger than what? But the advice was taken. Also, as corollary, keep off prime-time television those who do not support corporate America. During the 1960s and early 1970s I used, once a year, to do a 'state of the union' analysis on David Susskind's non-network, non-prime-time television programme. Many people watched. In the summer before the 1976 presidential election,

Susskind wanted to produce a series of one-hour interviews with the twenty or so leading candidates of the two parties. For one hour I would question each candidate about politics, history, economics – whatever came up. Since I favoured no candidate and neither party, I could not be said to be partisan. Public Broadcasting System agreed that this sort of programme was precisely why PBS had been founded and funded. All the candidates, save President Ford, affected delight. As we prepared for the first programme, the head of PBS affiliate WNET, Jay Iselin, cancelled the series without explanation. Then the intrepid producer Hillard Elkins took over. He had 'a good relationship' with Home Box Office, which was 'hungry for product'. HBO manifested delight in having its hunger so cheaply sated. Then, just before the first taping, Andrew Heiskell, the overall *capo* of Time-Life-HBO, cancelled us. In due course, I was advised that it was not in the national (that is, corporate) interest for so many *expensive* presidential candidates to be questioned by me in a – what was the phrase? – 'nonstructured format'. Now, of course, with the megacorporate ownership of the media becoming more and more concentrated in fewer and fewer hands, structure is total, indeed totalitarian, and the candidates can no longer be discerned through the heavy blizzard of thirty-second spots.

Currently, the principal dispenser of the national religion is Ted Koppel, a very smooth bishop indeed. Fairness & Accuracy In Reporting – noble, doomed enterprise – had a study made of just who appeared as Koppel's guests during a forty-month period from 1985 to 1988. White male Establishment types predominated. Henry Kissinger (Koppel's guru and a longtime cardinal in the national security state's curia) and Alexander Haig (by his own admission, in one of many moments of confusion at the White House, 'a vicar') each appeared fourteen times, the maximum for any guest. Yet the Cardinal's views on almost any subject are already known to anyone who might be interested in looking at *Nightline*, while Haig's opinions have never interested anybody in the course of a long busy career climbing ladders so that he could be close to those with power – in order to be close to them. The next two champ guests, weighing in at twelve appearances each, were the mendacious Elliott Abrams (Koppel assumes that although Abrams will lie to Congress, he won't lie to Koppel) and Jerry Falwell, a certified voice of God whose dolorous appearance suggests a deep, almost personal grief that the Thirteenth and Fourteenth Amendments to the Constitution are not yet repealed. Most of the other guests are hired guns for the National Security state.

The Koppel explanation for this bizarre repertory company is that, well, they are the folks who are running the country and so that's why they're on. Well, yes, Ted, that *is* why they're on, but there are other more interesting and more learned – even disinterested – voices in the land and, in theory, they should be heard, too. But theory is not practice in bravery's home. Of semi-dissenters, only Jesse Jackson and Studs Terkel have been honoured with solo interviews with the bishop, who insists, by the way, that the guest face not him but a camera in another room, preferably in another city, with an earphone but no monitor. Good television one-upmanship.

To my amazement, just before Mikhail Gorbachev spoke at the United Nations, on December 7, 1988, I was asked to contribute a tiny pre-recorded (and thus easily edited) cameo. I suppose that I was asked because I had attended Gorbachev's famous anti-nuclear forum in Moscow two years earlier. I spoke to a camera. I predicted, accurately, that Gorbachev would say that Russia was unilaterally disarming, and that we were now dangerously close to peace. To the question What will the United States do without The Enemy? – a pretty daring question from those whose livelihood depends on the demonising of Russia and Communism – I said that, thanks to television, a new demon can be quickly installed. Currently, the Arabs are being thoroughly demonized by the Israel lobby while the Japanese are being, somewhat more nervously, demonized by elements of the corporate state. But neither will do as a long-term devil because the Arabs are too numerous (and have too much oil) while the Japanese will simply order us to stop it; should we disobey them, they will buy the networks and show us many hours of the soothing tea ceremony. I suggested that the new devil will be the threat to our ecosphere, and the new world god, Green. None of this was used, of course, but a man who writes Russians-Are-Coming thrillers was shown, frowning with intense anguish at, What, *what*! does it all mean? Because you godda be real careful with these guys. Fine show, Ted.

The unloved American empire is now drifting into history on a sea of red ink, as I predicted in *The Nation* on January 11, 1986 ('Requiem for the American Empire'), to the fury of the few and the bewilderment of the many. Thanks to money wasted in support of the national religion, our quality of life is dire, and although our political institutions work smoothly for the few, the many hate them; hence the necessity of every corporate candidate for president to run against the government, which is, of course, the corporate state – good fun. In due course, something on the order of the ethnic rebellions in the Soviet Union or even of the people's uprising in China will take place here. Too few have ripped off too many for too long. Opinion can no longer disguise the contradiction at the heart of conservative-corporate opinion. The corporate few are free to do what they will to customers and environment while the many are losing their freedoms at a rapid rate. The Supreme Court, the holy office of the national religion, in upholding the principle of preventive detention got rid of due process two years ago, and now the Court is busily working its way through the Bill of Rights, producing, as it goes, a series of bright, crackling *autos-da-fé*, among them not only the hectic flag but children and mental defectives.

Significantly, our prison population is now among the world's largest. Certainly, it is right up there, per capita, with the Soviet Union and the Republic of South Africa. Now the few are proposing that if the war budget is to be, tragically, reduced, the army camps – perfect symbolism – can be used to house our criminal population, particularly weak-fibred drug users. Thus do the few now declare open war on the many, as millions of citizens are now liable to mandatory blood, urine and lie-detector tests, while an electronic bracelet has been invented that will make it possible to track its wearer wherever he goes. Theoretically, half a nation can now monitor the movements of the other half. Better we enslave ourselves, the priests chant, than *they* do.

Lately, the language of government, always revealing, grows more and more fierce and commanding (due to so many wars lost? so much money wasted?), and military metaphors abound as czars lead all-out wars on drugs. Yet, at the risk of causing both offence and embarrassment among even the not-so-faithful, I feel obliged to say that I do not accept the authority of any state – much less one founded as was ours upon the free fulfilment of each citizen – to forbid me, or anyone, the use of drugs, cigarettes, alcohol, sex with a consenting partner or, if one is a woman, the right to an abortion. I take these rights to be absolute and should the few persist in their efforts to dominate the private lives of the many, I recommend force as a means of changing their minds. In this, I echo Jefferson.

Meanwhile, let us hope that opinion will respond to recent events. For instance, despite millions of dollars spent in the last presidential election on trying – successfully – to obscure every political issue while demonstrating – unsuccessfully – that there was a dramatic difference between Dukakis and Bush, 50 per cent of the American electorate refused to vote. When a majority boycotts a political system, its days are numbered. The many are now ready for a change. The few are demoralised. Fortunately, the Messiah is at hand: the Green God. Everyone on earth now worships him. Soon there will be a worldwide Green movement, and the establishment of a worldwide state, which the few will take over, thus enslaving us all while forgetting to save the planet. That is the worst-case scenario. The best? Let the many create a *new* few.

*The Nation*
7–14 August 1989

# 5

# GODS & GREENS

For three days, at a long green baize-covered table littered with
microphones and translators' headsets, Graham Greene and I sat
side by side in a conference room of the Kosmos Hotel in Moscow.
Facing us, several hundred members of the cultural section of
Gorbachev's international conference on nuclear disarmament.
One look at this hanging jury and that one-time engineering
student, Norman Mailer, fled to the science section. Hour after
hour, Greene and I listened to long speeches, usually delivered in
flawed or, most chillingly, in flawless French.

As we did not break for lunch until noon, Graham would start
to get a bit edgy around 11 o'clock. On the third day, he muttered
in my ear, 'I have a flask. Dare I . . . ?' Since Gorbachev was
currently engaged in his doomed battle against vodka, I said we
must show solidarity, in public. 'But why not drop a paper on the
floor, reach down for it, and take a swig?' He shook his head sadly
(I use this tired adverb because Greene is hostile to the adverb and
I in love with it): 'I might not come back up again.'

At noon we went from conference to a room bright with
television lights. The world's journalists, east and west, were all on
hand and at their pert prettiest. Greene and I were promptly
interviewed by a number of television journalists, many from exotic
lands. At lunch, a bottle of vodka between our plates, Graham
observed, 'I never do television.' As he had clocked at least a dozen
appearances in three days, I asked myself, aloud, as the French

say, what did he mean by 'never'? 'But this is the East. That doesn't count. I don't live here,' he said. 'But in the West I don't want people to know my face.'

When I remarked that his face was perhaps the best known of any of the world's writers, the familiar pale face – like an adolescent boy's left out too long in a great cold – turned pink, and we changed the subject. But then, as we ate pale February watermelon from Georgia, he said, 'You like to go on television, don't you?' I said, yes, I did – very much, in fact. Why? Because how else could I talk politics and history and religion to the general public without the smothering intervention of a print-journalist bent on re-creating one to conform to his publisher's prejudices? This interested him. 'Then you don't talk about your work?' I said that as I assume no one is interested in anyone's writing, I only talk about what interests the viewer – and me. The grey-yellow eyes blinked (what about a 'thoughtfully', Graham?). Then he said, 'I saw Anthony Burgess on French television.' Graham frowned. There had been some sort of a chill between the two neighbours on the Côte d'Azur, and as I enjoy each, I have never inquired the reason. What, then, did Burgess talk about? Graham shuddered with true horror; then he whispered, 'He talked about *his* books.'

Two years later, I was asked if I would chat for 30 minutes into a television camera. Subject? Anything. Naturally, given so much freedom, I could think of nothing. Then the day, as it always does, came. On 13 April, 1989, a television crew arrived at my house in Ravello (province of Salerno, Italy), and I still had no text. I would ramble, I decided. See what, if anything, was in my head other than the fact that my father had been born on this day, 94 years ago. I panicked. Had I been thinking about anything lately, or merely thinking that I was thinking? What most disturbed me? That was easy. There had been no rain all winter. This had never happened before. In Salerno water was being rationed. Environment. Yes. But how to do it without every eye glazing over as the familiar statistics sound, merry as a leper's bell?

I take the camera into my confidence. Say where we are – on a balcony 400 metres above the Tyrrhenian sea. I live part of the year in Italy, part in Los Angeles. I am not a tax exile (this always astonishes the British who do not know that every American must pay full tax to his beloved country no matter where he lives or makes his living). I am also not a political exile – yet. On that note, a gust of wind topples the electrical equipment, and we retreat to my work room. I start over. When in doubt, grab *The Oxford Book of Greek Verse* (after all, we are in Magna Graecia). Quote Lucian: 'The world is fleeting; all things pass away;/Or is it we that pass and they that stay?' I say that the first line is now the correct one. We are killing our green world and everything will pass away. Question: what ought we to do so that they will stay?

Our lives are dominated by symbols of our own making. Once we had invented time by differentiating one year from another, we became in thrall to the notion of the decade, the century, the millennium. Every twenty years the middle-aged celebrate the decade of their youth. Hence the current preoccupation with the Sixties, while the elderly dote upon the Forties or even the Thirties.

But these arbitrary groupings mean nothing at all except in a subjective way. Nevertheless, such is the force of habit, we are now faced, most dramatically, with not only the century's end but with the end of the second Christian millennium. As the first joyous millennium was drawing to a close, the end of the world was regularly announced, as a sort of marker to celebrate the thousand years that had gone by since a sky-god had chosen unwisely to become a man who was then put to death, all the while predicting that the world would end within the lifetime of many of his contemporaries. Millennial fever is a bit like the madness of those citizens of Cavafy's Hellenic city who lived in terror of the Barbarians whose coming would destroy them. But the Barbarians never came. Possibly because the citizens themselves *were* the Barbarians and, in their waiting, they destroyed themselves within their own high gates.

Now, two millennia later, we are once again talking of final things. First eye-glazer: there are five billion people on a very small planet. At least four of those billions are too many, but which four? That is when the enlightened start talking of planned parenthood, while the dark souls contemplate with ecstasy the four horsemen cantering into view.

But if the four or whatever billions were to vanish or simply be unborn, what about the planet itself? Although the signs of disaster have been clearly visible for more than a generation, no one has thought to do much of anything to purify the water and the air, and to shut, if possible, those two great holes in the polar skies. Only a world crisis can focus our rulers' attention. This year's skewed harvests may do the trick.

David Hume once observed that all power is with the governed because they are many while the governors are few. How then do the few control the many? Through Opinion, as expressed from the pulpit and in the classroom. Today we can add that terrible word – media.

In my lifetime and country I have watched our governors manipulate Opinion with the greatest of ease. Certain races, arbitrary categories of human beings, political systems are demonised or trivialised on a daily and unrelenting basis. These are the carefully crafted subliminal *opinionated* messages that hiss through the airways and into the minds of everyone from the first switching on of the cathode tube to the last TV supper when the light goes out.

At a time of imperial crisis, Americans demonised the Germans and the Japanese. Then, once they were safely enclosed within our empire, we demonised the Russians and something called communism which was particularly evil because it was godless, while everyone knows that we have more than enough sky-god for two.

The present crisis is due not so much to the actual crisis – the destruction of the environment – but to a realignment of official enemies. Opinion is changing rapidly in every country. After the Second World War, the American empire decreed that the three conquered countries were not to maintain military establishments. As a result, Japan and Germany, unencumbered by military pretensions, now lead the world's economy while Italy is doing very well indeed. For almost half a century America's client states in western Europe have depended on American nuclear power to protect them from godless communism and brute Russia. Thanks to all those trillions of dollars spent to keep at bay phantom Barbarians, the United States has ceased to be the world's pre-eminent economic and industrial power. Worse, the Soviet Union has perversely lost all interest in playing Lucifer to America's nuclear god, and so by simply opting out of our peculiar version of Paradise Lost we are bereft of a beloved enemy.

Desperate attempts are being made to rally the American people and their European clients – soon to be non-clients – by redemonizing the Japanese. During the Second World War, I was assigned to the Pacific Theatre, as our Japanese war was called. We were regularly briefed on the inhumanity of the Japanese; luckily for us, we were told, they could never manage modern aircraft because their eyes were too narrow to see properly. Then they sank our fleet at Pearl Harbor.

Lately, redemonization has begun. But there is something half-hearted about the exercise because, each fiscal quarter, if the Japanese do not buy sufficient US Treasury bonds, there would not be enough money to operate the American government. In the end, I suspect that Japan will simply not allow us to make them the devil. If necessary, they can always buy up our television networks and show hour after hour of anodyne programmes celebrating the beauties of Kyoto and the tranquil pleasures of the tea ceremony. No pulpit, no God; no pulpit, no devil either.

Currently, another American candidate for demonization is the one billion Muslims in general and the Arabs in particular. Since America's Israel lobby controls American foreign policy in the Middle East, and since terrorist elements within Israel now control the Israeli government, we shall see Arabs more and more depicted as sub-human killers, never so happy as when blowing up a school. But, again, I don't think that the Muslims will make a suitable enemy. For one thing, there are too many of them. For another, they control too much of the world's oil supply. Finally, if the more thoughtful elements within Israel fail to make peace now, the Japanese may not give the Americans the money that they then give to Israel for its wars. So, let us rule out the Japanese and the

Arabs as demons to be used to frighten the governed. What is left? Just us – the human race which is now breeding like a virus under optimum conditions.

Think of earth as a living organism that is being attacked by billions of bacteria whose numbers double every forty years. Either the host dies, or the virus dies, or both die. That seems to be what we are faced with. The Reverend Malthus is often revived in order to show how wrong he was with his formula that population increases in a geometrical ratio, food in an arithmetical one; hence, the first must outgrow the second. So far it has not, but in order to feed so many, the damage to air, earth and water has been catastrophic. Until recently any attempt to recognise that we are all at risk has been ignored by our rulers because to acknowledge that things are wrong would hurt their short-term profits.

Governments are in place so that the few can take advantage of the many whom they control through Opinion. This explains the fierce tone of coercion assumed by the few when they give orders to the many. If ours were openly totalitarian societies, everything could then be justified in the name of the State or of the leader or of the all-powerful party of the people from which the actual people are excluded. But in the northern so-called democracies, we pretend that we are liberal societies where the many govern themselves and the few put down their plough, as it were, from time to time, to go to Washington or to Westminster.

The sad truth is that we live not in liberal democracies but in quasi-totalitarian patriarchies. This has been a gradual evolution since the eighteenth century's partial enlightenment. So great now is the indoctrination in the United States and so vast the ignorance due to the – calculated? – collapse of the general school system, that America's high school graduates when shown the Bill of Rights, unidentified, sternly reject all its guaranteed freedoms.

But then, paradoxically, despite our 'inalienable rights', we have always accepted, in principle, the right of the State to intervene in our private lives. It is taken for granted that we are allowed only one husband or wife at a time and always of the opposite sex. It is considered fitting and proper that the Government may seize the

children of anyone, except the rich, and incarcerate them in schools
where they learn very little, except how to become docile workers
and eager consumers. Although the few are also obliged to send
their children to school – expensive schools where they do learn a
good deal more than the many – their children are even more
fiercely indoctrinated than those of the many in Opinion.

It is a great joy to read the American or British press celebrating
their respective democracies. Apparently, a democracy is a place
where numerous elections are held at great cost without issues and
with interchangeable candidates. In the 1988 presidential election,
the only difference between Mr Bush and Mr Dukakis was that
Mr Dukakis, a liberal – which means a standard unthinking
conservative – would reduce the Pentagon budget to $292 billion
while the unthinking conservative, Mr Bush, would save the world
from Communism with a budget of $298 billion. Neither addressed
himself to the true issue, why waste so much money on war without
an enemy?

In America, we do not have political parties. The same people
pay for the Republicans who pay for the Democrats. At present in
Great Britain there might as well not be parties. As it is, the people
at large are in no way represented in either country. Great Britain
is governed by a sort of conservative – small c – oligarchy of
interchangeable careerists while the United States is governed by
the hugely wealthy military industrial complex. Citizens need not
apply for public office unless they agree to serve the famed
complex. As a result, in the last presidential election 51 per cent
decided, most sensibly, not to vote at all.

But with or without legitimacy the few who govern the United
States continue to acquire more and more powers in order to
control the many. Drugs are a natural target and weapon for
rulers. What better way to keep control than, first, prohibit various
substances; then allow organised crime to distribute them most
profitably; then hire hundreds of thousands of police to keep tight
control over the private lives of everyone. In freedom's land and
bravery's home, many millions are subject to mandatory blood
tests, urine tests, lie-detector tests. But then, it is the object of

governors everywhere to obtain as much power as they can over the governed, preferably through Opinion rather than through force, which is expensive and volatile. After all, the police may one day arrest the few.

Meanwhile, strident American voices – government-inspired? – want martial law declared and all rights suspended in order to wipe out those drugs which would, if legalised and sold at cost, be rather less of a problem than alcohol. But one cannot control the· many without fierce prohibitions. In order to prosecute the war on drugs and the battle against Aids and the fight for chastity – note all the military metaphors – the governments of the West are losing their ancient notions of freedom – notions which have often been not much more than fragile pieties but awfully good things to have to refer to.

Meanwhile, in the green and pleasant land, government hedges itself round with secrecy, guillotining parliamentary debate, manipulating the Australian press, while maintaining 'that the security services are essential to the safety of the State and they serve the nation best if they are not put under public scrutiny'. As Great Britain's national security is under no threat, this is the voice of a complacent fascism whose only interest is total unaccountable control of the many by the secret, unscrutinised few.

Where then does the battle – let us be warlike – to save the green planet fit in? In theory, it is the one cause that everyone on earth supports. In practice, those who profit by destroying rivers and forests are not going to do much of anything until something vividly goes wrong. Now the climate is changing – vividly. The next battle-plan will be an attempt to coordinate all efforts in order to reverse the greenhouse effect. This will mean demonizing some of our governors.

But they are shrewd enough to adapt to new necessities. Note the speed with which the 'mostest' ever British Prime Minister became the Lady Greensleeves. Thus far our own Bush is not yet ablaze (he belongs to the oil industry as well as to 'defence') but he will come around – and when the world's various fews all agree, we shall then end up with that most terrible of all utopias, a world government. There may be no alternative.

But let us anticipate the perils. After two thousand years of history, it is fairly evident that once the few have total charge of the many, they will forget to preserve the environment, and we shall perish as slaves rather than as what we are now, demi-slaves. It is not wise ever to be optimistic when it comes to the human race. Prometheus stole fire from Heaven so that we could cook not only dinner but one another. We create; we destroy. Balance is what we have always needed. Know thyself. Everything in moderation. Man is near, Heaven is far. Do unto others as you would have them do unto you. This last sentence everyone knows in the West as the words of Jesus. But five hundred years before Jesus, Confucius said exactly the same thing.

I suggest that those who create Opinion must address themselves – and us their victims – to a new way of looking at life. To a new religious sense that differs drastically from the truly terrible religions that we have suffered from for two millennia. Monotheism is easily the greatest disaster to befall the human race. By nature, the sky-god is totalitarian. You will have no other god but he. You will kill those who refuse to worship him, and you are free to destroy the earth because he has instructed us 'to be fruitful and multiply, and replenish the Earth, and subdue it; and have dominion over every living thing that moveth upon the Earth'. In today's context, the instruction is madness and its single god – Judaic, Christian, Islamic – is one of immaculate evil.

It is time for us in the West to look to more subtle religions and ethical systems, particularly those of China and India. Here there are many gods. There, there are no gods. For the Buddha, we are not here except to be gone from here. For Confucius, harmony within the State is all. When asked what happens after death, Confucius said, since we know so little of life why ask about death of which we know nothing? He thought there was a golden mean and, through education and right conduct, it could be achieved in public as well as in private life.

The technology now exists to change dramatically everyone's

way of looking at the world, past, present and future. One has only to think of Gorbachev's first four years in power. Seventy years of demonizing the Soviet Union was expertly undone by his masterful use of television and all the teacherly arts. The few can now create, rapidly, new Opinion so that we can make a proper marriage with the planet instead of an incontinent rape, in the name of dominion.

But, if I may give some advice to the Greens of the world, do not allow our totalitarian-minded governors in the West to coopt your movement. Start with the many. Let them convert the few. Meanwhile, the clock is ticking. The new millennium is at hand. Since you started to read this piece, $x$ thousand people have joined us on the planet. If you went to the loo or out in the garden, hordes were born. They will have a very hard time of it here. But, of course, if they are monotheists, they are just passing through. Heaven's their destination.

Meanwhile, let me note that just as I finished my chat to the camera on the Sahelian drought that has befallen southern Italy, it started to rain cats and dogs and we have had the wettest summer in years. Let us give thanks to the protean Green God.

*The Observer*
27 August 1989

# 6

# ON THE LAST DAY
# OF THE 1980's

Usually when a decade ends the know-it-all critic will first gaze
with superior but not unfriendly eye upon the used-up decade;
then he will look into the future and find – what else? More of the
same. For residents of these islands that means exciting political
speculation: whence Heseltine, whither Kinnock, or whence Kinnock, whither Heseltine? No hint of radical change because, by
and large, the island press bows low to those who exercise what
looks to innocent journalists very like power and those with power
want no change, ever, for what does change signify to nature's
conservative? Death. And on television, too, as Romania's Video-
cracy is presently demonstrating.

Already the minor changes required of the islanders in order to
make a more perfect union with the mainland have set all bells
tolling. Is monetary union the End of the Island Story? Will clean-
limbed English lads and lasses be flung without languages at
Babel's gates, armed only with metal-tipped boots in a world
where garlic makes foul the air and even the intrepid Thatcher can
be seen clutching her handbag bosom-close. Look! Here come
Andreotti and Gonzalez and Soares. Look! Her knuckles are
whitening even though the sterling within the bag is not worth
quite as much as that of the Mafia – that is, the other signatories
of the Treaty of Rome. No matter. The island story will either
continue as part of the main story or the story will indeed end as

the green and pleasant land drifts off to join those other islands that history has forgot – Wight, Man, Dogs – Staten too.

That is more or less the standard opening of the new-decade piece. But not this time. We are not what we were, any of us in any land, and if we don't understand the nature of recent changes, boats will be missed, even sunk. Although attentive observers have been aware for some years of the growing irrelevance of the great nuclear empires, the last twelve months have made it apparent to even the dullest that the Second War and its darling heir, Cold, are both well and truly interred. It is as if some great hand (let us hope not Anarch's) has suddenly shaken up all Earth's tribes and nations and cast them in a new combination upon the polluted globe that in my youth was not only much less polluted but mostly, on the map, British-pink. 'I never dreamed when I went to India as Prince of Wiles,' the Duke of Windsor used to moan in his Bois de Boulogne bunker, 'that I would be the last king-emperor.' But so he proved to be when his successor let go half the orb.

Now there is yet another twist to the screw, a new world in which Britain is mere spear-carrier and the Soviet Union and the United States – what? Gog and Magog, or perhaps, Rosencrantz and Guildenstern waiting for . . .?

Last summer a starry-eyed, apple-pie, neo-fascist American paper did a summing-up of the Eighties. Although our adolescent police state is not yet able to liberate angry rich from feckless poor, the editors claim that the collapse of Great Satan Communism is entirely due to unregulated capitalism; needless to say, the victory was not an easy one, and the true enemy, as always, was from within. Your humble end-of-decade preacher was named by the editor as 'the number one pain in the ass of the Eighties' with Sting and Noam Chomsky as runners-up. Immodestly, I note this tribute to my ability to deal in fundamentals.

Of course, the recent dramatic changes in the world are in no way related to the United States or to Western Europe or even to the shy children of the Rising Sun. But as it is our western habit to personalise – that is, trivialise – historic events, the top of history's iceberg, Gorbachev, has been given full credit for almost everything, just as he will be given full blame should things go wrong as, inevitably, they do anywhere, any time.

This is unfair. Worse, it is missing the point. For once, the human race can be said to be the star of its own continuing drama. I speak now not of Jungian archetypes whispering in our psyches or Lorenzian banshees howling in the collective blood-streams but only of a world that has been changed beyond all comprehension by technology.

In bravery's home, Joseph McCarthy was invented and destroyed on television while Nixon was invented, destroyed, re-invented, re-destroyed . . . But the most astonishing victory to date was the way TV brought to an end the mindless war in Vietnam, despite the manipulative skill of Corporate America which owns not only the politicians but, what really matters, the media. Happily, they did not suspect that each evening's pictures of Americans being killed in far-off jungles would turn the most passive viewer against a war whose only purpose was to give our National Security state something to do and justify the expenditure of two-thirds of the federal budget on war, even when there is no war. There is more money, of course, when a war has been cooked up as in Vietnam or, this week and last, Panama where our most advanced air power was used against a country with no air force. Such enemies are a proper treat for Byzantium-on-Potomac and its cutely-named 'just cause'. But now that Panama appears to be 'free' again, one wonders when, if ever, the United States will be freed of a suffocating and brutal military-industrial-political complex. The *last* shoe to fall?

Despite a geopolitical mind-set stuck in 1950, Americans are still very much in advance of everyone else. It can be argued that as we don't have official censorship our free institutions and press got rid of the thirteen-year Asiatic war that no one could ever explain. But our institutions – particularly the media – are strictly, if subtly, controlled, while no meaningful political party can be established, as I discovered when the anti-Vietnam-war People's Party's attempts to get on the ballot in Texas ended in anonymous gunshots through the Houston headquarters' windows.

Debate on prime-time television is between those who support wholly the policies of the Administration in office and those who would 'fine-tune' government policies. On *ABC Nightline*, the voice of Corporate America, (whose guru *gris* is Henry Kissinger), no voice will be heard that questions, let us say, the folly of the current war against drugs. Lately, British television has been catching up. In the US if a critic of the *status quo* does get to be interviewed on a programme that looks to be live, he will be refuted, but not censored or edited. Recently I appeared on a BBC Saturday evening programme where I was questioned by a woman whose inverted triangle of a face sported a wide, weird rictus of a smile that looked to be stapled on. She was eager to establish me as a bitter expatriate without any political experience – one doomed to the sidelines.

Briefly, I reminded her that in 1960 I had got 20,000 more votes for Congress in my New York district than Kennedy had got for president; that in 1964 I had turned down what was by then a 'safe' seat in Congress; that from 1968–72 I was co-chairman of the People's Party; while, in 1982, I got close to a half-million votes for Senator from California – rather more votes than Dr Owen here enjoys, I added, and the studio audience applauded. This line was cut, along with any number of other phrases that spoiled the negative image that the BBC wished to project. Can Murdoch be worse? Tell us, Clive.

Despite the open censorship of television, radio, press in the *ci-devant* Communist countries and covert censorship in the United States and Europe, word somehow gets through to interested parties. That is why, for once, the human race is suddenly a protagonist in today's upheavals.

The fact that *Time* and *Newsweek* have come to the same conclusion is only a minor lapse. At the moment when Gorbachev was changing the politics of the world, in December 1986, *Time*, the original Cold War propagandist, passed him over for the dubious honour of its personage of the year for the pointless Cory Aquino. But eventually, even in *Time*, all things shall come to pass (*Ecclesiastes*). For four years I have compared Gorbachev's improvisatory artful-dodger style to that of Franklin Roosevelt. I was called outrageous. Today (*Time*, 1 January 1990 leader): 'Improvisation corrected by feedback, that was Roosevelt's way ... [Gorbachev's] political style resembles Roosevelt's.' In time ...

Simultaneously, in a number of countries living under austere and unsuccessful regimes, news of consumer goods to be easily had in a world elsewhere was spread by television leaking from excessive West to deprived East across the small crowded borders of Europe. Even more interesting, the Middle Kingdom, now in its third millennium of proud celestial isolation, got the same word, presumably from a few radio sets which Dr Conor Cruise O'Brien has held responsible for the doomed uprising in Tiananmen Square: the United States, he claimed, had raised the hopes of a billion auditors and then let them down. But Western propaganda played only a minor part in what was a kind of spontaneous combustion. The issue was freedom, and the heirs of Confucius do not need us to tell them where resides the mandate of Heaven.

Strictly speaking, there is hardly a free country on earth (recall the Danish lady writer who was obliged, one year, to pay tax of more than 100 per cent on her income); but the desire for a better life in a material way is universal, as well as a distaste for bureaucracy and nepotism, whether centred upon smiling Copenhagen or brutal Peking. The always sensible Alexander Herzen rejected his contemporary, Marx, on the ground that each generation was a world unto itself alone and evil was he who would sacrifice a generation, making them caryatids, bleakly supporting floors for unborn others to dance upon in a building not yet designed.

In 1980 I took the position, needle held against fleshy national parts, that the sort of communism practised by the Soviet Union and its client states was a failure and that there was no danger of contagion. I also noted that nuclear world war was not probable except by accident. But 90 per cent of the press and close to 100 per cent of those whom Corporate America pays to go to the Congress and live in the White House are dedicated not only to the arms race (of the roughly 70 per cent of the federal war budget, a sizeable commission goes to politicians, universities, the press), but also to the war of angry rich against feckless poor. I had said the unsayable. If Communism was not predatory, no arms race. If Communism was not insidiously attractive to the 40 millions clinging to either side of the poverty line, what then could be used to keep the tax money – not to mention the loans – coming to the government? How to replace the evil empire with another bogyman in whose awesome Satanic shadow the few could continue to collect the money of the many?

Currently in audition for America's Public Enemy Number One (alas, our public enemies become yours too) are the Arabs, bestial, sub-human terrorists. The American Israel lobby can take full credit for this particular campaign and their canny investment in American politicians is so astute that this year 65 out of 100 Senators, acting on the lobby's orders, forbade the Administration to allow Arafat on American soil long enough to address the United Nations.

This is nothing compared to the 'spontaneous' protectionist mood of the country as the Japanese buy more and more of our alabaster cities, our amber waves of grain. The late poet-philosopher Paddy Chayevsky, in his masterpiece *Network* (where the oil cartel OPEC was the villain), wrote a superb aria for a television mogul to the effect that the money that has gone out of the country due to the higher price of oil is now returning home where it belongs as the Arabs (today, read the Japanese) buy up America, and we get our own money back to play with while they are stuck with crumbling towers and a sullen workforce. To stand in the way of this inevitable round is to act, the mogul thundered, against nature.

Nevertheless, the anti-Japanese tide is rising and if it goes too far then the authors of Pearl Harbor are quite apt, this time, to drop an economic bomb. If for two consecutive quarters they do not buy American Treasury bonds, the American economy, not to mention empire, will shut down. *Tora, tora, tora!* Japan also has other cards to play and other markets, as the world now rearranges itself.

Finally, most sinister of the putative national enemies is drugs. Drug-sellers and users have no lobby and their legalisation only a small one. Through the prohibition of drugs, government is given extraordinary police powers over everyone. On 3 November our Justice Department determined that the Federal Bureau of Investigation and our military forces have the 'legal right' to arrest any drug-dealer in any country on earth with or without the consent of the host country involved. So much for the idea of sovereignty. The sooner the United States is invited to leave Europe altogether, the better for Europe and for those of us who would like to see a restoration of the American republic.

In this year of the people and their near-bloodless – until Romania – revolutions, one observes two quite contrary forces at work. The first is centrifugal.

Everyone consciously or unconsciously detests the nation-state as we know it, and what we know is the nineteenth-century invention of Lincoln, who welded together the loose confederation of the American states into a centralised, industrialised, militarised, federal state, and of Bismarck, who was doing much the same for the German states. In due course South Carolina has learned to put up with New York, while Bavaria put up with, first Prussia, now Hesse-Darmstadt. But the old states of Europe are still proudly tribal, and dialects, customs, religions differ from the states to which they have been, often capriciously, assigned. It is no coincidence that the only truly successful modern state is Switzerland, with its four languages, four races and two religions, all peacefully and prosperously flourishing together. Since this confederation is easily the most democratic and prosperous in the world, no good or non-derisive word is ever said of Switzerland in our protective media.

Today the tribes are gathering around their standards – Armenians, Basques, Croats, Scots. The nation-states that contain these tribes are too confining and too stupid to be borne. The tribes want out – or perhaps one should say they want *in*, in to themselves. For a degree of autonomy, they will accept vague Brussels if that means an end to, say, oppressive Madrid. The managers of the nuclear empires are puzzled by all this because, simultaneously, there is a centripetal force at work in the world. One sees it most vividly in Europe where the Twelve prepare for 1992, where the two fragments of the German tribes are being drawn together like bits of mercury where, finally, everyone's life is dominated economically by undomiciled conglomerates. These vast corporations instinctively centralise in order to sell more software and hamburgers. But their kingdom is not of this world. They belong to the Book – in this case, the ledger, and any government unwise enough to try and curb them will either be punished through often witty secret sanctions or simply, as in the case of the American government, bought off.

The tone of most of the end-of-the-decade, century, millennium, pieces that I have read is: we live in dangerous times. This covers every prophecy, and Gorbachev is bound to fail if he is not bold enough to set up a golden calf in Red Square. The sectarian press of the West is nothing if not predictable. Even so, it is curious that none has yet suggested the terrible possibility that what began as Roosevelt may yet end as Lincoln. But, personalities and ingenious software to one side, the obvious is not addressed head-on. I wrote in *The Observer* in August: 'Think of Earth as a living organism that is being attacked by billions of bacteria whose numbers double every forty years. Either the host dies, or the virus dies, or both die.' I then pointed out that the Reverend Malthus's figures and timing may have been off, but his formula is undeniable. I am happy to say that many of last week's leader writers are *Observer* readers. *Newsweek*: 'Like any parasite, we have the potential to kill our host, the planet – or at least to change the conditions that favour our existence, and thus kill ourselves. Unlike other para-sites, however, we can't send our children off to find fresh hosts when this one dies.'

I like this addition. Due to a certain delicacy about the deeply-cherished beliefs of others, and respect for religion, any religion, and a need for votes, governments do not dare take on the Catholic Church and those fundamentalist Protestant organisations who have said No to birth control and abortion. Without a lead – and money – from the prosperous nations, the second and third worlds will continue to breed into oblivion while destroying their environment in order to stay alive.

The leader writers do note, approvingly, that population is dropping in the industrialised world; disapprovingly, that births are often below replacement levels and that there is a 'greying' of the only world that really matters to us – us. It would seem to me that a great work for the coming European Confederation will be not only an integration of the less-developed countries with our own but an all-out campaign to help those who want to be helped (just about everyone) in curbing population. Although Western politicians shudder at the thought of disciplining religious leaders obsessed with sex, particularly those officially celibate, I would with extremest unction, *urbi et orbi*, propose to these divines that, for once, they imitate in matters sexual and reproductive Our Lord, who never said a word on the subject other than a single wisecrack to the effect that only those without sin may condemn ladies of easy virtue.

All in all, I would not have missed this century for the world. Let us hope that our ingenious race does not manage to miss out on the next century as a result of nuclear fireworks in, let us say, the Middle East or as a result of the planet suddenly gone bald in its arid greenhouse, the few human survivors existing beneath plastic domes, munching hydroponic veg while dreaming, as proper viruses must do, of space, planets, worlds elsewhere, furiously to infest.

*The Observer*
31 December 1989

# 7

# ITALIAN FOOTNOTE

On April 11, Bernardo Bertolucci and his Italian associates won nine Academy Awards for the film *The Last Emperor*. The press made much of the fact that Italy had, at last, made a successful, international, 'epic' film. Bertolucci did his best to reassure us: the picture really wasn't all that Italian. He had got financing from everywhere, even from far Cathay. But he was too tactful. The victory really was one of Italian talent and entrepreneurship, which includes the ability to get international financing. The success of this movie is yet another outward and visible sign of the Italian re-Renaissance. Italy has now moved to fourth place in the world's gross national products; only West Germany leads in Europe. The Italian commercial presence is everywhere. Recently, an Italian businessman almost bought Belgium, leading to a sulphurous European debate on what is *nationality*. Can one Carlo De Benedetti own 51 per cent of the shares of Société Général de Belgique, which controls most of Belgium's financial assets? Meanwhile, Pirelli bids for Firestone, and the fire sale continues. What's going on?

As a longtime, part-time resident of Italy and honorary citizen of the town of Ravello, I have watched, in half a century, Italy go from a Third World agricultural country to its current position atop the economic and cultural ladder down which the United States is painfully stumbling, while the Soviet Union is still unable to negotiate the bottom rungs. The origin of Italy's re-Renaissance is due, in part, to the special relationship between us and them. When the Allies defeated Germany, Japan and Italy in 1945, Italy came under our rule and, to this day, we occupy, militarily, the peninsula with close to a dozen air, ground, sea and nuclear bases. But then, since the Second World War, the West has come full circle. For more than 2,000 years, the 'known' world was centred upon a small sea called the Mediterranean – or Midland – by the Romans, China and India were known to be out there somewhere; and that was about it. All that mattered was the doings of the white race – a minority race even then – cooped up in Europe, Asia's wild west. For 2,500 years we have been, to ourselves at least, centre-stage. Now, in the twentieth century, the world has grown very small (jet travel brings us much too close together), as well as very large: five billion people now crowd the planet. Asia dominates the world's economy while Europe is, literally, 'eccentric'; and our own imperial republic, once Europe's salvation – and human landfill – has entered its listless Manchu phase.

Although in the West there is a general sense of drift, one finds at least in what was, for most of our civilisation, the very centre of our boutique – I mean culture – Italy. Thanks to toll-roads, creative litigation, and the happy invention of cement, ancient Rome became the first world power. Since the empire was most of Europe and much of the Middle East and North Africa, it is pointless to generalise about the Roman character, much less about the Italian character when Italy, as such, was just a name. But today the nation-state of Italy has become the West's principal centre of entrepreneurial energy, combined with a cultural life considerably richer than that of any of those nations which once were Rome's provinces.

Fashion is a form of art in which Italians now lead the world. One sees Italian fashion in the streets of Chiang Mai as well as in Duluth. Factories, prefabricated in Italy, rest now on the steppes of Russia, like intricate works of metal sculpture. During the last half-century, Italy has produced perhaps the only major world novelist, Italo Calvino, while the late Primo Levi, in marked and bitter contrast to certain American contemporaries, was able to define the true nature of twentieth-century genocide. Since Anglophones, by and large, do not like to read foreigners, it is a source of surprise, even to our schoolteachers, that the most brilliant and original critic of nineteenth-century English literature was Mario Praz, whose *The Romantic Agony* is the definitive study of romanticism's disorders and discontents. Then, to be right up to date, the most unlikely world best-seller, *The Name of the Rose*, was the work of one Umberto Eco, a professor of semiotics at the University of Bologna, who decided to apply the arcana of his discipline to popular fiction, with a most astonishing result. In film, where directors are taken far too seriously in all countries, Italy has gone through a golden age from Roberto Rossellini and Federico Fellini to Michelangelo Antonioni to Elio Petri and Francesco Rosi and Bertolucci. In music, Luciano Berio is a master like no other. Theatre – well, a country with so vivid a piazza-life does not need to go indoors for drama.

In journalism, Italians are more politicised than Americans. But then they have political parties, which we don't. As for their politics, contrary to the legend that Italy is an unstable republic with governments falling, if not right and left, right and centre, Italy has been governed by the same group for forty years. When Benito Mussolini was asked whether he found it difficult governing so restless a people, he said, 'No, it's not difficult, it's just pointless.' Where the American political genius is the separation of state from church, the Italian genius is the separation of state from people. The government does not bother the people; and the people leave the government alone. For reasons that deny reason, Italy's combination of the worst aspects of capitalism with the worst aspects of socialism works.

I think the chief Italian virtue can be summed up in a word – curiosity. It is no accident that Marco Polo made it first to the court of Kublai Khan. It is no accident that the western hemisphere is named for Amerigo Vespucci, having been discovered, more or less, by Christopher Columbus. It is no accident that we might never have had atomic power if Enrico Fermi hadn't broken the first atom.

*Los Angeles Times*
1 May 1988

Why did I write this little piece for the *Los Angeles Times?* Because, in all my life, I have never read in the mainstream American press a story favourable to any other society. It was a first-time experience for Los Angeles readers. A last time, too, as Mafia stories keep coming and how the Swedes, with better health care and quality of life and education than Americans, all commit suicide because – well, they aren't Americans, are they?

# 10

## REFLECTIONS ON
## GLORY REFLECTED
## AND OTHERWISE

I

Although the New York family of Auchincloss is of 'recent arrival' (1803), as Sitting Bull used to say, they have managed, through marriage, to become related to everyone in the United States who matters – to everyone in the United States who matters, that is. For idle hypergamy and relentless fecundity there has not been a family like them since those much less attractive Mittel-Europa realtors, the Habsburgs. Although the family has produced neither a great man nor a fortune ('each generation of Auchincloss men either made or married its own money' – Louis Auchincloss in *A Writer's Capital*), there are, aside from the excellent novelist, numerous lawyers, stockbrokers, and doctors whose Cosa Nostra is the Presbyterian (*not* Episcopalian) Hospital in New York. By the mid-twentieth century, the clan's most notorious member was Hugh D. Auchincloss, Jr. A bulky man who stammered, 'Hughdie' (usually known as 'Poor Hughdie') was heir to a Standard Oil fortune, thanks to his father's marriage to the daughter of a Rockefeller partner named Jennings. This worldly, I think the adjective is, match, sharply separated Hughdie's line from those of the brownstone cousinage (fifty-seven male Auchinclosses in 1957), content with their snail-like upwardly mobile marriages to Old as well as Older New York.

Early in life, at Yale, in fact, Hughdie's originality was revealed;

218

*he was unable to do work of any kind.* Since the American ruling class, then and now, likes to give the impression that it is always hard at work, or at least very busy, Hughdie's sloth was something of a breakthrough. The word 'aristocrat' is never used by our rulers, but he acted suspiciously like one; certainly he was inert in a *foreign* way. Would he move to England? But Hughdie's originality in sloth was equally original in ultimate choice of venue. He moved not to London but to Washington, DC. Not only had no Auchincloss ever moved to Washington, DC; *no one* had ever moved there without first undergoing election or appointment. As if this was not original enough, he started a brokerage firm with a million dollar gift from his oleaginous Jennings mother, and settled into an Italian palazzo next to the Japanese embassy in Massachusetts Avenue. Since the partners did all the work at the brokerage house, he had a great deal of time to woolgather and to fret whether or not he was happy. In fact, each day would end with a careful analysis of the preceding not-so-crowded hours and whether or not others – specifically, the wife of the moment – had contributed sufficiently to his happiness, a somewhat vagrant bluebird with other errands that took precedence in the nation's capital.

As the city had no life other than the political, Hughdie became a 'groupie' even though he had little interest in politics as such. He believed in the virtue of the rich and the vice of the poor and that was as far as introspection ever took him. But Hughdie very much believed in celebrity (one of his most attractive monologues was of the date that he had had in youth with the film star Kay Francis) and of all celebrities the politician most fascinated him, and of all politicians the members of the United States Senate were the most visible and glamorous.

For a long time, before and after Franklin Roosevelt, presidents tended to be nonentities kept hidden in the White House while senators were always centre-stage. They were, literally, the conscript patriciate of the nation until they were elected directly in 1913. After that, though hereditary nobles continued to sit in the chamber (today one finds a Rockefeller, a Dupont, a Pell, a Heinz, all in place, as well as such recent hustlers as the Kennedys), outsize tribunes of the people joined them and, along with Byrds, Hales, Frelinghuysens, there were Borahs, LaFollettes, and Longs.

From Lincoln's murder to FDR's first inaugural the Senate was the great stage of the republic. At our own century's quarter time there were ninety-six senators, and the whole country observed these paladins with awe if not pleasure. When a powerful senator spoke, the galleries would be full. Everyone understood exactly what Borah meant when he said that he would rather be right than president, or did *Senator* Clay say it first? For Hughdie, the Senate's Reflected Glory was sun enough for him. But few political magnificos came to his Massachusetts Avenue palace during the time of his Russian-born first wife. There was a grim divorce in which an airplane propeller surreally figured. With Hughdie's second wife, the 'beauteous' (*Time* magazine's adjective) daughter of the blind Senator Gore, he hit the jackpot, and she filled Merrywood, his new house – or 'home' as the press liked to say even then – across the river, with senators and the Speaker, Sam Rayburn, and the likes of Walter Lippmann and Arthur Krock: my mother had persuaded Hughdie that if one wanted true Reflected Glory, certain Jews would have to be invited to the house if only to set up the reflectors.

In due course, after two children, Nina Gore Vidal Auchincloss left Hughdie for Love, and he was promptly married for his money by one of her ladies-in-waiting, who brought him two very poor but very adorable frizzy-haired step-daughters to take my place in his ample heart. For a long time there was no RG, much less G, to illuminate the sad Merrywood until one of the adorable girls married. . . . But let Hughdie state his victories in Caesarean plainstyle, written for an Auchincloss family publication: 'Hugh D. Auchincloss (golf and chess) has twice been connected with the U. S. Senate through marriage; once as the son-in-law of the late Thomas Gore, senator from Oklahoma, and now as step-father-in-law of John F. Kennedy, junior senator from Massachusetts.' That was it. All of it, in fact. At the end, there was to be absolute RG.

A decade later Hughdie was acclaimed 'the first gentleman of the United States' by Mr Stephen Birmingham, a society chronicler who should know. But by then Reflected Glory had so paid off that as he and I stood face to face in the Red Room of the White House, he could ask himself rhetorically, 'What am I doing here? I am a Republican and I hate publicity.' I have never seen anyone so happy but then, next to limelight, RG is best. At the American empire's zenith, there was poor Hughdie, a dusty mirror at the dead center of The Sacred Way.

*Tout ça change*, as the French say, but with us, unlike the French, the specifics never remain as they were. The actors are constantly changed at our capital; plays, too. I am put in mind of my native District of Columbia and its turbulent clubhouse, the Senate, by Patricia O'Toole's *The Five of Hearts*, by Joseph Alsop's various published reminiscences, by the two Henrys, Adams and James, neither ever very far from my thoughts. In *The Five of Hearts* O'Toole describes that eponymous coven of Henry and Clover Adams, of John and Clara Hay, of Clarence King, the five who, in 1882, came together in Washington as friends and so remained until the last died in 1918, their lives illuminated – indeed set ablaze – by Reflected Glory to which Hay, as Secretary of State, gained some of the real thing; while Adams, by constantly saying that RG hurt his eyes, achieved a degree of True Glory not to mention all sorts of Last Words.

2

In youth, one does not bother with one's own relatives much less their social and historical connections. Even so, although I was unaware at mid-century of the existence of an Annapolis-bound seventh cousin, who would one day achieve Glory as our thirty-ninth president, I was very much aware that my grandfather with whom I lived was Glory; and that my father, much newsreel-ized as the Director of Air Commerce and airlines-founder, was also Glory (most glorious, in my eyes and probably everyone else's, as an All-American football player at West Point). I was also aware that when I was transported at ten from the house of the Gores in Rock Creek Park to trans-Potomac Merrywood, I had left Glory for Reflected Glory, and though Hughdie maintained a lavish, by Washington standards, household with five *white* servants, it was very clear that Senator Gore and Gene Vidal were the people that everyone read and talked about as opposed to the army of shadowy Auchinclosses and their equally dim to me (if not to Mr Birmingham) connections up there in dirty New York City and dull Newport, Rhode Island. Give me Rehobeth Beach, Delaware, any day.

Although I, too, was RG, I knew from the start that I was out for Glory. So, too, was Henry Adams at my age. But as grandson and great grandson of two presidents, he was positively blinded at birth by RG; later, by settling in a house opposite the White House, he was incessantly bombarded by RG waves. Unlike Adams, I got out at seventeen, and vowed that if I was not elected to anything, I would not come back to live in the capital when there were so many other worlds and glories elsewhere. At seventeen, I enlisted in the army and, Mr Birmingham to the contrary, I was delighted to get my own life started and be rid of all the RGs of Merrywood, whom Jack Kennedy, years later, characterized to me as 'the little foxes,' a phrase taken from that perennial favorite, *The Old Testament*, by Lillian Hellman.

In later years, Adams's friend and mine, President Theodore Roosevelt's daughter, Alice Longworth, congratulated me every time we saw each other: 'You got out. So wise. It's a mistake to end up here, as a fixture. Like me. Like Joe,' she added once, gazing with benign malice at her cousin, Joe Alsop, across the room. When I was in my early teens, Joe had been a fat, bibulous journalist in his twenties who often came to Merrywood, and several times watched me as I played tennis with a schoolmate. Years later, when Joe was involved with an Italo-American sailor, Frank Merlo (soon to enter RGdom's all-time Hall of Fame as the inamorato of Tennessee Williams), he told me, 'Of course I know *all* about *The City and the Pillar*. The Who, and Where, and the . . . What?' For the great majority that has since joined us, *The City and the Pillar* was a 'glorious' *roman* of the Forties, whose *clef* was much sought by interested parties.

As I read with some pleasure *The Five of Hearts* I was struck, as always, by what a small world the American one was – and is. For Henry Adams at the end of the last century, the country was 'a long straggling caravan, stretching loosely toward the prairies, its few score of leaders far in advance and its millions of immigrants, negroes, and Indians far in the rear, somewhere in archaic time.' Today there are more millions at the rear and a few score more leaders but the ownership of the country is as highly concentrated as ever, and at the capital of the country there are still ruling families, connected by politics and marriage and bed. Like papal Rome, each old Washington family descended from a president or senator who'd come to town and stayed. The Gores were an aberration: in the eighteenth century much of that part of Maryland which is now the District of Columbia had belonged to them before they moved west, buying up sequestered Indian lands. When Thomas Pryor Gore came to the Senate in 1907, he was actually returning to the family's original homestead; also, as a senator, he was the Hearts' toga-ed enemy.

Twenty-five years earlier, Henry Adams had published anonymously the novel *Democracy*, whose villain was a powerful, corrupt United States Senator and whose protagonist, Madeleine Lee, was attracted to Glory, rather like the Five, but, unlike them, was horrified by 'democracy' up close. In many ways, this novel is still one of the best about capitoline ways. Nevertheless, it was that energetic dilettante genius, Clarence King, who saw the flaw in Adams's rendering: 'The real moral is that in a Democracy, *all* good, bad and indifferent is thrown in the circling eddy of political society and the person within the whole field of view who has the least perception, who most sadly flaunts her lack of instinct, her inability to judge of people without the labels of old society' was Adams's heroine. One rather wished that King had got round to excelling at the popular novel as easily as Hay and Adams had. Certainly he had a better grasp of the whole than either Hay or Adams. Also, the gift of phrase. Of England, King wrote: 'a big hopeless hell of common people to whom all doors are shut save the grave and America.'

John Hay's problems with the Senate began when he first came to town as assistant to President Lincoln's secretary; later, as Assistant Secretary of State to President Harrison and, finally, most spectacularly, as Secretary of State under William McKinley and Theodore Roosevelt, when he ceased to be entirely lunar and became solar – but a sun outshone by the national sun of that huge spotted star, TR, and bedazzled as well as tormented by the ninety competitive capitoline suns clustered at the wrong end of Pennsylvania Avenue. Unlike Henry Adams, Hay was Glory by the end; but he had had to pay for his distinction in a series of pitched battles with the Senate, specifically with the arrogant senator from Massachusetts, Henry Cabot Lodge (known as 'Pinky'), a one-time protégé at Harvard of the then professor Henry Adams. Cabot, with his wife, Nannie, was practically a Heart himself; and this made the duels with Hay all the more bitter.

Hay had proved to be a marvellous manager of his wife's money while Adams had inherited a fortune from his mother. As a result, they were able to build and share a joint 'Neo-Agnostic' Romanesque building in Lafayette Park; here they maintained the most civilized pair of establishments in the city until . . . I suppose Mr Birmingham would say Merrywood, which was not as unintellectual in the Thirties and Forties as it became later when the not-so-merry house in the Virginia woods was loud with girlish shrieks, slammed doors, the thud of great feminine feet on the stairs, and poor Hughdie's sighs. But then, even at its zenith, Merrywood's Reflected Glory was never much more than old limelight; certainly nothing was ever generated on the premises. There was no intelligence at the centre, only a Meredithian heroine on temporary loan from the Senate.

The love-hate of Hearts for Senate took a powerful turn when widower Henry Adams became the lover – or 'lover' – of the splendid Elizabeth Sherman Cameron, wife of Senator Don Cameron from Pennsylvania, while John Hay became the lover (without quotation marks) of the wife of his senatorial nemesis, Henry Cabot Lodge.

As a young journalist in Washington, Adams wrote, 'To be abused by a senator is my highest ambition.' With *Democracy*, the anonymous author was much abused by many senators, among them the suspected model for Senator Ratcliffe, James G. Blaine. On the other hand, by his love for Lizzie, Adams probably earned not the abuse but the complaisant admiration of the hard-drinking, sad senator from Pennsylvania. Certainly the triangle was a balanced one and gave Henry James the shivers – of excitement and total interest in the oddity, the sheer *American*ness of it all.

O'Toole strikes a balance between today's mindless prurience and what really matters (which once actually mattered to our mindful Protestant founders), the public life of the republic. Sex lives of the glorious and their reflectors are no more interesting in themselves than are those of the bamboozled masses that now crowd our alabaster cities and cover over with cement our fruited plains. In a society with an hereditary monarch the comings and goings of the night are duly noted for their effect upon Grace and Favour and the conduct of public affairs. But as the American oligarchy selects, at what often looks to be absentminded random, its office-managers, the private lives of these public functionaries arouse no particular interest unless there is comedy in it.

On the other hand, the private lives of the actual rulers of the country are as out of bounds to American historians as they are to all of the other paid-for supporters of that oligarchy which controls the sources of information and instruction, that is, the 'media' and Academe. What is fascinating *inter alia*, in any story of the Hearts, is that the reader, often quite unprepared, is placed at the heart of the oligarchy that he has been told all his life does not – indeed cannot – exist in a 'democracy.' Yet the whole point to the enchanting Five is that, by birth or design, they are central to the ruling class. As in England, promising plebes have always been absorbed into the oligarchy. Although a fortune is a necessity somewhere in a patrician family, the visible players on the national stage are either plebes for sale (McKinley, Reagan, or that hypergamous railway lawyer, Lincoln) or they are energetic members of the oligarchy who take to public life in the interests of their class: the Roosevelts, the Tafts, currently Mr Bush of Kennebunkport, Texas. From time to time, regional oligarchies contribute to the national establishment – members of such old clans as the Byrds and the Gores, not to mention more recent combines like the Kennedys and the Longs. But as the First Gentleman of Entropy, Henry Adams, knew, all the clans wear out, usually more soon than late.

Of the Five, only Clarence King was doomed because he was merely brilliant as a geologist and talker. There was no King fortune. When he decided to make one, almost alone among his generation, he failed. The fact that he had secretly married a black nursemaid by whom he had a number of children was no help. The fact that King could not, like Hay, marry a fortune makes one suspect that, for all his potency with dusky women of the lower class or exotic foreign primitives, he could not function sexually with women of his own class. This is a common condition too little explored in our democratic orgasm-for-all-the-folks self-help (often literally) books. It might explain Clover Adams's suicide and Henry's chaste passion for Lizzie Cameron not to mention the Virgin of Chartres.

The Five set up shop in Washington, and there they remained, except for the peripatetic King. Pleased but not satisfied with the anonymous Glory of *Democracy*, Henry Adams settled in to write a history which was really autobiography, or at least family chronicle; but as he was subtle, he did not write of the administrations of the two Adams presidents – he wrote instead of their coevals and rivals, Jefferson and Monroe. Then, perversely, when he came to write a memoir, he was more historian than memoirist. In any case, Adams's writing is full of tension. To write of the deeds of others, though an act of a sort, is not *action* in the sense that Glory requires. He was permanently soured not so much by the risible republic or its imperial spin-off in whose ruins we have our dull being, but by his own inability to set foot on the national stage as had such sub-Hearts as the awful Theodore Roosevelt or the far worse 'Pinky' Lodge. Even Hay was able to turn his great gift for flattering the glorious into high office.

In 1885 Clover abruptly killed herself; grief over her father's death was the official line. But somewhere in Adams's latest – last – novel, *Esther*, there are clues. The protagonist notes how 'everything seems unreal' while, in real life, Clover says to her sister in that last year, 'Ellen, I'm not real . . . Oh, make me real – you are all of you real!' Clover's death killed off Henry Adams. But his ghost continued to haunt Washington, where he never ceased to worship the beauteous Lizzie, or act as sardonic chorus to the American empire, enjoying, all the while, the respectful love of those young women he liked to have about him, his 'nieces,' as he called them. Finally, he set himself up as a sort of marriage-broker between Virgin and Dynamo, faith and machine; but that match could not be made. Happily, there were Washington politics to delight in, and the Spanish-American War, and an unruly campaign in the Pacific, and the First World War, when so many of his worst prophecies were confirmed. Next to 'I win,' 'I told you so' are the sweetest words.

Meanwhile, Adams and Hay had the best seats to observe the national comedy. In their letters, they were so often to the witty point about the actors that two of the mummers struck back when Hay's letters were published posthumously. Theodore Roosevelt deplored Hay's 'close intimacy with Henry James and Henry Adams – charming men but exceedingly undesirable companions for any man not of strong nature – and the tone of satirical cynicism which they admired . . . impaired his usefulness as a public man.' TR then took full credit for everything that Hay had accomplished, while Lodge solemnly blamed Hay's problems with the Senate on Hay's bad-mouthing of that collective body. Meanly, Lodge even denied Hay's brilliance as a conversationalist, so reluctantly attested to by TR. Apparently, O. W. Holmes and J. R. Lowell were better at meal-time autocracy than Hay.

\* \* \*

Twenty years after the death of the last of the Adams Circle I can remember half-hearing their names spoken as if they were still contemporary in a city where office-holders are constantly changed but the oligarchy never. I thought of all this recently when I spoke on alumnus John Hay at Brown University, and saw in the audience John Hay's face, the current possession of a great-grandson who wears it almost as nicely as the original Johnny Hay, who was, according to Mark Twain, 'a picture to look at, for beauty of feature, perfection of form, and grace of carriage and movement.'

As I described Hay's career, I thought of my own mother's involvement with Hay's grandson, John Hay Whitney, known as Jock, while, simultaneously, my symmetrically-inclined father was involved with Jock's wife, another Liz like Cameron. In fact, it was Liz Whitney who taught me how to ride in the Virginia hills during that far too short 'long summer' before the Second War when my half-sister was born to grow up to marry Jock's first cousin, while summer's end – apotheosis, too – took place in 1939 when the King and Queen of England arrived in town and all of us Reflected Glory extras took to the streets and cheered them while our parents attended the garden party on the lawn at the British Embassy, presided over by the handsome, tactless Sir Ronald Lindsay, whose wife was Lizzie Cameron's niece, Elizabeth Hoyt, a small dark woman often at Merrywood that summer, where she did her best to influence the gathered magnates to come to England's aid in a war that most Americans wanted to stay out of. My grandfather was an 'isolationist' and so was I. In fact, I did my part so well as an America-Firster at school that, one night at Merrywood, Alice Longworth left the dinner party to come sit on my bed, and give me ammunition to use in her war against foreign entanglements in general and cousin Eleanor in particular.

Although the oligarchy occasionally splits on the no-turning-back issues, taking their positions to one side or the other of the Jefferson-Hamilton fault line that runs through our history when it is not, indeed, our only history, war has always united the oligarchy and it is then that their house-servants, the teachers and communicators, are set to work redecorating the American interior, removing old furniture like the Bill of Rights to the attic, or romanticizing England and demonizing Germany and Japan in those days, the Arab world in these. The First World War was largely a matter of the Hamiltonian oligarchs feeling their oats while the Jeffersonians fell glumly into line.

The Second War, a continuation of the First, hurtled us into the nuclear age as king – a harvest king as it turns out – of the castle. But since so simpleminded a game cannot be so bloodily played by a serious people, our domestics have been hard at work trying to disguise what really happened. As a result, the American people now believe that the Second World War was fought by two teams. The bad team wanted to kill all the Jews, for reasons unknown; the good team was anti-genocide and pro-Zion. As a veteran of that war and of the debates that led up to it, I can only say that the fate of the Jews had no more to do with American policy in 1941 than the ideals of democracy had to do with the First World War. Hitler's treatment of the Jews was not known to the American public when it was placed at war by the oligarchy in order to stop German expansionism in Europe and Japanese in Asia, a pointless enterprise since they have now superseded us anyway.

Henry Adams was the first to anticipate and articulate the *realpolitik* behind the wars: Germany, he said, was too small a power 'to swing the club,' and prevail. He predicted the division of the world between the United States and Russia, and as much as he disliked the English he never ceased to favour an 'Atlantic Combine' from 'the Rocky Mountains on the West' (could he have, presciently, already surrendered the California littoral to Japan?) 'to the Elbe on the East.'

## 3

The short, superficial biography written to be read not taught is an agreeable English speciality. The practitioners are often ladies whose research is often adequate to their task, which to my mind is a most useful one: to tell people something about the interesting or still relevant dead. After all, no one not institutionalized is expected to read, as opposed to teach or quarry, Dumas Malone's six-volume life of Jefferson, but should anyone still at large actually read it, as I did, every page, he will know profound despair. There is no sign of intelligent life anywhere in an artifact comparable only to Gutzon Borgland's Dakota cliff. True, close readers will delight in the footnotes, the work of often inspired graduate students, but the actual dead lunar text exists not to be read but to be worshipped. So there is room for another kind of book between the charming but light *Five of Hearts* and Dumas Malone. Unfortunately, those few Americans who can make sense of history can't write while those who can write usually know nothing at all. For any sensible oligarch, this is a fine arrangement; and will never be altered as long as one American university stands, endowed.

The fact that Henry Adams was not only a gifted writer but a uniquely placed historian carries no particular weight in today's world, where a field is a field, as a book editor of yesteryear used to say, assigning for review the latest biography of Queen Elizabeth I to her last biographer, with predictable (either way) results. Honourably and gracefully, O'Toole covers her complex subject, but without much sense of what they – Adams, above all – were about. Here one must trust to a biography that is literature as well as good academic scholarship, Ernest Samuels's *Henry Adams*.

At times, one senses that O'Toole has not read with sufficient care or interest Adams's Jefferson-Madison volumes, without which the Adams literary character is not graspable; but she is Gibbonian when compared to her reviewer in the Sunday *New York*

*Times*, an Englishwoman who is also known for writing light readable books about complex figures. The reviewer's confusion about the United States in general and the Hearts in particular would have given joy to the Five, none of whom took very seriously the English who, even then, were turning into eccentric Norwegians as their once-glorious day waned. Although it is plain that the reviewer had never read or, perhaps, heard of any of the Five before she got the book to review, she pluckily strikes the notes that she thinks an American paper like the *New York Times* would want struck. She deplores but does not demonstrate the male sexism that drove Clover Adams to suicide and Clara Hay to fat; affects astonishment over Henry Adams's 'anti-semitism,' as nothing compared to that of jolly *Private Eye*, which doubtless gives her a real giggle; even uses the word *zaftig* to show she knows what's what at the *Times* – rather like her ambitious compatriot, a novelist, who recently told an American interviewer that he might have been a much better writer had he been even slightly Jewish.

Genuflections to dumb Americans completed, she mounts her Norse horse. O'Toole had compared the Hearts to Bloomsbury. This is too much for the reviewer, who writes that the Hearts 'had an emotional gaucheness that has no counterpart in the England of the 19th century. . . . Bloomsbury would not have gone in for those enameled Five of Hearts pins, worn as the badge of friendship. Virginia Woolf would not have been caught dead using their heart-embossed paper on which the Five wrote their sentimental missives.' None of this is true, of course. There were no pins. The note-paper with the hearts was the joke of a season. There were no sentimental missives. There was a tragedy when Clover killed herself and Adams lost his world; when Hay's son died and he shattered. Otherwise, there were splendid, ironic 'missives' full of splendid jokes.

Humour is more definitive of a class than anything else. The English instinctively grade humour on class lines, and the one who fails to get the joke gets a one-way ticket back to where he came from. If nothing else, Bloomsbury knew its place: at the very top of the educated middle class. They aspired no higher, and if they had it would have done no good. (Maynard Keynes was the exception, and much resented by the Woolf-pack.) Certainly, they would never have had access to the Hearts, who were too high above them, except for the Hearts' 'cousin,' Henry James, who lived close by, and since he treated them sweetly, they called him 'Master,' and not always with the humorous quotation marks.

The point to the Five is that they were far more civilized than their American, much less English, contemporaries. They cannot be compared, finally, to Bloomsbury because, reflected or true glory, they were ruling class, while the Bloomsburyites were simply educated, powerless, middle-class folk who, like Mrs Dalloway, came all over queer when a great one drove by, pearl-grey kid-gloved hand visible at a back-seat window. American grandees have always mystified the English with their easy manners. They treat Bloomsburyites or taxi drivers as if they were equals, but it would have to be an uncharacteristically dull Bloomsburyite to remain unguarded, if not uncovered, in such a presence.

True aristos as well as idle artists, the Hearts did not take seriously the busyness of the contemporary arts, particularly as commodities. They preferred works of the past; they trafficked with Berenson. The reviewer displays a true Norse envy, when Hay hangs a Botticelli on his wall. She has also found a target. This is a 'book about things: the acquisition of the marvelous art objects with which the friends stuffed their houses,' and about 'dependence on possessions and buildings as a source of inspiration and shame, almost a substitute for spiritual life.'

Norwegians like to talk about spiritual life which, in Blooms-bury, meant Friendship, as the Hearts perfectly exemplified. Although they could afford pictures that Virginia and Leonard and Vanessa and Quentin and poor Lytton could not, their interests were not in possessions but in each other and their common, curious nation, whose history they not only recorded but helped direct, in office like Hay; in the study, as historian, like Adams; or in the drawing-rooms of Clara and Clover.

O'Toole is perhaps wise to deal as superficially as she does with the intellectual life of her characters because it is hard to dramatize something that does not exist for today's uncommon, alas, common reader, or someone like the *Times* reviewer who thinks that the Hearts wrote 'sentimental' letters to each other when their letters are mostly sharp and shrewd and engaged in the world in a way quite alien to sentimentalists. She finds a lack of spiritual life (can she be born-again?) in Henry Adams, whose last decades were spent in profound spiritual meditation upon the Virgin. But then she cannot have read *Mont Saint-Michel and Chartres* or even *The Education of Henry Adams*.

The Hearts, she tells us, 'lived on a knife edge between taste and tastelessness.' Proof? Poor Clara Hay tried to wear a too-tight wedding dress at her wedding anniversary. But the English mind (to the extent that one can say such a thing exists, Henry Adams mutters in my ear) needs desperately to believe that its American masters are emotionally gauche yet elitist and snobbish, buyers-up of old culture to stuff houses with. When it comes to getting things wrong, the English are born masters. In fact, I was once so impressed by their inability to sort things out that I used Madame Verdurin as a prototype for their professional book-chatterers, only to find myself defeated yet again: they hadn't heard of Madame Verdurin either.

# 4

Today literature enjoys a certain prestige in the First World, and much is made of successful writers in the press and in the schools. It is salutary to find that neither Adams nor Hay took writing, as such, very seriously. Hay was one of the most popular light-verse writers of his day, and his life of Lincoln, with John Nicolay, was – well, as monumental as a Dakota mountain. But, pseudonymously, inspired by Henry Adams, Hay wrote a novel called *The Breadwinners* which was a huge success with both general public and reactionary critics.

As so many of today's celebrities and journalists seem to be born knowing, it is a very easy thing to write a popular novel if one has an exploitable name. But even today it is hard, if not impossible, to reach a wide audience with no name at all, as anonymous John Hay and Henry Adams did. But then the ease with which these two, and Clarence King, too, wrote so very well makes one suspect that education might actually play a part in a process we are taught to think of as charismatic – *creative* writing as a silver spring that gushes miraculously from the psyche's mud. Perhaps if one has learned to speak well, one can probably think well, too, and if one can then coordinate thought and speech one might be able to write it all down in a way that is agreeable for others to read. But I am sure that this is far too simple; in any case, *high* art, even for them, was elsewhere, and they revered their honorary Heart, Henry James, who had chosen to settle in backward England for reasons which they could never appreciate, though Clover Adams thought he'd be better off running a hog ranch in Wyoming. Hog ranch is bad enough, but what Clover really meant was even worse; that is, better: 'hog ranch' was period slang for a whore house.

Henry James was very conscious that he had got out and that the Hearts, particularly Clover, were not entirely approving. Yet with them, as with so many American grandees of the period, Europe was just a pleasanter extension of their usual life; and far less foreign than Wyoming. It has often been noted (and never explained) why so many American writers who could get out of the great republic did so and how even those most deeply identified with the republic and its folkways – Mark Twain, Bret Harte, Stephen Crane – all managed to put in quite a lot of time on the other side of the Atlantic. *Douceur de la vie* was one reason. Also, God was doing well, extremely well, altogether too well in the last great hope on earth, while in Europe He was giving ground, if not to reason's age, to societies more interested in cohesive social form than Final Answers to All Questions. Edith Wharton believed that everything published in the States must first be made acceptable to an imaginary Protestant divine in Mississippi – probably named Gore.

In 1882, Henry James made the mistake of confiding to Clover his feeling for their native land, an emotion which had not much love in it. He was also tactless enough to regard her as America incarnate; to which her sharp response: 'Am I then vulgar, dreary and impossible to live with?' But James's eye was never so cold and penetrating as when it was turned upon those he loved, and he did coolly love the Hearts if not the Republic for which they sometimes stood. From his not-yet-Norwegian outpost in the North Sea and its still splendid world metropolis, London, he could generalize of things American – of Adamses, too. 'I believe that Washington is the place in the world where money – or the absence of it, matters least,' he wrote Sir John Clark. As for the Adamses, 'They don't pretend to conceal (as why *should* they?) their preference of America to Europe, and they rather rub it into me, as they think it is a wholesome discipline for my demoralized spirit. One excellent reason for their liking Washington better than London is that they are, vulgarly speaking, "someone" here, and they are nothing in your complicated kingdom.' This was written in the last days of our austere, deliberately *un*precedented republic. Then, in 1898, the American empire emerged with eagle-like cries (not least a mournful chirp or two from James), and in that year John Hay was recalled as ambassador from London to take over the State Department as well as such new imperial acquisitions as the Philippines. During this time of glory, Hay was aided and abetted by the English magnates; and subsequent visits to London were state affairs for the Hays, who were, most vulgarly, 'someone' in the complicated, declining Kingdom; for Henry Adams, too, if he chose. But he chose not to be someone, even though the raffish Prince of Wales as well as that ultimate someone, Gladstone, had admired *Democracy*.

Adams lived long enough to attend the birth of what he had conceived as 'The Atlantic Combine,' the bringing together of the United States and England, with the old country as the junior partner. When England ran out of money in 1914, the wooing of America began in earnest. Before, the British had encouraged their 'cousins' to acquire a Pacific empire in order to contain the

Russians, the Germans, and the Japanese. The Hearts, particularly Hay, played a great part in the making of this new alliance with a series of arrangements and treaties that culminated in the Hay-Pauncefote Treaty. Ironically, an adverb which sometimes does duty in these lives for 'inevitably,' Hay's principal antagonist in the Senate – England's, too – was Henry Cabot Lodge. Did Lodge know that Hay had so elaborately antlered him? O'Toole thinks not. But I think that he did on the ground that totally self-absorbed men, dedicated to their own glory, notice anything and everything that impinges on them.

Henry Adams records an edgy scene between the two when Lodge told Hay that he wished that he 'would not look so exceedingly tired when approached on business at the department.' It was Adams's view that the worn-out Hay had been 'murdered' by Lodge and his senatorial allies. Certainly, after Hay's death, there was little traffic between Adams and Lodge, much less with the great presidential noise across the park. The comedy was grim, Adams wrote Lizzie Cameron. Of himself and the bereft mistress, Nannie, he observed, 'We keep up a sort of mask-play together, each knowing the other to the ground. She kept it up with Hay for years to the end.' Then Nannie, too, was dead and Lizzie settled in Paris, besotted by the young American poet Trumbull Stickney (friend of Cabot Lodge's poet son, Bay), whom I dutifully read at school because my favourite teacher was writing a dissertation on his work.

5

Not long ago, I paid my last visit to Joe Alsop. As always, I telephoned and asked him, yet again, for his address in Georgetown. He gave me, yet again, the numbers and the street: 'N Street, "N" as in Nellie', he thundered. The new house was smaller than the one of his heyday; but, as ever, he was comfortably looked after by friends. I found him rather too small for my taste. The body had begun its terminal telescoping. But the brain was functioning and the large face was a healthy puce, like the brick of a Georgetown house, and the huge clown glasses magnified eyes only slightly dulled by a lifetime's reflection of (more of than on) Glory. Nevertheless, Joe was seriously unravelling and we knew that we were meeting, somewhat self-consciously, for the last time. With loved ones, this can be painful, or so the world likes to pretend, but with a life-long acquaintance, the *envoi* can be rather fun, particularly if you are dying at a slower rate than the other.

As always, Joe was for war anywhere any time in order to 'maintain the balance of power.' He had used this phrase so long that no one had any idea what – or whose – power was to be balanced. I was for the minding of our own business. He sounded like his great uncle; I sounded like my grandfather. So much for development in political attitudes or increased wisdom among the subsequent generations. As always, we played roles for each other. I was Henry James, returning to the collapsing empire from wicked, thriving Europe, and Joe was Henry Adams, weary with absolute wisdom. We gossiped: this was Washington, after all, Henry James's 'city of conversation.'

Joe told me how he had made up with cousin Eleanor Roosevelt, the only presidential widow ever to matter, to those who matter, that is. He had spent several decades attacking her dreadful husband and mocking her nobility of character and Sapphic tendencies; but there had been a sea-change before she died, and he spoke with affection of having seen her. I doubt if the affection had been returned. 'I forgive,' she once said to me, small gray eyes like hard agate, 'but I *never* forget.' Joe had been part of the Alice Longworth circle of TR devotees and FDR disdainers, and their wit was murderous, and Eleanor a preordained victim. But she had her own murderous quality, which Joe caught nicely in the *New York Review of Books*, when he likened her sweet nursery-school teacher manner to that of his 'Auntie Bye' who 'had a tongue that could take the paint off a barn, meanwhile sounding quite unusually syrupy and cooing.'

Joe was writing his memoirs and so unusually reflective of the past. I was undergoing the attentions of a biographer and in a most uncharacteristically down-memory-lane mood. He remarked that my father was the handsomest man he ever saw, adding, 'A colonel, wasn't he?' I took the trick with: 'No, a first lieutenant when he left the army.' In Washington the military have no status at all. To old Washington, a 'colonel' suggests someone lodged in a boarding house in E Street, with a letter to a senator as yet unacknowledged; while generals and admirals are not invited out anywhere except when they are hypergamous, as Robert McAlmon (in *Village*) notes bitterly of my father's marriage with the wealthy daughter of a United States Congressman, giving 'him enough of a start so that he would become quite a figure in the army some day.' But my father's wife was not wealthy, and he became quite a figure in civil aviation. Still, he was forever a colonel to Joe, while I always referred to Joe's admiral-grandfather as, 'Wasn't he something in the *regular* Navy?'

We spoke of the days of our youth and just before. He was convinced that Franklin Roosevelt could never have had an affair with the Roman Catholic Lucy Mercer *before* she had married someone else. Afterward, when she was no longer virgin, she could then commit adultery with an absolvable conscience. We discussed Henry Adams's special status in the city, which Joe had somewhat taken over. Adams never left his card with anyone, something unheard of in those days. He also never invited anyone to his daily breakfasts. The right people (those who were interesting), somehow, turned up. In later life, he almost never went out to other people's houses, including the white one across the road; *they* came to him. I recalled Eleanor's approving comment that though he would not come *into* her house when he took his drive, he insisted that the children come out and get in his carriage for a rough-house.

Joe and I stayed pretty much away from the subject of Jack Kennedy, since amongst the chroniclers of our time, Joe was chief mourner, even widow. I did remember the amusement that 'the old thing' aroused in Jack's vigorous breast, and I was present when someone said that Joe was getting restive, and it was time to have him over for lunch and 'hold his head,' an odd expression.

Joe shared with me a liking for the English that one could – how to put it without awakening shrieks of 'elitist snob' from both sides of the irradiated Atlantic? – 'relate to', combined with no particular liking for the fallen big sister nation. But then as the Hay-Adams generation marked the beginning of our national primacy in the world, our generation marked the actual mastery of the whole works, and our disdain for those who had preceded us was unkind, to say the least. Once, at Hyannisport, the thirty-fifth president was brooding on the why and the what of great men; he thought, not originally, that great political figures were more the result of the times in which they lived and not so much of character or 'genius.' I mentioned Churchill as a possible exception. Jack's response was worthy of Joe, his father: 'That old drunk! How could he lose? He always knew we were there to bail him out!'

In the fragment of memoir that Alsop has so far published, he did do a bit of a Henry Adams number when he diffidently told us how 'the WASP ascendancy,' to which he belonged, was at an end, and that he himself spoke now as an irrelevant relic of a quaint past when Washington was, in James's phrase, 'a Negro village liberally sprinkled with whites,' and one wore so very many clothes and changed them so often in a day. But Joe was putting on an act. He knew that the WASP ascendancy is as powerful as it ever was. How could it not be? They still own the banks. Head for head, they may be nearly outnumbered by Roman Catholics at the polls and by Jews in show biz and the press, but they still own the country, which they now govern through such non-WASP employees as Henry Kissinger, or through insignificant members of the family, like George Bush, who are given untaxing jobs in government.

Joe did manage to take a gentle swipe at cousin Eleanor, reminding us that in the old days 'Eleanor Roosevelt was not only anti-Semitic, which she later honorably overcame' (like klepto-mania?), 'she was also quite obstinately anti-Catholic, which she remained until the end of her days.' This is disingenuous, to say the least. Like everyone else, Eleanor was many people, not one. But the most important of her personae was that of politician, and no politician is going to be anti *any* minority if he can help it; unless, of course, his constituency requires that he make war on a minority, as George Wallace, say, used to do on blacks and Ronald Reagan always did on the poor. Neither Jews nor Catholics nor blacks, *as such*, figured in Eleanor's private world, which was exclusive of just about everyone or, as she explained to her husband's political manager, Jim Farley, when he complained that he was never asked to private Roosevelt functions, 'Franklin is not at ease with people not of his own class.' She was the same as a private person. But as a public one, she was there for everyone; hence, her implacable war with the Roman Catholic hierarchy over federal aid to education, which came to a head when that rosy Urning, Cardinal Spellman, denounced her as an unnatural mother, and she turned him into a pillar of salt in her column.

I fear that our imitations of the two Henrys were not much good at my last meeting with Joe Alsop. For one thing, Henry James could not bear his native land and he had, most famously, given reasons (but not the right ones) why. On his last trip to Washington to see the other Henry, he wrote: 'There is NO "fascination" *whatever* in anything or anyone . . .' And he was worn out with 'the perpetual effort of trying to do justice to what one doesn't like.' I, of course, am fascinated by my native land and my only not-so-perpetual effort involves restraining myself from strangling at the dinner table those Washington oligarchs who have allowed the republic to become a 'national security state' and then refused to hold their employees to account. 'Why didn't you impeach Reagan over Iran-Contras?' I asked a very great personage, indeed, a press lord. 'Oh, we couldn't! It would have been too soon. You know, after Nixon.'

Joe was an absolute romantic, and differed from Henry Adams in that he thought of himself as a participant on the battlefield as a brave journalist, which he was, and in the high councils of state, where he liked to bustle about backstage to the amusement of the actors. As avatars, Joe and I were not much. But we had had a very good time, I thought, as I left the N Street house for the last time.

Happily, for Henry Adams, and all other Hearts, the problem of Glory did not persist after middle age, when acceptance, if not wisdom, traditionally begins. Of himself and friends, Adams wrote: 'We never despised the world or its opinions, we only failed to find out its existence. The world, if it exists, feels in exactly the same way toward us, and cares not one straw whether we exist or not. Philosophy has never got beyond this point. There are but two schools; one turns the world into me; the other turns me into the world; and the result is the same.' Finally, not they but their great friend, Henry James, united the reflection of glory with the thing itself in a life that was all art, and it is no accident that he should have worked the proposition through not only in his unconscious but in the imagination, the only world there is, finally, that is graspable, artful.

On James's death-bed, he became Napoleon Bonaparte, and in his last coherent but out-of-self raving spoke in the first person as the emperor who personified for the Hearts' century the ultimate worldly glory.

From James's last dictations:

. . . we hear the march of history, what is remaining to that essence of tragedy, the limp? . . .

They pluck in their tens of handfuls of plumes from the imperial eagle . . .

The Bonapartes have a kind of bronze distinction that extends to their fingertips . . .

across the border
all the pieces
Individual Souls, great of . . . on which great perfections are If one does . . .

Later:

Tell them to follow, to be faithful, to take me seriously.

The secretary, Miss Bosanquet, wrote, after the end: 'Several people who have seen the dead face are struck with the likeness to Napoleon which is certainly great.' Thus, Glory and its Reflection had at last combined – not so much in death, where all things must, but in the precedent art and its true sanity.

*The Threepenny Review*
Spring 1991